LAUTERBACHER
ANNO 1651
ERDINGER
WEISSBRAU
ALKOHOLFREI
ERDINGER
Weißbier
ERDINGER
ALKOHOLFREI
Andechs
DOPPELBO
DUNKE
Franziskaner
Hefe-Weissbier
KAPUZINER
Weißbier
MIT FEINER HEFE
SEIT 1674
Das gute
Zirndorfer
LANDBIER

BEERS
OF THE WORLD

BEERS

OF THE WORLD

OVER 350 CLASSIC BEERS, LAGERS, ALES AND PORTERS

DAVID KENNING

Parragon

Bath New York Singapore Hong Kong Cologne Delhi Melbourne

This edition published by Parragon in 2010

Parragon
Queen Street House
4 Queen Street
Bath BA1 1HE, UK

ISBN 978-1-4454-0878-1

Editorial and design by
Amber Books Ltd
Bradley's Close
74–77 White Lion Street
London N1 9PF
www.amberbooks.co.uk

Project Editor: James Bennett
Design: Graham Curd
Picture Research: James Hollingworth
Additional Text: Robert Jackson, Chris McNab

Printed in China

Contents

Coors

FULLERS
ESB
EXTRA SPECIAL BITTER

MOUSEL
PREMIUM PILS

ER'S LAGER
F
ALIA'S CLASSIC
R SINCE 1888
355mL
FOSTER'S
CARLTON & UNITED BREWERIES LTD
77 SOUTHBANK BOULEVARD SOUTHBANK VIC 3006
BEER - PRODUCT OF AUSTRALIA

Introduction

'Beer is proof that God loves us and wants us to be happy' **– Benjamin Franklin**

It is hard to say for sure when exactly the first true beers were brewed, but it is likely that they originated in the Middle East and Egypt. The first detailed reports of brewing as we understand it were recorded more than 5,000 years ago by the Sumerians, who lived in the land between the Rivers Tigris and Euphrates, which roughly equates to modern-day Iraq. Even then, beer came in many different styles. The Sumerians recorded at least 20 different varieties, which each had a different role in their daily lives. Sikaru, for example, was used in their religious ceremonies and for medicinal purposes. It was made by soaking a type of bread made from emmer wheat and barley and fermenting the liquid that ran off in earthenware jars for several days, then flavouring it with honey and dates. The nutritional properties of beer were key to its initial development, though its intoxicating effects were also appreciated by early beer drinkers. One of the main reasons for brewing and drinking beer was simply that it was often unsafe to drink untreated water.

Beer Through the Ages

After the Sumerians, the ancient Egyptians developed the art of brewing on a large scale to supply the pharaoh's armies with a daily ration, and also refined the process of malting. The rise of Islam in the Middle East in the seventh and eighth centuries AD saw a corresponding decline in beer production, but by this time beer was already well established in Europe.

Around the fifth century AD, brewing was adopted by monasteries across Europe. These self-sufficient communities grew their own barley and were able to sell surplus supplies of ale to provide financial support for their religious activities. Over the centuries, the monks were responsible for many important developments in brewing, refining the process to the same basic form that is still used by commercial brewers to this day.

Until the sixteenth century all beers were top-fermenting ales, in which the yeast floated on the surface of the beer during fermentation. In the 1530s the monastic communities of Bavaria, Germany, started storing their fermenting beers deep underground in cool cellars, enabling them to continue brewing throughout the summer when the warm weather made brewing unpredictable. This cool storage had a remarkable effect on the

nature of the yeast, causing it to sink to the bottom and ferment at a much slower rate, allowing the beer to be stored for considerably longer periods. This process became known as lagering, from the German for storage (but note that in Germany the term lager is not used to designate a style of beer as it is in many English-speaking countries).

Outside of the monasteries, most brewing took place in the home on a very small scale. Successful home brewers attracted visitors, who eventually became customers, giving rise to the tradition of public houses. Some families developed a tradition for brewing, and by the fourteenth century the first commercial breweries were coming into existence. Due to the bulky nature of beer, it was still brewed and sold locally, even if the raw ingredients were imported from elsewhere. Until the late eighteenth century and the onset of the industrial revolution, beer could not be transported in significant quantities, and this only really changed with the coming of the railways from the 1840s onwards. Further scientific and technological developments in that period led to the increasing automation and mechanisation of brewing, enabling brewers greatly to increase their output. These new developments turned brewing into a major industry, and the brewing companies into international businesses.

The last major changes in brewing came in the middle of the nineteenth century. Until then, all beers were dark brown or amber-red and tended to be rather murky, but in 1842 in the Bohemian town of Plzen a brewer named Joseph Groll happened upon a way of making crystal clear golden lagers. His discovery was most probably an accident, a coincidence created by a chance combination of malt, water and environmental conditions. It helped that Bohemia was at that time also famous for its glass-making. Most beer at that time was drunk out of stone, metal or earthenware tankards, but Bohemian glassware was ideal for showing of the bright, clear colours of Groll's new beer, which quickly caught on.

By the 1870s, mechanical refrigeration had been introduced, allowing beer to be kept fresh for longer and also for it to be served chilled, making beer the perfect refreshing drink for a hot day.

Beer Ingredients: Water

Water, known to brewers as liquor, constitutes around 90% of the volume of beer, so it is not surprising that the mineral balance of a water source can have a huge impact on the flavour of the beer. The soft water of the Czech town of Plzen, for example, proved ideal for its famous golden lagers, while the hard, sulphurous waters of the River Trent in England played a large part in defining the character of the pale ales for which the town of Burton-upon-Trent is famous.

Beer Ingredients: Malt

Many different types of grain are used to make beer – wheat, rye, maize and oats among them – but one thing they all have in common is that raw grains will never produce satisfactory fermentation, so first they need to be malted. Barley is traditionally favoured by brewers because it is easiest to malt and produces a higher quantity of fermentable sugars. It is turned into malt by soaking the grains for two to three days until they start to germinate. The grains are then spread out on a malting floor and allowed to germinate for up to five days. It is at this stage that the starch in the grain is turned into the fermentable sugars that are essential to brewing. Germination is then halted by heating the grains in a kiln.

The heat the grains are subjected to and the length of time they spend in the kiln affects the colour and flavour of the malt, which in turn has a defining impact on the colour and flavour of the beer. Pale malt is the most commonly used form, being ideal for all types of beer. Amber and brown malts are made by heating barley to higher temperatures, giving a copper-red colour to any beer that they are used in. Chocolate malt is kilned longer to create an even darker colour and a more complex flavour, and black malt is darker still with a powerfully bitter flavour. Most malts are produced by gradually raising the temperature over a period of several hours, but for crystal malt the grains are introduced to higher temperatures almost immediately, creating a crystalline grain that imparts a fuller, sweeter flavour to beer.

Beer Ingredients: Hops

The first mention of hops being used in beer comes from monastic records of the eighth century AD. Even then, the monks understood the preservative qualities of hops, though initially their bitter flavour was not popular. Both qualities come from a resinous oil called lupulin. Before hops were introduced, many different alternatives were used, such as the blend of herbs and spices known as gruit. But beer drinkers eventually developed a taste for the bitter flavour of hops, despite the efforts of various influential figures like the Archbishop of Cologne, who enjoyed a monopoly on the production of herbs used for flavouring beer and attempted to ban the growing of hops. Hopped beers were first introduced to England in 1400 and here too ran into political difficulties because of the perceived threat to English brewers, but by 1600 the use of hops in beer was widespread throughout Europe and today many different varieties are used to provide subtle differences in aroma and flavour.

Beer Ingredients: Yeast

Early brewers were completely unaware of the existence of yeast

RIGHT
Belgian Lambic beer is brewed using only wild yeasts grown from airborne spores.

and even the medieval brewing monks had a very limited understanding of its effects, regarding it as a form of divine intervention that they called God-is-Good. Yeast was first observed in beer by a Dutch man named Leeuwenhoek in 1685 but it was not fully understood until the renowned scientist Louis Pasteur started to study beer in 1871.

Pasteur was the first person to observe the process by which yeast feeds on the malt sugars dissolved in the brew, turning them into alcohol and carbon dioxide. One of the down sides of yeast is that if the brewing conditions are not carefully controlled it can start to behave erratically, ruining the beer. Pasteur was able to determine the cause of many of the problems suffered by brewers. His work led the Danish brewer JC Jacobson to build a laboratory at his Carlsberg brewery in Copenhagen dedicated to breeding pure strains of brewing yeast. But as well as causing fermentation, yeast also has an effect on the flavour of beer, and many brewers prefer to use blends of different strains of yeast, while the lambic brewers of Belgium trust to the wild yeasts carried in the air.

Other Ingredients

Countless variations on the basic recipe for beer exist, using all manner of ingredients. Some of these added ingredients are considered 'adjuncts', used as a cheap alternative for malted barley, predominantly in mass-produced industrial lagers. Common examples are sugar, rice, maize, corn syrup and malt extracts. However, other grains like wheat and oats have a more legitimate claim for use in traditional beer styles, and some other ingredients can be considered genuine flavour enhancers. These might be blends of herbs and spices, such as juniper, coriander, ginger, and orange and lemon peel. The tradition of using honey to flavour beer stretches back centuries, while in Scotland, heather is used by one brewery to flavour its beer.

The Brewing Process

The key to brewing remains, as it has been since the earliest days, the conversion of sugar into alcohol by fermentation. Though the earliest Sumerian brewers did not fully understand the processes at work when they made their beers, they were still perfoming the same basic process as we do today in our computer-operated, high-tech, stainless steel, mega-capacity brewing plants.

The first stage of brewing is the mash, in which the fermentable sugar is extracted from the malt by boiling it in water until it creates a runny porridge. There are two methods of mashing: infusion, in which the sugar is simply left to dissolve, and the more complex decoction, in which the liquid is drawn off little by little and returned to the mashing vessel in controlled stages, using different temperatures to extract the maximum possible amount of sugar.

The liquid that is drawn off after mashing is called the sweet wort. The next stage is to transfer the sweet wort to the brewing kettle, where it is boiled for several hours, with hops added, either at the beginning to impart bitterness or towards the end to impart aroma. The spent hops are then removed using a filter called a hopback and the wort is then cooled before being transferred to fermentation vessels. It is now that the yeast is added and fermentation begins.

After the initial burst of fermentation, the brewer is left with a product known as 'green beer'. This needs to be given a secondary period of gentler fermentation (usually at lower temperatures) in conditioning tanks in order for it to develop its final character.

After conditioning, most beers are filtered and pasteurised, though some 'bottle-conditioned' ales are 'racked' into wooden casks or bottles still containing live yeast, which allows them to continue to develop depth and complexity right up to the point at which they are served.

Although the basic process is much the same for every beer, the endless variations in proportions of ingredients, types of water, malts, yeast and hops, not to mention the various other ingredients used, plus the different conditions under which each beer is brewed, give rise to a highly diverse and varied product. The positive side to this is that there you need not be restricted to calling a single beer your favourite. The truth is that there is a different beer for every occasion, whether it be a simple refreshing thirst-quencher on a hot summer's day, or the strong, dark beer to serve with a celebratory meal in winter.

ABOVE

Molson is one of the world's largest brewers with operations in Canada, Brazil and the United States. Molson Canadian, a crisp, easy-drinking beer, is one of its most popular brands. Other beers in the Molson Canadian family include Molson Canadian Light and Molson Canadian Ice, the best-selling ice beer in Canada. Molson traces its roots back to 1786, making it North America's oldest beer brand.

Canadian Beers

While the story of brewing in Canada shares many similarities with that of its neighbour to the south, there are several key differences. Most significant of these has been in the impact of prohibition. Although prohibition in Canada was repealed in 1932 – the same time that it was repealed in the United States – it was replaced with strict rules controlling the production and selling of alcohol that continue to restrict the market today.

ABOVE

Canadian cities have a thriving pub and bar culture, providing a ready market for local microbreweries.

TAXES ON ALCOHOL ARE AMONG the highest in the world, making beer in Canada expensive, and local laws prevent selling of beer across provincial boundaries.

As a result, beer production in Canada has traditionally been dominated by a handful of large brewing groups. Molson, the largest, was founded in Montreal in 1786 by Englishman John Molson. The next largest, Carling, was established in Ontario by Sir Thomas Carling in 1840 and merged with local rival O'Keefe in 1862 to form Carling O'Keefe, which was ultimately taken over by Molson in 1989. The other major Canadian player, Labatt, was founded by Irishman John Labatt in 1847. Both Labatt and Molson are now owned by foreign interests – Labatt has been part of the Belgian conglomerate Interbrew since 1995, and in the summer of 2004 Molson merged with giant US brewer Coors.

These big, powerful companies have been able to circumvent the local laws by opening regional brewing plants across the country, often by swallowing up smaller local brands. On a more positive note, the restrictions have also enabled many small microbreweries to spring up that are content to operate within their provincial boundaries and produce interesting craft beers on a small scale, though the market is still dominated by light, bland lagers. However, in spite of draconian licensing laws, Canadian brewers have always led the way in advancing brewing technology, Labatt in particular leading the way with its Ice Beer, which it introduced in 1993.

STATISTICS

Total production: 23,443,000 hectolitres (619,299,000 gallons) per year

Consumption per capita: 60 litres (16 gallons) per year

Famous breweries: Big Rock; Brick Brewing Co.; Budweiser Canada; Creemore Springs; Labatt Breweries; McAuslan Brewing; Molson Breweries of Canada; Moosehead Breweries; Unibroue

Famous brands: Brick Premium; Creemore Springs Premium; Labatt's Ice Beer; Moosehead; Big Rock Grasshopper; Molson Canadian

Alexander Keith's IPA

Brewed in Halifax, Nova Scotia, Alexander Keith's India Pale Ale originated in 1820, when the brewery owner decided to produce quality beers and ales that could be enjoyed across a wide cross-section of the community.

This particular India pale ale is a clear, light yellow ale with a small but distinctly fizzy head. The flavour is a pleasant combination of tangy and sweet, and there are additional hints of apricot, honey and butterscotch. The ale also gives an excellent, nutty aftertaste, and in general is greatly refreshing. Some critics, however, suggest that Alexander Keith's IPA is not a traditional India pale ale because it is not malty enough. Others also recommend the drink more as a draught rather than a bottled product. Whatever the varying opinions may be, the IPA certainly has a solid following among the ale drinkers of Canada.

SPECIFICATIONS

Brewery: Oland Brewery (Labatt/Interbrew)
Location: Halifax, Novia Scotia
Style: India pale ale
Colour: Light yellow
Alcohol: 5%
Serving temperature: 5°–7°C (41°–44.6°F)
Food: Bread with mature Cheddar cheese

Amsterdam Nut Brown Ale

Amsterdam was originally the name of a brewpub on John St, in the heart of Toronto's trendy nightclub district.

However, this brewpub was sold and converted into Al Frisco's (which still does do some sporadic house brewing). Amsterdam was also the name of the brewery above the Rotterdam bar, at 600 King St W, its present location. Amsterdam Nut Brown Ale is described as a classic British-style brown ale, with a deep chestnut colour and a medium body. It is brewed with chocolate malt from Belgium and balanced with continental hops to complement the rich malt flavour.

SPECIFICATIONS

Brewery: Amsterdam Brewing Company
Location: Toronto, Ontario
Style: Nut brown ale
Colour: Rich brown
Alcohol: 5%
Serving temperature: 5° (41°F)
Food: Bread, strong cheese and pickles

Big Rock McNally's Extra Ale

Big Rock was named after a local geological feature – an 18,000-ton boulder believed to have been deposited by a glacier – in the brewery's home town of Calgary. It was founded in 1984 by Ed McNally, a Canadian of Irish descent, and a beer enthusiast who wanted to provide a more flavoursome alternative to the bland, mass-produced beers that dominated the local market. Having no previous beer-making expertise himself, he appointed Bernd Pieper, an experienced Swiss brewer, to take care of the hands-on side of production, and the brewery was soon turning out three brews: mild, well-balanced traditional ale, which is still produced today, plus a bitter and a porter.

In the summer of 1986, the mild-flavoured thirst-quenching pale ale was introduced to the range. Coincidentally, several of the bigger brewers were hit by strikes at the same time, so Big Rock Pale Ale was willingly received by a thirsty public. By the Christmas of 1986, McNally's Extra Pale Ale was added to the repertoire and became the first – and only – Big Rock beer to bear the name of McNally himself. It is a robustly flavoured bright amber-coloured ale brewed in the typical Irish style. Powerful aromas of roasted malt with fruity, toasty notes are followed on the palate by a similarly rich bread-like malt flavour which carries hints of caramel and raisins.

SPECIFICATIONS

Brewery: Big Rock
Location: Calgary, Alberta
Style: Irish red ale
Colour: Clear, deep amber-red
Alcohol: 7%
Serving temperature: 10°–13°C (50°–55.4°F)
Food: Roast pork with apple sauce

Big Rock Grasshöpper

A unique wheat ale that is easy to drink and exceptionally refreshing, Grasshöpper is delicately hopped and delivers a smooth, bright finish.

Grasshöpper is influenced by Germany's Kristall Weisen. It is one of several popular products of the Big Rock Brewery, which was founded in the mid-1980s by Ed McNally, a native of Lethbridge, Alberta. McNally originally trained as a lawyer, but eventually abandoned that trade to become a farmer, then a beverage entrepreneur. Grasshöpper is a clear ale which has a slightly lemony aroma, and is crisp and sharp on the palate. The ale, which has a sunny ambient yellow colour, retains its head for quite some time after pouring.

SPECIFICATIONS

Brewery: Big Rock Brewery
Location: Calgary, Alberta
Style: Wheat ale
Colour: Golden-yellow
Alcohol: 5%
Serving temperature: 5°C (41°F)
Food: Any spicy oriental dish

Brick Red Baron

Red Baron is brewed to a similar recipe as Brick Premium Lager, but with a less pronounced hop profile, making it more of a thirst-quenching 'session' beer.

It is not to be confused with Red Cap, a revival of a popular beer of the 1950s and 1960s, which comes in a short 25cl (8.5oz) 'stubby' bottle with a distinctive red cap. Both of these, however, are part of an extensive range of beers produced by the Brick Brewery, including Waterloo Dark. Named after the brewery's home town, this is a rich, dark mahogany-coloured Munich-style lager with a mild malty character.

SPECIFICATIONS

Brewery: Brick Brewing Co.
Location: Waterloo, Ontario
Style: Lager
Colour: Pale straw yellow
Alcohol: 5%
Serving temperature: 8°C (46.4°F)
Food: Hot spicy food such as Thai curries

Brick Premium Lager

Since its founding in 1984, Jim Brickman's Brick Brewery has become one of the largest in Canada. It started on a small 'microbrewery' scale, with a selection of beers devised after five years of research across 29 countries and 68 breweries, and eventually opened in a former furniture factory dating from the mid-nineteenth century.

Its first beer and still its flagship brew was Brick Premium Lager, brewed using all-Canadian malt and two varieties of imported European hops. The aroma is dominated by a sweet malt profile with hints of herbal, lemony hops in the background. The hops become more forthright on the palate, balancing well with the soft, buttery malt flavours. With its medium body and spritzy carbonation, this is a crisp and refreshing beer. Its quality is attested to by the fact that it has five times been the winner of the Monde Selection Gold Medal.

Currently, Brick offers one of the widest ranges of beer of any brewery in North America, including a mildly hopped, lighter flavoured lager, and a range of 'competitively priced' lagers under the Laker label. Brick has a second brewing plant in the hamlet of Formosa (from where it obtains the spring water used in the Premium Lager), the site of one of Canada's oldest breweries, and produces one beer under the Formosa label, Cold Filtered Draft. Most Brick beers are lagers, but Conners Best Bitter is a traditional English-style amber ale with a robust hop aroma and a bitter finish. Also in the range is Andechs Special Hell Lager, which is brewed to the same recipe as used by the Andechs monastery brewery in southern Bavaria, Germany.

SPECIFICATIONS

Brewery: Brick Brewing Co.	**Alcohol:** 5%
Location: Waterloo, Ontario	**Serving temperature:** 8°C (46.4°F)
Style: Lager	**Food:** Grilled or smoked seafood
Colour: Pale straw yellow	

Creemore Springs Premium Lager

Available in both bottled and draught form, Creemore Springs Premium Lager has a good balance of hops with a touch of honey in the malt.

It has a pleasant, homely quality with a slight citrus aroma and a fresh, crisp taste reminiscent of a good Pilsner. The brew is sweet, but not overwhelmingly so. It pours a golden orange colour, with a small head that soon disappears to leave a pleasing lacy effect. The brewery, located in the village of Creemore, has the advantage of access to pure spring water bubbled through a limestone bed and used in the brewing process. Creemore publicity emphasises that 'our unique amber lager is fire brewed in small batches and delivered fresh weekly.' Devotees of the Creemore beers can belong to an official fan club run by the brewery and known as the 'Frothquaffers'.

SPECIFICATIONS

Brewery: Creemore Springs
Location: Creemore, Ontario
Style: Premium lager
Colour: Golden-orange
Alcohol: 5%
Serving temperature: 5°C (41°F)
Food: Beef or pork

Labatt Blue

John Kinder Labatt was an Irish immigrant who settled in London, Ontario, in the 1830s.

After giving the matter some consideration, in 1847 he set up a brewery in partnership with a fellow Irishman, Samuel Eccles, and by 1853 had become the brewery's sole proprietor. Labatt is now one of the largest two breweries in Canada, and Labatt Blue is the best-selling Canadian beer in the world. Introduced in 1951 as Labatt Pilsner, it was unofficially renamed by fans of the Winnipeg Blue Bombers Canadian football team. Brewed using imported German hops, it is a well-balanced beer, matured for a smooth body and a full, fruity flavour.

SPECIFICATIONS

Brewery: Labatt
Location: Toronto, Ontario
Style: Pilsner-style lager
Colour: Clear golden yellow
Alcohol: 5%
Serving temperature: 6°–8°C (42.8°–46.4°F)
Food: Grilled mildly flavoured sausages

Labatt Ice

When it was introduced in 1993, Labatt Ice was the world's first ice beer. It is created using a unique process in which the beer is chilled to around -4°C, at which temperature ice crystals begin to form.

These ice crystals are then removed, leaving a smoother, lighter beer; as water freezes at a higher temperature than alcohol, the beer's alcohol content also increases. Extra smoothness is achieved through lengthy maturation, and selected North American and European hops are used to create a full yet delicate flavour. Today the Labatt 'family' of brands incorporates a wide range of styles.

SPECIFICATIONS

Brewery: Labatt
Location: Toronto, Ontario
Style: Ice beer
Colour: Pale golden yellow
Alcohol: 5.6%
Serving temperature: 6°C (42.8°F)
Food: Spicy chicken dishes

McAuslan Griffon Extra Pale Ale

In 1989, Toronto man Peter McAuslan, believing that he could brew a beer better than any of the others that were available locally, set up the McAuslan brewery.

His products fall into two groups, each with its own branding: St-Ambroise and Griffon. The two Griffon beers are the Irish-style red ale, made with roasted barley and crystal malt for a nutty, malty flavour, and Extra Pale Ale, a golden ale with a well-balanced hop and malt flavour. Both have won several awards, including a gold medal at the 1996 World Beer Cup for Extra Pale Ale. McAuslan Griffon is keen to promote cooking with its beers, and recommends using its products in recipes which include soda bread, carrot and sweet potato soup, apricot chicken pilaf with almonds, and chocolate stout mousse.

SPECIFICATIONS

Brewery: McAuslan Brewing
Location: Montreal, Quebec
Style: Pale ale
Colour: Bright, clear golden yellow
Alcohol: 5%
Serving temperature: 8°–10°C (46.4°–50°F)
Food: A hearty vegetable soup

McAuslan St-Ambroise Oatmeal Stout

Among the many awards to come the way of Toronto's McAuslan brewery has been a Platinum medal for its St-Ambroise Oatmeal Stout at the 1994 World Beer Championship, along with the second-highest rating of more than 200 beers.

A high proportion of dark malts and roasted barley give this rich black ale a powerful aroma redolent of coffee and chocolate, while the oatmeal produces a remarkably smooth and full-bodied texture. A light balancing hop bitterness, with a hint of grass in the aroma and a crisp, dry finish, makes this a very well rounded beer and surprisingly light and easy drinking.

SPECIFICATIONS

Brewery: McAuslan Brewing
Location: Montreal, Quebec
Style: Oatmeal stout
Colour: Deep opaque black
Alcohol: 5%
Serving temperature: 12°C (53.6°F)
Food: Rich chocolate cake

McAuslan St-Ambroise Pale Ale

McAuslan Brewing began its operations in 1989 in the St Henri district of Montreal and is now the leading microbrewery in the province of Quebec.

St-Ambroise Pale Ale, named after the street on which the brewery stands, was the first beer produced there, and it remains one of its most popular. It is a beer that is driven by hops, with a crisp, fresh, floral, apple-like aroma, followed by an initial citrussy hop bitterness on the palate that mellows into sweet caramel, fruity maltiness before a dry, lingering bitter finish in which hops once again take control. To celebrate the brewery's 15th anniversary in 2001 McAuslan also launched Vintage Ale. Designed to improve with keeping, this is a rich, strong and malty barley wine made with wheat and Munich malt.

SPECIFICATIONS

Brewery: McAuslan Brewing
Location: Montreal, Quebec
Style: Pale ale
Colour: Amber red
Alcohol: 5%
Serving temperature: 10°C (50°F)
Food: Bread with a strong-flavoured cheese

Molson Canadian Lager

Molson, North America's oldest brewery, produces this classic lager using only the finest hops, crystal-clear water and malted barley.

Established in 1786 by John Molson, who founded a brewery on the St Lawrence River near Montreal, Molson produces a great many popular brews. The lager is smooth, with a hint of bitterness; it is an 'easy' drink, very popular at parties, and should never be served warm. Served cold, its taste is crisp, modern and extemely refreshing.

SPECIFICATIONS

Brewery: Molson Breweries of Canada
Location: Toronto, Ontario
Style: Lager
Colour: Golden yellow
Alcohol: 5%
Serving temperature: 5°–7°C (41°–44.6°F)
Food: Cold chicken salad

Molson Rickard's Red

Rickard's Red, another offering from Molson, has remained Canada's top-selling red beer for over 10 years.

First brewed in Vancouver at the original site of the Capilano brewery in the early 1980s, Rickard's Red is made with a unique blend of three different malted barleys. The result is an unbelievably smooth and delicious red beer with exceptional drinkability. A very well balanced drink, creamy and malty, with just the right amount of flavour and carbonation to last until the end. Rickard's Red comes occupies the mid range of alcohol content in the Molson brands. At the bottom are beers such as A Marca Bavaria (4.5%) and Molson Ultra (4.5%), while climbing above Rickard's Red are the Molson Dry (5.5%) and the potent alcomalt (available in a range of flavours) Tornade (6.0%).

SPECIFICATIONS

Brewery: Molson Breweries of Canada
Location: Toronto, Ontario
Style: Dark ale
Colour: Reddish-brown
Alcohol: 5.2%
Serving temperature: 5.6°C (42°F)
Food: Roast beef or pork salad

Moosehead Lager

The history of the Moosehead Breweries, now located in Saint John, New Brunswick, began in 1867, when Susannah Oland first brewed a solitary batch of brown October ale in her backyard in neighbouring Nova Scotia.

Encouraged by friends and family, Susannah and her husband, John James Dunn Oland, began to market the beer. Since then, the firm has survived a succession of disasters, including the explosion that wrecked Halifax in 1917, to produce one of the finest premium lagers in North America. Moosehead Lager is a smooth, clean-tasting lager well balanced between malt sweetness and hop bitterness. It is brewed from a blend of Canadian Barley malt, two types of hops to balance aroma and bitterness, and fresh water from nearby Spruce Lake. The lager is then aged a full 28 days.

SPECIFICATIONS

Brewery: Moosehead Breweries Ltd
Location: St John, New Brunswick
Style: Classic American lager
Colour: Golden yellow
Alcohol: 5%
Serving temperature: 5°C (41°F)
Food: Curries

Sleeman Cream Ale

Sleeman Cream Ale was the first brand produced by the two Guelph breweries in the late nineteenth century by George Sleeman, whose ambition was to combine the qualities of a German lager with the distinctive taste of an English ale without actually combining the two.

This bottled beer has a remarkably smooth texture for a full-flavoured brew, and tastes best when only slightly chilled. Sleeman Cream Ale has a pronounced cream bite, which may be enhanced by adding some fresh lime.

SPECIFICATIONS

Brewery: Sleeman Brewing & Malting Co.
Location: Guelph, Ontario
Style: Strong ale
Colour: clear yellow
Alcohol: 5%
Serving temperature: 5°C (41°F)
Food: Cold meat pies, sandwiches

Unibroue Eau Bénite

A spicy aroma and a soft, fruity flavour characterise this Belgian-style golden triple ale, which despite its high original gravity is brewed to a relatively modest alcohol content, making it light and easy to drink.

At the other end of the flavour scale in the Unibroue range is Quelque Chose (French for 'something'), which is heavily flavoured with wild cherries that have been soaked for several months in a bitter ale before being blended into the base beer, a dark ale made with roasted whisky malts. The end result is particularly good gently heated with fruit and spices.

SPECIFICATIONS

Brewery: Unibroue
Location: Chambly, Quebec
Style: Belgian triple ale
Colour: Golden yellow
Alcohol: 7.7%
Serving temperature: 10°–12°C (50°–53.6°F)
Food: Pork with beans, or meat pies

Unibroue Blanche de Chambly

Blanche de Chambly is a naturally cloudy, unfiltered Belgian-style golden wheat beer.

Its aroma and flavour are redolent with zesty orange and lemon and light fruity malts, backed up by hints of coriander, ginger and other spices, while the high level of carbonation gives this beer a Champagne-like appearance and a spritzy mouthfeel, while light hopping provides it with a refreshingly dry finish. It comes from Unibroue in the town of Chambly in Quebec, and it is no coincidence that this brewery's products have a Franco-Belgian character as the company was founded in 1991 by Belgian-beer enthusiast André Dion, with guidance through its early stages from the highly regarded Liefmans and Riva breweries of Belgium. Unibroue is now the most successful microbrewery in the province, producing a large range of characterful bottle-conditioned beers, and has even been able to open subsidiary breweries in the United States and France. Some of its beers can even be found on sale in Belgium – tribute indeed to the way Unibroue has learned from its mentors.

SPECIFICATIONS

Brewery: Unibroue
Location: Chambly, Quebec
Style: Witbier / Belgian wheat beer
Colour: Pale golden
Alcohol: 5%
Serving temperature: 8°–10°C (46.4°–50°F)
Food: Poultry, fish and shellfish

Unibroue La Fin du Monde

Unibroue's La Fin du Monde (French for 'the end of the world') is inspired by the Belgian triple ales produced by the Trappist monks.

Traditionally, these rich, spicy ales were brewed to drink on special occasions, and this example – made with pale Pilsner malt and imported German and Belgian hops – has a typically powerful aroma of spicy hops balanced by rich fruity malt and citrus notes. On the palate, hops and malt vie for attention, although the flavour is well balanced and surprisingly subtle, enhanced with wild spices. La Fin du Monde has a smooth, creamy body and a long finish that becomes increasingly dry and bitter.

SPECIFICATIONS

Brewery: Unibroue
Location: Chambly, Quebec
Style: Belgian abbey triple
Colour: Deep golden yellow
Alcohol: 9%
Serving temperature: 14°C (57.2°F)
Food: Fine cheeses and desserts

Unibroue Raftman

Brewed using peat-smoked whisky malt, Raftman has a robust yet smooth flavour with a subtle but persistent smokiness and hints of vanilla over a background of toasty, fruity malt and a hint of hop dryness.

It is brewed, in Unibroue's own words, 'to commemorate the legendary courage of the forest workers' and is one of a range of speciality beers from Unibroue with unusual characteristics. Others include Ephémère, a green-tinged straw-coloured ale made with a blend of barley malt, wheat and Granny Smith apples, to give it a fresh green apple aroma.

SPECIFICATIONS

Brewery: Unibroue
Location: Chambly, Quebec
Style: Smoke beer
Colour: Red-brown with a coral sheen
Alcohol: 5.5%
Serving temperature: 10°–12°C (50°–53.6°F)
Food: Smoked fish and meat, and lightly spicy dishes

Upper Canada Lager

Established in 1984, the Upper Canada Brewing Company was Toronto's first microbrewery.

The public got its first taste of Upper Canada Lager, a light lager offering the rich flavour of a German Pilsner, in 1985. Unlike many contemporary lagers, Upper Canada Lager employs the traditional handcrafted lagering methods of a century ago. The result is a balanced lager of exceptional flavour: slightly sharp on the palate, but with a subtly smooth finish. Upper Canada Lager is brewed with Hallertau Nortbrau and Hersbrücker hops. Only the finest Canadian two-row pale malt is selected for each brew.

SPECIFICATIONS

Brewery: Upper Canada Brewing Company
Location: Guelph, Ontario
Style: Lager
Colour: Clear yellow
Alcohol: 4%
Serving temperature: 5°C (41°F)
Food: Bread and mature cheese with pickles

Wellington Iron Duke Strong Ale

Wellington Iron Duke is an English-style strong ale, a product of Wellington County Brewery.

SPECIFICATIONS

Brewery: Wellington County
Location: Guelph, Ontario
Style: English strong ale
Colour: Dark ruby
Alcohol: 6.5%
Serving temperature: 6°C (42.8°F)
Food: Roast beef, steak and kidney pudding, mature Cheddar

Dark ruby colour with a fully diminishing fizzy and frothy tan head, it has a dark fruit, toffee and cherry aroma, as well as dark fruit, plum, raisin, light toffee and alcohol flavours. The ale is full bodied, with a dry and lightly fizzy mouthfeel. The small head has a rather nutty taste, and the aftertaste is malty and mellow. From the start, Wellington County used some North American raw materials, but also British malts and traditional English hop varieties such as Fuggles and Goldings. The brewery's strong ale was named after the Duke of Wellington, the British military leader who defeated Napoleon at Waterloo.

Above

A new generation of craft brewers has also given a new lease of life to the traditional pub. Establishments such as this, in Seattle, Washington, now stock a huge range of flavoursome and unusual beers, both home-brewed and imported. Some notable US microbreweries featured in this book include Hale's of Seattle and Saint Arnold, based in Houston, Texas.

American Beers

The United States is the world's largest brewing nation. The story of how it arrived at this position begins in 1612, with the establishment of the first brewery by early colonial settlers. Waves of immigrants from Britain, Ireland, the Netherlands and Germany all brought a love of beer with them and set up numerous breweries, with over 4000 in operation by the late nineteenth century.

ABOVE
MacTarnahan's is one of the pioneers of the craft brewing revival in the United States.

THE IMPORTANCE OF BEER in the history of the United States cannot be overstated. Several of America's key figures in history were brewers, including George Washington and Thomas Jefferson, and British taxation imposed on colonial breweries was one of the triggers for the Revolution.

The efforts of the puritanical temperance movement led to prohibition in several states in the 1850s, although this ended with the American Civil War. Later, during World War I, prohibitionists argued that alcohol production should be banned to conserve grain. By 1919, prohibition was national, ruining most of the breweries and forcing liquor production underground. In 1933 Franklin Roosevelt was elected President on the strength of a pledge to repeal Prohibition.

After Prohibition, brewing came to be dominated by a small handful of long-established breweries. Names such as Anheuser-Busch (Budweiser) and Miller gained a dominance that they hold to this day, their beers accounting for around 80% of all domestic sales. Most of this is light lager, which has little in the way of character to distinguish one brand from the next, but since the late 1970s a new generation of enthusiasts has begun to re-establish small-scale craft brewing in the United States. Some of these new brews hark back to the traditional European beer styles brewed by their ancestors, while others are the result of a more innovative approach, producing full-flavoured modern American beers characterised by exciting use of new varieties of hops. Compared to 1980, when there were fewer than 100 breweries in the United States, the industry is now flourishing, with well over 1000 microbreweries, ranging from tiny brewpubs producing beer for consumption on the premises to larger concerns with the capacity to distribute their beers across the nation. Some breweries, such as Anchor and Sierra-Nevada in California and Sam Adams in New York, are even gaining a foothold in foreign markets.

STATISTICS

Total production: 232,216,000 hectolitres (6,134,498,000 gallons) per year

Consumption per capita: 84 litres (22 gallons) per year

Famous breweries: Anheuser-Busch; August Schell Brewing Co.; Boston Beer Co.; Brooklyn Brewery; Coors Brewing Co.; Latrobe Brewing Co,; SAB Miller; Stoudt's Brewing Co.

Famous brands: Budweiser; Coors Original; Miller Genuine Draft; Michelob; Milwaukee's Best; Pabst Old Style; Rolling Rock; Samuel Adams Boston Lager

Anchor Steam Beer

The Anchor Brewery dates back to 1896, but nearly went out of business in the 1960s, a difficult period when traditional hand-made beers from small-scale craft breweries were unfashionable and at risk of dying out altogether.

Fortunately, a well-heeled student by the name of Fritz Maytag stepped in to rescue his favourite beer. He soon moved it to its current premises in an elegant 1930s coffee warehouse and installed traditional hand-built copper brewing equipment. The brewery's flagship beer is the same one that it first brewed in 1896, a distinctive local style known as steam beer that was popularised by Californian gold prospectors in the late 1800s. Early steam beers were brewed with lager yeasts, but fermented at warmer temperatures due to the lack of means to cool the tanks in California's warm climate. Cooling was brought about by the use of wide, shallow fermenting vessels. The resulting beer was very lively and, when the casks were tapped, they were said to 'steam' with carbon dioxide. Throughout most of the twentieth century, Anchor was the only company brewing steam beer (the term is now an Anchor trademark), although a number of other breweries are now helping to revive the style.

An earthy malt character dominates the aroma, while on the palate an initial burst of sharp, citric hop bitterness mellows as the well-balanced light fruity, caramel malt background flavours come through before giving way to a dry, bitter finish. Its clean, crisp flavours and light refreshing fruitiness make this an ideal beer for quaffing.

SPECIFICATIONS

Brewery: Anchor Brewing
Location: San Francisco, California
Style: Californian steam beer
Colour: Bright, golden amber
Alcohol: 4.9%
Serving temperature: 8°–10°C (46.4°–50°F)
Food: Simply grilled fish

Anchor Liberty Ale

San Francisco's Anchor Brewing produces a range of seven regular and seasonal ales. One of its most popular is Liberty Ale, which was first brewed in 1975 to commemorate the bicentennial of the famous ride made by Paul Revere in 1775 that marked the start of the American War of Independence.

It became a regular fixture in the Anchor repertoire in 1983. American pale ales are inspired by classic British bitters; typically a bright, clear bronze or copper colour and well flavoured with hops to give them a characteristically dry flavour. Liberty Ale is a fine example of the style, with a rich, complex aroma redolent with floral, resiny, citric hops combined with sweet, biscuity malts. The flavour is dominated by slightly astringent hops balanced with light, fruity maltiness, and the finish is dry and refreshing with hints of lemon zest. Other beers in the Anchor range include a special Christmas Ale, which is brewed to a different top-secret recipe every year, and a heavily hopped barley wine called Old Foghorn. Anchor Small is a vestige of the ancient English tradition of sparging a mash (sprinkling it with warm water) after the first batch of wort has run off, to produce a second brew.

SPECIFICATIONS

Brewery: Anchor Brewing Co.
Location: San Francisco, California
Style: American pale ale
Colour: Clear amber
Alcohol: 6.1%
Serving temperature: 10°C (50°F)
Food: Steak and ale pie

Alaskan Smoked Porter

In 1881, gold prospectors arrived in the Alaskan town of Juneau seeking their fortune and it didn't take long before several breweries sprang up in the town. Between 1899 and 1907 the Douglas City Brewing Company produced a beer called Alaskan Amber that proved to be very popular.

The brewery was forced to close when the prospectors moved on to the next strike, and the beer was lost until 1986 when the Chinook Alaskan Brewing Company was established, using the original Alaskan Amber recipe for its first beer, a dry, malty altbier. The company now produces a range of regular and seasonal beers, including this highly individual Smoked Porter. The malt is roasted over alder wood at a nearby smoked salmon processing plant, picking up a smoky flavour that gives the finished beer great depth and complexity. The smokiness is apparent in the aroma, along with dark fruit and caramel, plus a hint of briny oiliness. On the palate, it feels rich and creamy, and the roasted malts give it a bitter chocolate, coffee and burnt fruit character. Alaskan Smoked Porter is brewed in a small quantity every autumn.

SPECIFICATIONS

Brewery: Alaskan Brewing Company
Location: Juneau, Alaska
Style: Smoke beer
Colour: Opaque dark mahogany brown, almost black
Alcohol: 5.9%
Serving temperature: 12°C (53.6°F)
Food: Smoked fish

Budweiser

Self-styled as the 'King of Beers', Budweiser is the single largest-selling beer brand in the world, a title it has held since 1957.

It is the epitome of smooth, easy-drinking American lager, brewed using rice as well as malt, and only lightly hopped, to create a beer with a crisp, clean, refreshing taste. Extra smoothness is achieved by maturation over beechwood chips for a period of four weeks. For a beer so light in flavour it is surprisingly strong, coming in at just under 5% alcohol by volume. Budweiser was launched in 1876, and Budweiser beer was named after the small Czech brewing town of Budweiser, a decision that has in recent years been at the heart of a bitter rights battle with the tiny, independent Czech brewer Budvar, which also calls its beer Budweiser. What's more, by coincidence, the Czech Budweiser is subtitled 'Beer of Kings'.

SPECIFICATIONS

Brewery: Anheuser-Busch
Location: St Louis, Missouri
Style: Lager
Colour: Pale straw colour
Alcohol: 4.9%
Serving temperature: 6°–8°C (42.8°–46.4°F)
Food: Burger and fries

August Schell Doppel Bock

A large part of the population of the Minnesota town of New Ulm can claim to have German roots. It is therefore hardly surprising that such a characteristically German style of beer should be brewed here.

A seasonal beer available from January to March every year, the Doppel Bock – recognised by its distrinctive double drinking ram label – is a strong, dark amber-coloured double bock made with a blend of five different malts and three varieties of hops and matured in cold storage ('lagered') for a full 12 weeks. The end product is a smooth, rich malty beer with a long malty finish balanced by dry, citric hoppiness. It is a particularly powerful brew, with an alcohol content of 6.8%.

SPECIFICATIONS

Brewery: August Schell Brewing Co.
Location: New Ulm, Minnesota
Style: Double bock
Colour: Dark amber
Alcohol: 6.8%
Serving temperature: 9°C (48.2°F)
Food: Salty French fries

August Schell FireBrick

The August Schell brewery, the second-oldest brewery in the United States, was founded in 1860 and is still run by members of the Schell family to this day.

Its beers are hand-crafted according to traditional methods and styles, including being brewed in 100-year-old kettles. Schell's Original is a pale lager that has been brewed to the same recipe for over 140 years. Schell FireBrick is a more recent addition, launched in 1999 and named after the bricks that line the brewery's old boilers. This Viennese-style amber-red lager is a highly drinkable beer with a pleasantly mild, sweet malty flavour and a light hoppy finish. It is produced from a mix of four speciality malts and Vanguard, Chinook and Hallertau hops.

SPECIFICATIONS

Brewery: August Schell Brewing Co.
Location: New Ulm, Minnesota
Style: Vienna red lager
Colour: Amber-red
Alcohol: 5%
Serving temperature: 8°–10°C (46.4°–50°F)
Food: Mild smoked cheese

Bear Republic Hop Rod Rye

Bear Republic started out as a small home-brewing outfit run by Richard Norgrove and his wife, Tami, at their home in Healdsburg, California.

They soon realised that in order to be able to develop the kind of beers they were interested in they needed to increase the scale of their operation, and so with the aid of Richard's parents the Bear Republic Brew Pub and Restaurant was opened. All the beers are hand-crafted using traditional brewing methods and ingredients carefully selected by Richard himself. Hop Rod Rye is a strong American-style IPA made with 20% rye malt. The extremely high hop content gives this beer an IBU (International Bitterness Units) rating of more than 90, making it around twice as bitter as a typical English-style IPA, but while the hops certainly dominate both the aroma and the flavour with their citrus and piney resin notes, they are not overwhelming, and this remains a well-balanced beer with hints of caramel and luscious berry fruits, while the rye adds a spicy element.

Hops play a large part in several of Bear Republic's other beers, including its Red Rocket Ale, a full-bodied Scottish red ale made with Belgian malts and given aroma and bitterness with Centennial and Cascade hops. This beer won a silver medal at the 1999 Great American Beer Festival, one of many awards won by Bear Republic.

SPECIFICATIONS

Brewery: Bear Republic Brewing Co.
Location: Healdsburg, California
Style: American IPA
Colour: Deep mahogany red-brown
Alcohol: 7.5%
Serving temperature: 12°C (53.6°F)
Food: Rich, spicy food

Bert Grant's Fresh Hop Ale

Grant's Brewery Pub, founded by Scottish-born Bert Grant, was the first brewpub to be opened in the United States following the repeal of prohibition legislation and is widely regarded as the home of modern American craft brewing, reintroducing long-lost classic beer styles to the nation.

His famous Imperial Stout, for example, is a deeply complex ale with roasted coffee and chocolate balanced with hops and a touch of sweetness. The brewery is situated in Yakima, which is the leading hop-growing region in the United States, producing 80% of all hops used in brewing in the country, and Bert Grant himself is one of the leading experts on the subject of hops. All his extensive know-how has been poured into creating this Fresh Hop Ale, which is made, as the name suggests, with fresh Cascade hops straight from the vine, plunged into the brew kettle just 20 minutes after being picked. This gives the beer a very fresh floral aroma and a somewhat 'green' flavour, reminiscent of grass, leaves and even a hint of mint.

SPECIFICATIONS

Brewery: Bert Grant's Ales / Yakima Brewing Co.
Location: Yakima, Washington
Style: Pale ale
Colour: Copper
Alcohol: 5.2%
Serving temperature: 10°–12°C (50°–53.6°F)
Food: Irish stew

Bert Grant's Lazy Days

Another of Bert Grant's award-winning seasonal beers, Lazy Days is a light, refreshing ale designed for summer drinking, as reflected in the sunny beach scene depicted on the beer's label.

Mild buttery malt and a hint of hops come through in the aroma, while the palate is given a dose of light, grainy malts balanced against a gentle bitterness and the lemon character of Amarillo hops. The companion beer for winter is Grant's Deep Powder, a rich, robust and warming dark beer with a deep, chocolatey flavour and a hint of spice.

SPECIFICATIONS

Brewery: Bert Grant's Ales / Yakima Brewing Co.
Location: Yakima, Washington
Style: American pale ale
Colour: Golden amber
Alcohol: 5%
Serving temperature: 8°C (46.4°F)
Food: Ham or chicken salad

Breckenridge Trademark Pale

The original Breckenridge Brewery was founded in the 1990 in the ski-resort town of the same name in Colorado's Rocky Mountains.

Breckenridge's beers are now brewed at three locations, the main site now being the Breckenridge Brewpub in downtown Denver, which opened in 1996 and unusually has the brewery open to view in the middle of the pub. Trademark Pale is one of the original recipes created by the brewery's founder, Richard Squire. Brewed with three kinds of malt and five varieties of hops, this is a well-balanced and easy-drinking beer which possesses a soft maltiness and sweet floral hop notes.

SPECIFICATIONS

Brewery: Breckenridge Brewery
Location: Denver, Colorado
Style: American pale ale
Colour: Deep golden
Alcohol: 5%
Serving temperature: 10°–12°C (50°–53.6°F)
Food: Shepherd's pie

Brooklyn Black Chocolate Stout

Throughout the nineteenth century Brooklyn was home to a great number of breweries, many set up by German immigrants who brought their brewing traditions with them when they settled in the United States. Prohibition of the 1920s had a devastating effect on the brewing industry, from which it never fully recovered, and the last remaining brewery in Brooklyn closed in 1976.

Then in 1987 former foreign correspondent Steve Hindy and former banker Tom Potter got together to establish the Brooklyn Brewery. In 1996 it moved to its present site in the artistic Williamsburg district, occupying a former steel foundry building, and has since been at the forefront of the New York brewing renaissance. This immensely powerful black stout, the brewery's seasonal winter beer, is as black and opaque as oil. Aromas of roasted mocha coffee, bitter chocolate and roasted malt are followed on the palate by a smooth, rich, spicy malt character with a hint of caramel sweetness and a dry, subtly bitter hop finish. A deeply warming 8.3% alcohol keeps out the winter chill, but despite its strength this is a very drinkable beer. The brewery's first beer was an unfiltered, fruity flavoured Bavarian-style wheat beer called Brooklyner Weisse, and today it produces a wide range of regular and seasonal beers, including the award-winning East India Pale Ale, noted for its intensely dry hop flavour.

SPECIFICATIONS

Brewery: Brooklyn Brewery
Location: Brooklyn, New York
Style: Russian imperial stout
Colour: Black
Alcohol: 8.3%
Serving temperature: 13°C (55.4°F)
Food: Chocolate-based desserts

BridgePort India Pale Ale

Founded in 1984 as Columbia River Brewing, BridgePort is the oldest established craft brewery in the Pacific Northwest city of Portland, one of the focal points of American microbrewing.

No fewer than five varieties of hop are used in this award-winning India Pale Ale – Cascade, Chinook, Golding, Crystal and Northwest Ultra. It is a creamy, rich and full-flavoured beer naturally conditioned in the bottle to give it a resiny hop aroma with grapefruit notes, a robust hoppy palate with hints of vanilla and orange fruit, and an intensely bitter hop finish.

SPECIFICATIONS

Brewery: BridgePort Brewing Company
Location: Portland, Oregon
Style: India pale ale
Colour: Pale amber-gold
Alcohol: 5.5%
Serving temperature: 12°C (53.6°F)
Food: Duck in orange sauce

BridgePort Old Knucklehead

As a beer is not a wine, the authorities have dictated that the traditional term 'barley wine' be replaced with 'barley wine style ale' to describe beers such as BridgePort's Old Knucklehead, a brewery tradition since 1989.

Brewed with double the usual amount of malts and four varieties of hops, it is a strong, complex, warming ale with an assertively fruity malt character balanced against spicy hop flavours. The annual Knucklehead vintage is released every November in a bottle bearing the image of the current holder of the honorary title Knucklehead, which changes every few years. The eleventh vintage features the face of craft brewing pioneer Fred Eckhardt.

SPECIFICATIONS

Brewery: BridgePort Brewing Company
Location: Portland, Oregon
Style: Barley wine
Colour: Deep red-brown
Alcohol: 9.1%
Serving temperature: 13°C (55.4°F)
Food: Sausage casserole

Celis White

Few brewers can claim to have been a major influence on brewing in two different countries, never mind two countries as significant in world brewing as Belgium and the United States, but that is exactly what Pierre Celis has done. Celis, who learned the art of brewing as a child living next door to the Tomsin brewery, started brewing in the Belgian town of Hoegaarden in 1966, producing the famous cloudy wheat beer of that name, flavoured with herbs and spices.

Following the sale of the Hoegaarden brewery to Interbrew (now InBev), Celis moved to the United States to take part in the brewing revolution that was introducing more characterful beers to a nation raised on bland lager. Celis White is close to the original Hoegaarden (qv) recipe, brewed with coriander spice and orange peel for a light, refreshing taste. As is appropriate for an authentic Belgian wheat beer, the beer pours with a natural cloudy haze and a deep foaming head. Celis White went out of production for a few years, but has recently been revived by the Michigan Brewing Company with the blessing of Celis himself. The reborn Celis White won a gold medal at the 2003 Great American Beer Festival. The Michigan Brewing Company, founded in 1995 in Webberville, has won great respect for its own range of fine craft-brewed beers, including the well-balanced Mackinac Pale Ale, a classic English-style refreshing bitter.

SPECIFICATIONS

Brewery: Michigan Brewing Company
Location: Webberville, Michigan
Style: Belgian wheat beer
Colour: Hazy copper-orange
Alcohol: 4.9%
Serving temperature: 8°–10° C (46.4°–50°F)
Food: Spicy American-style pizza

Climax Extra Special Bitter Ale

The original ESB was created by London brewery Fuller's, but the popularity of the style in the United States has seen many imitations produced by the new generation of small craft brewers.

This deliciously smooth, fruity version comes from the Climax brewery, one of New Jersey's first microbreweries, founded in 1996 in Roselle Park, south of Newark. Like all the brewery's beers, it is hand-crafted in small batches using a blend of domestic and imported Belgian malts. Others in the range include a mild, malty Nut Brown Ale and an intensely hoppy IPA.

SPECIFICATIONS

Brewery: Climax Brewing Company
Location: Roselle Park, New Jersey
Style: Strong bitter / extra special bitter
Colour: Bright copper-orange
Alcohol: 5.5%
Serving temperature: 10°–12°C (50°–53.6°F)
Food: Summer fruits pudding

Coors Original

The Coors brewery in Golden, Colorado, is the largest single brewing site in the world. It was founded in 1873 by the 26-year-old German immigrant brewer Adolph Coors on a site chosen for the cool, clear Rocky Mountain spring water that flowed nearby.

Coors Original has a sweet malty aroma and a smooth, grainy flavour, and the beer took gold medals at the Great American Beer Festival in both 1996 and 2004. Coors Extra Gold is a full-flavoured lager brewed with lightly roasted malts, and the latest addition to the range is Aspen Edge, a crisp, light-flavoured low-carbohydrate beer. Another beer in the Coors range is Blue Moon, defined by the company as 'an unfiltered wheat ale spiced in the Belgian tradition for an uncommonly smooth taste'. In 2002, Coors bought a large part of Bass from Interbrew to become the second largest brewer in the United Kingdom and one of the top 10 brewers in the world.

SPECIFICATIONS

Brewery: Coors Brewing Company
Location: Golden, Colorado
Style: Lager
Colour: Pale gold
Alcohol: 5%
Serving temperature: 8°C (46.4°F)
Food: Risotto and pasta

Killian's Irish Red

George Killian Lett began brewing his famous Irish red ale in his home town of Enniscorthy, Ireland, in 1864.

The Lett's brewery closed in the 1950s, but the name lives on in this version of his beer created by Coors, which was launched in 1981. Unlike the original Killian's, a top-fermented ale made with ruby malts, this is a bottom-fermented lager with a fruity, slightly sweet malt aroma and flavour. Killian's is one of Coors' speciality premium brands, along with Blue Moon, an unfiltered Belgian-style cloudy wheat beer with a refreshingly fruity, spicy flavour. Alcohol content is kept at a very respectable 4.9%. Popular beer reviews tend to give the Irish Red a high rating, and many also attest that the beer is eminently suited to drinking with spicy Indian, Thai or Chinese food. The distinctive Irish Red bottle has its ancestry in the bottle used by Lett to hold his original amber lager, and it forms an attractive addition to any collection.

SPECIFICATIONS

Brewery: Coors Brewing Company
Location: Golden, Colorado
Style: Dark lager
Colour: Deep golden amber
Alcohol: 4.9%
Serving temperature: 8°–10° C (46.4°–50°F)
Food: Spicy Indian, Thai and Chinese cuisine

Full Sail Ale

Full Sail Ale, a seven-time gold medal winner at the World Beer Championships, is a superbly balanced amber-coloured pale ale.

Rich malty aromas with background hints of hops are followed by a medium malty body on the palate, ending with a long, dry, spicy, floral hop finish balanced by an underlying malty sweetness. It comes from one of the leading craft brewers in the United States, which has been making beer since 1987 at its scenic site in the Columbia River Gorge, where the Hood and Columbia rivers meet. From its small origins in the former Diamond Fruit Cannery, Full Sail has expanded to become one of the largest businesses in the region. As well as its three regular beers – the others being Pale Ale and Rip Curl – Full Sail produces four seasonal beers, among them the warming Wassail Ale. In 2003, following an agreement with Miller, Full Sail began brewing some of that company's Henry Weinhard brands.

SPECIFICATIONS

Brewery: Full Sail Brewing Co.
Location: Hood River, Oregon
Style: American amber ale
Colour: Reddish amber
Alcohol: 5.5%
Serving temperature: 10°C (50°F)
Food: Pies and fries

Great Lakes Dortmunder Gold

This smooth, well-balanced and full-bodied lager is typical of the strong 'export' lager that became popular in Dortmund, Germany, in the mid-nineteenth century, when seven different breweries simultaneously started brewing the style.

A Dortmunder tends to be less dry than a Pilsner, but more hoppy than a pale Munich lager, and it is stronger than either. This multiple award-winning example of the style, full bodied with a deep golden colour and a grainy dry malt flavour, comes from the Great Lakes brewery and dining pub, which was founded in downtown Cleveland in 1988. The pub is said to have been popular in a previous incarnation with Cleveland's most famous resident, the 'untouchable' Eliot Ness, in whose honour the brewery has created a fragrant, full-bodied and malty amber Vienna-style lager. Several of Great Lake's other beers have won many awards in national and international competition. The Edmund Fitzgerald Porter, named after a ship which sank in 1975 with many Clevelanders on board, has twice won a gold medal at the Great American Beer Festival. It has a complex, roasty malt aroma with dry, bittersweet flavours of chocolate and coffee. Among the brewery's seasonal beers, its Christmas Ale is highly popular, brewed with cinnamon and ginger for a truly festive spicy flavour, with honey added for extra strength and complexity.

SPECIFICATIONS

Brewery: Great Lakes Brewing Co.
Location: Cleveland, Ohio
Style: Dortmunder export
Colour: Deep golden amber
Alcohol: 5.6%
Serving temperature: 9°C (48.2°F)
Food: Salads, fish and chicken

Geary's Pale Ale

One of the early pioneers of craft brewing in the United States, David Geary learned his trade during spells at various British breweries, including Ringwood in Hampshire, southern England, before setting up his own brewery back home in Portland, Maine.

He produces three regular beers available all year round – Pale Ale, London Porter and American Ale – plus two seasonal beers – Hampshire Special Ale and Summer Ale. Geary's Pale Ale is a classic, smooth, full bodied and full of big malty flavours with hints of zesty orange fruit and a refreshingly dry, bitter hop finish.

SPECIFICATIONS

- **Brewery:** Geary's Brewing Co.
- **Location:** Portland, Maine
- **Style:** English pale ale
- **Colour:** Bright, clear copper
- **Alcohol:** 4.5%
- **Serving temperature:** 12°C (53.6°F)
- **Food:** Salad and cold meats

Hale's O'Brien's Harvest Ale

Mike Hale's microbrewery and pub has led the way in introducing classic British beer styles to northwest United States for 20 years. His inspiration was a holiday in 1981 which was spent cycling around southern England, sampling the local beers.

After returning to the United States, he decided to set up his own brewery, releasing his first beer – Hale's Pale Ale – on Independence Day 1983. Alongside Hale's year-round beers are four changing seasonal beers – for the autumn, the line-up is completed by O'Brien's Harvest Ale, a beer that celebrates the hop harvest with the use of freshly picked hops grown nearby in central Washington. It is a distinctively rich and flavourful beer with a sweet, fruity aroma and a dry, floral hop flavour. Mike Hale's love of all things English has led to him refurbishing an old red London bus, which he uses to promote his beers.

SPECIFICATIONS

- **Brewery:** Hale's Ales Brewery & Pub
- **Location:** Seattle, Washington
- **Style:** Strong ale
- **Colour:** Copper-red
- **Alcohol:** 4.5%
- **Serving temperature:** 12°C (53.6°F)
- **Food:** Stews and casseroles

Hair of the Dog Adam

The tiny Hair of the Dog microbrewery was founded in 1993, inspired by a talk on extinct beer styles by the brewing historian Fred Eckhardt.

Its first beer was a re-creation of a long-lost style known as Adambier, a strong, dark top-fermented ale that was brewed in Dortmund, Germany in the middle of the nineteenth century. Famously, when King Frederick William IV of Prussia visited Dortmund and was presented with a tankard of this immensely strong ale, he downed it in a single gulp and passed out. The legend runs that such was the power of the beer that he remained unconscious for a full 24 hours. No one today knows for sure what the original Adam beers were like, but this interpretation is a rich, peppery and full-bodied, almost syrup-like, beer with a complex flavour of roasted coffee and chocolate. It is given a lengthy period of maturation and is unfiltered to allow natural conditioning in the bottle. Other beers in the brewery's limited range are also given names more commonly associated with people than beer. Fred, named in honour of Fred Eckhardt, is an aromatic deep golden lager made with rye malt and 10 different varieties of hops. Ruth is a light and refreshing ale named after the grandmother of brewery founder Alan Sprints, while Rose is a fruity Belgian-style triple named after the brewery's home city of Portland, Oregon, 'the Rose City'.

SPECIFICATIONS

Brewery: Hair of the Dog Brewing Co.
Location: Portland, Oregon
Style: Adam beer / old ale
Colour: Dark chocolate brown, almost black
Alcohol: 10%
Serving temperature: 12°–14°C (53.6°–57.2°F)
Food: Chocolate-based desserts

Left Hand Black Jack Porter

The Left Hand and Tabernash breweries both opened in the Colorado town of Longmont, 48km (30 miles) north of Denver, in 1993 and merged their operations in 1998, although the two brands retain distinct identities.

While Tabernash beers have a traditional German character, Left Hand ales follow English styles. This multiple award-winning Black Jack Porter is a robust, full-bodied beer with a rich roasted malt flavour and hints of chocolate. An initial sweetness on the palate is balanced by a judicious dose of Kent Goldings hops that give it a smooth, dry finish. Many porters are heavy drinks which can only be sustained in moderate amounts. Black Jack Porter is no slouch itself, the alcohol content standing as it does at 6.8%, but it has a drinkability which means it can be sustained as the sole beverage for a night sipping in front of the fire.

SPECIFICATIONS

Brewery: Left Hand & Tabernash Brewing Co
Location: Longmont, Colorado
Style: English porter
Colour: Dark brown, almost black
Alcohol: 5.8%
Serving temperature: 13°C (55.4°F)
Food: Sticky toffee pudding

Left Hand Sawtooth Ale

Sawtooth Ale is a strong English-style bitter, brewed with hard water to re-create the distinctive mineral character of the famous pale ales of the city of Burton-upon-Trent in the English Midlands.

It is a well-balanced, medium-bodied beer with a moderately sweet malt aroma, contrasting with a pronounced hoppy sharpness on the palate over a soothingly fruity, nutty malt background, leading to a refreshingly crisp, citrussy, bitter finish. The malty texture of the beer emerges more clearly as the beer warms itself towards room temperature. Also in the Left Hand brewery's range is a rare example of an English-style milk stout, made with lactose for an extra sweet, creamy and mild flavour.

SPECIFICATIONS

Brewery: Left Hand & Tabernash Brewing Co
Location: Longmont, Colorado
Style: Strong bitter / extra special bitter
Colour: Dark amber
Alcohol: 4.75%
Serving temperature: 10°–12°C (50°–53.6°F)
Food: Peanuts and crisps

Leinenkugel's Red Lager

'Leinie's' started in 1867 when Jacob Leinenkugel, the son of an immigrant German brewer, set up the Spring Brewery to provide beer for Chippewa Fall's local brigade of thirsty lumberjacks.

Though it is now owned by Miller, the brewery still has connections with the Leinenkugel family and remains one of the most popular beer brands in the region. Its flagship beer is this traditional full-bodied dark Munich-style lager, made with roasted caramel malts for a mellow yet malty flavour, balanced by a subtle dry bitterness provided by two varieties of hops.

SPECIFICATIONS

Brewery: Jacob Leinenkugel Brewing Company
Location: Chippewa Falls, Wisconsin
Style: Munich dark lager
Colour: Deep ruby red
Alcohol: 4.9%
Serving temperature: 6°–8°C (42.8°–46.4°F)
Food: Pancakes

MacTarnahan's Mac's Amber Ale

Founded in 1986, MacTarnahan's is one of the pioneers of the craft brewing revival in the United States. It was named after the brewery's patriarchal figurehead 'Mac' MacTarnahan, now in his eighties, but still involved with the business of brewing.

His award-winning signature beer is a rich, smooth, full-bodied, amber-coloured ale with a sweet, roasted, caramel malt flavour tempered with citrussy, floral Cascade hops. It also claims to include a secret ingredient that gives it an especially Scottish character – could this secret ingredient perhaps be the brewery's own single-malt scotch whisky?

SPECIFICATIONS

Brewery: MacTarnahan's Brewing Company / Portland Brewing Co
Location: Portland, Oregon
Style: Scottish amber ale
Colour: Deep amber red
Alcohol: 4.2%
Serving temperature: 10°–13°C (50°–55.4°F)
Food: Grilled and smoked meats, such as beef, lamb or venison

MacTarnahan's Uncle Otto's Oktoberfest

MacTarnahan's plays heavily on its Scottish heritage with tartan-liveried packaging and beers with names such as Black Watch Porter and Highlander Pale Ale, which is infused with a hint of Scottish heather to give it a slightly sweet herbal flavour.

However, for this seasonal favourite, a gold-medal winner at the 2001 Great American Beer Festival, the brewery looks to Germany for inspiration, re-creating the strong dark lager traditionally drunk at Munich's Oktoberfest. It has a sweet malty aroma and a full-bodied, assertively malty palate with nutty, caramel and raisin flavours and a gentle hop finish.

SPECIFICATIONS

Brewery: MacTarnahan's Brewing Co / Portland Brewing Co
Location: Portland, Oregon
Style: Märzen / Oktoberfest
Colour: Copper-red
Alcohol: 6%
Serving temperature: 10°–12°C (50°–53.6°F)
Food: Hot dogs

Magic Hat Blind Faith IPA

While many of the new generation of craft breweries in the United States aim to create a traditional image, Magic Hat prefers a distinctly alternative New Age style with labels that reflect the brewery's mystical philosophy and spirituality.

The Blind Faith is a fine example of the India pale ale style with a powerful malty aroma and pungently spicy hop flavours dominating on the palate over a smooth, full-bodied caramel malt background. During brewing, the beer is dry hopped with Cascade hops to give it a refreshingly bitter 'bite' in the finish. Magic Hat brews an extraordinarily wide range of regular and seasonal beers, such as Mother Lager, an authentic German-style Pilsner marketed with revolutionary propaganda, the unusual and refreshingly fruity '9', described on the label simply as 'not quite pale ale', and Miss Bliss, which is brewed with malted rye and spiced with coriander and orange peel.

SPECIFICATIONS

Brewery: Magic Hat Brewing Company
Location: South Burlington, Vermont
Style: India pale ale
Colour: Deep golden amber
Alcohol: 5.6%
Serving temperature: 10°–13°C (50°–55.4°F)
Food: Caramel puddings

Michelob

Michelob was launched by Anheuser-Busch in 1896, marketed as a 'draught beer for connoisseurs', a 'premium' beer alternative to its mainstream Budweiser brand.

Like Budweiser, Michelob is named after a famous old brewing town in the former Bohemia, now part of the Czech Republic. It is brewed with a higher percentage of two-row barley malt and imported hops to create a fuller-bodied beer with a mouth-filling richness. It has a light, sweet malty aroma, and the mild, grainy sweet malt flavour also dominates on the palate, backed up with a gentle hop astringency without any bitterness. The finish is crisp and refreshing.

SPECIFICATIONS

Brewery: Anheuser-Busch
Location: St Louis, Missouri
Style: Lager
Colour: Pale straw colour
Alcohol: 5%
Serving temperature: 6°–9°C (42.8°–48.2°F)
Food: Cooked meats and sausages

Michelob Ultra

Created directly in response to the fashion for low-carbohydrate diets, Michelob Ultra bears a label that proudly proclaims just 95 calories and 2.6 grams of carbohydrates per bottle.

The low-calorie content of Michelob Ultra attests to the brewery's reach to non-traditional beer consumers, particularly women, who typically want a lighter beverage. The reduced carbohydrate level is achieved by using a carefully selected blend of grains in the mash, including a proportion of Munich malt, as well as a specially chosen strain of yeast. The result is a smooth, light-flavoured lager. It is also pitched fairly low down the alcohol scale, coming in at only 4.2%. Michelob Ultra is part of a 'family' of beers that also includes Michelob Honey Lager, a full-bodied, floral-scented lager flavoured with a touch of honey, and Michelob Amber Bock, a rich, hearty, malty dark bock-style beer.

SPECIFICATIONS

Brewery: Anheuser-Busch
Location: St Louis, Missouri
Style: Low-carbohydrate lager
Colour: Pale golden yellow
Alcohol: 4.2%
Serving temperature: 6°–9°C (42.8°–48.2°F)
Food: Grilled steak

Miller Genuine Draft

Frederick John Miller started brewing in his native Germany in 1849 before emigrating to the United States, where in 1855 he bought the Plank Road Brewery in Milwaukee and started brewing beer using yeast that he had brought with him from Germany.

Miller has gone on to become the United States' second-largest brewer. Miller Genuine Draft is produced at Miller's state-of-the-art brewing facility in Eden, North Carolina, using an exclusive cold-filtering process. It has a light, grainy malt aroma, a slightly sweet and sharp flavour and a smooth, dry, lightly hopped finish.

SPECIFICATIONS

Brewery: SAB Miller
Location: Milwaukee, Wisconsin
Style: Lager
Colour: Bright, clear golden yellow
Alcohol: 4.6%
Serving temperature: 6°–8°C (42.8°–46.4°F)
Food: Barbecued meats

Miller High Life

Subtitled 'the Champagne of beers', Miller High Life was first launched in 1903.

Its immediate widespread popularity was largely responsible for the fast growth of the company in the early part of the twentieth century, which enabled Miller to survive the prohibition period while many other breweries failed. It remains Miller's premium brand 100 years later and is still the same medium-bodied, refreshing and very drinkable beer. Soft, sweet malty aromas on the nose are followed by smooth, sweet malty flavours and a slightly creamy texture on the palate balanced with a moderate hop bitterness.

SPECIFICATIONS

Brewery: SAB Miller
Location: Milwaukee, Wisconsin
Style: Lager
Colour: Pale golden yellow
Alcohol: 5%
Serving temperature: 6°–8°C (42.8°–46.4°F)
Food: Ham sandwiches

Milwaukee's Best

Aside from its three core brands – Miller Lite, High Life and Genuine Draft – Miller also owns a number of other beer brands, including 'Leinie's' speciality German beers and Henry Weinhard of Oregon, whose beers are currently brewed under licence by the Full Sail Brewing Company.

Closer to home, Milwaukee's Best was first brewed in 1895 by the A. Gettlman Brewing Company of Milwaukee and purchased by Miller in 1956. It has a fruity malt aroma with a light, clean, refreshing flavour. Many reviewers also point out the beer's cheap price tag, which is perhaps reflected in the 4.3% alcohol content. Indeed, the brewery's website describes the beer as 'Miller Brewing Company's lead brand in the economy beer segment'. However, it is a beer that has won many converts, not least because its low cost makes it ideal for kitting out everything from student parties to family barbecues.

SPECIFICATIONS

Brewery: SAB Miller
Location: Milwaukee, Wisconsin
Style: Lager
Colour: Pale golden straw colour
Alcohol: 4.3%
Serving temperature: 6°–8°C (42.8°–46.4°F)
Food: Curries

North Coast Ruedrich's Red Seal Ale

Mark Ruedrich is the brewmaster of the North Coast Brewing company and it is his job to devise the recipes for most of the brewery's beers.

The full-bodied copper-red ale that bears Ruedrich's name is a fitting testament to his craft, providing a fine balance of fruity malt and bitter hop flavours on the palate, while generous hopping provides a long, dry, spicy finish. The popularity of this particular beer is one of the reasons why North Coast has been named one of the ten best breweries in the world by the Beverage Testing Institute in Chicago.

SPECIFICATIONS

Brewery: North Coast Brewing Co.
Location: Fort Bragg, California
Style: Pale ale
Colour: Amber
Alcohol: 5.5%
Serving temperature: 10°C (50°F)
Food: Fish pie

New Belgium Fat Tire Amber Ale

Returning home to Colorado following a cycling holiday in Belgium, Jeff Lebesch had been so impressed with the Belgian beers he sampled that he tried to re-create them for himself. And so in 1991 the New Belgium brewery was launched, operating from a small plant in the basement of Jeff's home, with his wife, Kathy, running the marketing side of the business and an artistic neighbour providing labels for the bottles. Fat Tire Amber Ale is named after the bike ride that started it all and was the first beer to come out of the brewery.

This rich, complex amber ale exhibits toasty malt flavours balanced against crisp, citric hoppiness and has a smooth, well-rounded texture. The brewery's range also includes 1554, a rare example of a Brussels-style black ale, which has the blackness of stout, but is in fact a refreshingly zesty lager, and the highly unusual Transatlantique Kriek, a blended ale made with authentic imported Belgian lambic (beer that is spontaneously fermented with wild yeast) and flavoured with Polish cherries. With these pioneering beer styles, it is no wonder that the brewery soon enjoyed great success and by 1995 the brewery had outgrown Jeff's basement. New premises were built, designed according to environmentally friendly principles – and in 1998 New Belgium became the first wind-powered brewery in the United States.

SPECIFICATIONS

Brewery: New Belgium Brewing Company Inc.
Location: Fort Collins, Colorado
Style: Amber ale
Colour: Bright copper-brown
Alcohol: 5.3%
Serving temperature: 12°C (53.6°F)
Food: Spicy grilled fish or meat dishes

New Glarus Wisconsin Belgian Red

Unlike many fruit beers that are flavoured with preserved fruit or syrups, this Belgian-style wheat beer has whole locally grown Montmorency cherries added during brewing to give it the finished product a genuine cherry flavour and colour.

This is hardly surprising, as New Glarus is a brewery that does not take shortcuts. After brewing, the Belgian Red is given a lengthy period of maturation in oak tanks, and aged Hallertau hops are added for extra aroma. With its high level of carbonation and its complex and intensely fruity flavours and aromas, the brewers suggest serving this beer as an aperitif in Champagne flutes as an alternative to a sparkling wine, and with its bright red colouring it certainly looks the part. Belgian Red is one of seven regular year-round brews, also including Edel-Pils, a smooth, full-bodied Pilsner; Fat Squirrel, a nutty-flavoured brown ale; and an intensely aromatic India pale ale called Hop Hearty Ale. There are also eight seasonal beers, ranging from the full-bodied Coffee Stout in winter, a rich, dark beer made with highly roasted malts for a smooth, bitter coffee flavour, to Solstice Weiss in the summer, an authentic Bavarian-style wheat beer with a cloudy golden colour and a soft, fruity flavour. New Glarus beers have won many awards at all the major national and international beer festivals.

SPECIFICATIONS

Brewery: New Glarus Brewing Company
Location: New Glarus, Wisconsin
Style: Fruit beer
Colour: Ruby red
Alcohol: 5.1%
Serving temperature: 10°–12°C (50°–53.6°F)
Food: Strawberries

North Coast Old Rasputin Russian Imperial Stout

Despite the name, Russian Imperial Stout is an English beer style. It was first developed in the nineteenth century as a fortifying winter-warmer, and quickly became popular with the Russian Czars who had it imported in vast quantities. The infamous 'Mad Monk' Rasputin was reputedly among its devotees, and so it is that the North Coast brewing company decided to name its version after him.

With 75 IBUs (International Bitterness Units) this rates as one of the hoppiest stouts around. The aroma is all roasted coffee and chocolate with a hint of caramel, while on the palate it offers a smooth body and a complex blend of burned toffee and citric, resiny hop flavours, leading to a fairly sweet finish. It is one of the most popular beers from this multiple award-winning brewery, which opened in 1988 in Fort Bragg on the rugged Mendocino coast of California with an adjacent taproom and grill restaurant. Other beers in the brewery's range include PranQster, a Belgian style golden ale brewed using traditional techniques and an ancient strain of yeast imported from Belgium, which gives it a heady floral aroma and refreshingly fruity flavours. Old Stock Ale, meanwhile, is a dark chestnut brown ale brewed with maris otter pale malt and flavoured with imported English Fuggles hops, and designed to improve with ageing, mellowing like a fine wine.

SPECIFICATIONS

Brewery: North Coast Brewing Co.
Location: Fort Bragg, California
Style: Russian imperial stout
Colour: Very dark red-brown, almost black
Alcohol: 8.9%
Serving temperature: 13°C (55.4°F)
Food: Rich chocolate cake

Odell's 90 Shilling

Doug Odell, an American with Welsh ancestry, brews his beers using imported British malt and hops.

The inspiration for his recipes stems largely from visits to Scotland, where in the nineteenth century beers were named according to the tax charged per barrel. The weakest beers would be rated at 60 shillings, while stronger ales could reach 90 shillings. Odell's flagship beer, first launched as a seasonal (winter) beer in 1989, is an authentically rich and satisfying amber ale with a full malt aroma and a blend of nutty, fruity and caramel flavours on the palate, finishing with a crisp hop dryness. The malts used in the beer are two-row barley malt, Vienna Malt, Crystal Malt and Chocolate Malt, and the finishing hops are Northern Brewer and Cascade. In 2004, 90 Shilling remained as one of Odell's most popular beers, accounting for a full 40% of Odell Brewing's sales.

SPECIFICATIONS

Brewery: Odell Brewing Company
Location: Fort Collins, Colorado
Style: Amber ale
Colour: Deep copper-red
Alcohol: 5.3%
Serving temperature: 10°–13°C (50°–55.4°F)
Food: Steak

Odell's Cutthroat Porter

Cutthroat Porter was introduced as a house beer for the Mountain Tap Tavern in Fort Collins, but due to its immense popularity was soon re-launched on a wider scale and has been available in bottles since 1997.

Although named a porter, it is more of a cross between a porter and a stout, with a higher roasted barley and dark malt content than a typical porter, giving it a strong roasted flavour balanced with dry bitterness provided by two varieties of hops. The Cutthroat name is also applied to a zesty, floral and spicy flavoured pale ale. The company attests to the creation of Cutthroat Pale as 'a tribute to independent brewers in England that had gone by the way'. Cutthroat Pale is also a stronger beer than the porter, having an alcohol content of 5.3%.

SPECIFICATIONS

Brewery: Odell Brewing Company
Location: Fort Collins, Colorado
Style: English porter
Colour: Black
Alcohol: 4.5%
Serving temperature: 10°–12°C (50°–53.6°F)
Food: Lamb casseroles

Tupper's Hop Pocket Ale

A hop pocket is a long sack into which hops are packed after they have been dried and it is an appropriate name for this hop-laden ale and its counterpart Pilsner. The ale has a powerfully floral hoppy aroma which is balanced with a solid malt background, while the Pilsner has intensely fruity hop character.

Both are named after the man who devised the recipes, Bob Tupper, a school history teacher who also holds lectures and beer tastings at the famous Brickskeller bar in Washington DC. They are brewed by the Old Dominion Brewing Company, which has been in operation since 1989, producing a wide range of hand-crafted lagers, ales and stouts, including many traditional seasonal specialities. All of its beers are brewed according to the ancient German Reinheitsgebot purity laws, using the characteristically soft local water. Dominion Lager, the company's flagship beer, has a smooth, mild flavour, while Dominion Oak Barrel Stout is conditioned in oak barrels that have previously been used for maturing bourbon, which gives it a rich vanilla scent along with a dry, roasted bitter flavour and a silky smooth texture. The range also includes a regular dry stout with a mellow, sweet roasted malt flavour, and Old Dubliner Amber in the style of a traditional Irish red ale with a well-rounded malt flavour.

SPECIFICATIONS

Brewery: Old Dominion Brewing Company
Location: Ashburn, Virginia
Style: Pale ale
Colour: Deep golden amber
Alcohol: 6.0%
Serving temperature: 10°C (50°F)
Food: Chicken salad

Ommegang Abbey Ale

The Ommegang is a colourful annual procession which is held every July in the Grand Place (main market square) of the Belgian capital city of Brussels, a tradition that dates back to the fourteenth century.

The Ommegang brewery was founded in 1997 by Don Feinberg and Wendy Littlefield who, inspired by a visit to Belgium in 1980, started out as importers of Belgian beer, but then decided they wanted to create their own brews. The company has since been taken over, but as the new owner is the Belgian brewer Moortgat, creators of the famous Duvel, it is safe to assume that the brewery will continue to produce authentic Belgian-style beers. Its flagship ale is this Belgian Dubbel ale, brewed to resemble a beer from the famous Trappist abbeys of Belgium, in the same way that the brewery itself was built to look like a Belgian abbey. It is a beer with richly complex fruit and spice aromas containing hints of cloves, cinnamon, liquorice and figs, followed by a full-bodied blend of honey, toffee, chocolate, raisins and plums on the palate. The finish is lingering, sweet and only lightly influenced by hops. Ommegang's other two regular brands are the spicily hoppy, deep golden-coloured Hennepin and Rare Vos, an amber ale named after a famous Brussels bar which has a spicy, zesty orange fruit character.

SPECIFICATIONS

Brewery: Brewery Ommegang
Location: Cooperstown, New York
Style: Belgian Dubbel
Colour: Dark chestnut brown
Alcohol: 8.5%
Serving temperature: 16°C (60.8°F)
Food: Slow-cooked meat or game stews

Pabst (Heileman's) Old Style

Old Style is the Chicago version of Pabst beer, a clean refreshing lager with a light malty flavour.

It was originally launched in 1902, brewed by a German immigrant by the name of Gottlieb Heileman at his small brewery in the town of La Crosse, Wisconsin. The popularity of his beer quickly spread across state lines and Old Style was soon adopted by the people of Chicago as their own brand, which led to the sponsorship of the Chicago Cubs baseball team, an association that endures to this day. Heileman Brewery became part of the Pabst family in 2000. The beer has also given its name to a design font, which was created specifically for the Pabst Brewing Company by the American typographer Frederic Goudy.

SPECIFICATIONS

Brewery: Pabst Brewing Company
Location: San Antonio, Texas
Style: Lager
Colour: Deep golden
Alcohol: 4.5%
Serving temperature: 6°–8°C (42.8°–46.4°F)
Food: Chicago-style pizza

Pabst Old Milwaukee

Pabst was founded in 1844 when German immigrant Jacob Best and his four sons set up a brewery in Milwaukee.

One of the sons, Philip, married the daughter of a local steamship captain, Frederick Pabst, who in 1864 bought half the company and later became its president. Today Pabst brews a vast range of beers, offering a range of regional styles to suit local markets. Although the brewery is now located in Texas, Old Milwaukee, a light, uncomplicated, easy-drinking lager first launched in 1955 as a 'popular' beer, remains as a link with its past.

SPECIFICATIONS

Brewery: Pabst Brewing Company
Location: San Antonio, Texas
Style: Lager
Colour: Pale golden
Alcohol: 3.6%
Serving temperature: 7°C (44.6°F)
Food: Spaghetti carbonara

Penn Gold Lager

Proud brewers of authentic German beers, Pennsylvania Brewing Company was founded in 1986.

It was established in the historic Eberhardt and Ober brewery building, dating from the 1880s, in the Deutschtown district of Pittsburgh. All of the equipment and ingredients used in the brewery are imported from Germany, and naturally all the beers are brewed according to the ancient German Reinheitsgebot purity laws. The German links run even deeper: head brewer Tom Pastorius is a direct descendant of Francis Daniel Pastorius, the German scholar who was a contemporary of William Penn, after whom the state of Pennsylvania is named. Penn Gold is a medium-bodied Munich-style lager with a full malty flavour and a delicate hop aroma. There is also a dark version of the beer, again brewed to a style typical of the city of Munich, with a good balance of soft, fruit and dark, slightly burnt malt flavours, plus a subtle dose of hops. The brewery also produces two Pilsners, one called simply Pilsner based on Tom Pastorius's favourite beer, a smooth, full-bodied amber Vienna-style lager; the other called Kaiser Pils, a crisp, clean, refreshing lager in the north German fashion, with a pronounced hop bitterness, brewed with a triple decoction process. Seasonal brews include the dark, malty and deliciously strong St Niklaus Bock Bier, a Christmas speciality, and a smooth, mellow, golden-coloured Oktoberfest, which has a nutty, fruity malt character.

SPECIFICATIONS

Brewery: Pennsylvania Brewing Company
Location: Pittsburgh, Pennsylvania
Style: Munich lager
Colour: Pale golden
Alcohol: 5.0%
Serving temperature: 8°–10°C (46.4°–50°F)
Food: Battered fish and squeezed lemon

Pete's Wicked Ale

Pete Slosberg began brewing as a hobby in 1979, choosing beer over wine because it didn't take as long before he could enjoy the results of his endeavours. But it wasn't long before Slosberg was completely hooked on beer, and in 1986 he formed Pete's Brewing Company, which has since become one of the leading craft brewers in the United States. His Wicked Ale is a mellow, malty nut-brown beer with an aroma of roasted malt and floral hops, and a slightly sweet malt flavour leading the way on the palate, tempered by a gentle hoppy dryness.

Overall, there is very little bitterness to this beer, with Brewers Gold hops used for their floral aroma. Pete's also produces three other brews: Strawberry Blonde, Rally Cap and Wanderlust Cream Ale. Strawberry blonde is a light-bodied, golden-coloured, bottom-fermented wheat beer naturally flavoured with strawberries, along with Yakima Cluster and Tettnang hops to create a clean, well-balanced beer with a slight strawberry sweetness. Wicked Ale and Strawberry Blonde are available all year round, while the other two are seasonal. Rally Cap is a more straightforward refreshing wheat beer for summer drinking, flavoured with a hint of lemon, while Wanderlust is a velvet-smooth amber ale for winter drinking, made with Munich and pale malts, as well as some malted wheat.

SPECIFICATIONS

Brewery: Pete's Brewing Company
Location: San Antonio, Texas
Style: Brown ale
Colour: Ruby red-brown
Alcohol: 5.3%
Serving temperature: 12°–14°C (53.6°–57.2°F)
Food: Game pie

Pike Pale Ale

This highly quaffable pale ale provides a well-balanced blend of flavours featuring a smooth, fruity maltiness that contrasts with a fresh, floral, herby hop character.

It is the flagship beer of the Pike brewery, which started out in 1989 in tiny premises in the storefront of the LaSalle hotel building in Seattle's Pike Place market. In 1996, to meet popular demand, a new, larger brewery opened just two blocks away, enabling the brewery to greatly extend its range. New beers included Naughty Nellie's Ale, like a soft, easy-drinking English mild, and KiltLifter, a Scottish-style 'wee heavy' with rich toasted malt flavours.

SPECIFICATIONS

Brewery: Pike Pub and Brewery
Location: Seattle, Washington
Style: Pale ale
Colour: Deep amber
Alcohol: 5.3%
Serving temperature: 13°C (55.4°F)
Food: Grilled salmon or mussel stew

Portland Oregon Honey Beer

Oregon Honey Beer comes from the same brewery that produces MacTarnahan's Scottish style beers, but this one has more of a genuine homegrown character to its flavours and aromas.

Oregon Honey Beer is a crisp and refreshing ale which has a hint of sweetness provided by the addition of clover honey. The beer also has a soft, mellow malty character balanced by the judicious use of Willamette hops. It is ideal as a light, easy-drinking summer beer, in stark contrast to another of the brewery's beers, Mac Frost, a strong, rich winter beer made with five types of malt and aromatised and bittered with three varieties of hops, or the MacTarnahan's Black Watch Cream Porter, which uses malted barley, unmalted grains and oatmeal.

SPECIFICATIONS

Brewery: MacTarnahan's Brewing Company / Portland Brewing Co.
Location: Portland, Oregon
Style: American pale ale
Colour: Pale golden straw yellow
Alcohol: 4.2%
Serving temperature: 8°–10° C (46.4°–50°F)
Food: Shellfish

Post Road Pumpkin Ale

This autumn seasonal ale from the Brooklyn Brewery is a revival of a style of beer brewed by early colonists.

During the autumn in this part of the world, pumpkins were an excellent and abundant source of nutrition. Each brew is blended with several hundred pumpkins, which is clearly evident in the orangey colour of the beer, as well as in the warming, comforting aroma, deeply infused with cinnamon and nutmeg. At the heart of the beer is a light, biscuity maltiness, and the finish is crisp and clean. The brewery claims that 'Post Road Pumpkin Ale is a revival of a beer brewed by the early American colonists. Pumpkins were plentiful, flavorful and nutritious, and they blended nicely with barley malt.'

SPECIFICATIONS

Brewery: Brooklyn Brewery
Location: Brooklyn, New York
Style: Pumpkin ale
Colour: Amber orange
Alcohol: 5%
Serving temperature: 8–10°C (46.4–50°F)
Food: Pumpkin pie

Redhook ESB

The Pacific Northwest is home to the United States' major hop-growing regions and many of its finest craft brewers. Redhook is one of the very earliest, established in 1981 to provide a homegrown alternative to the quality imported European beers that were gaining in popularity.

It was the start of a new movement in small-scale brewing that has since gained massive momentum. The first Redhook ale was modelled after dark, spicy Belgian-style abbey beers and was given a mixed reception. It then launched Ballard Bitter (named after the district where the brewery was located), which proved much more popular. But by far the most successful of the brewery's beers to date is its ESB, the first American beer to use the term, which it borrowed from Fuller's of London to describe its strong, complex and well-balanced bitter. Hops dominate the aroma, while on the palate toasted malt flavours lead to a soft, sweet lingering finish tempered by floral hop bitterness. Redhook now brews its beers at three sites across the northwest and since 1994 a selection of Redhook beers, including ESB, have been distributed nationally by Anheuser-Busch.

SPECIFICATIONS

Brewery: Redhook Ale Brewery
Location: Woodinville, Washington
Style: Strong bitter / extra special bitter
Colour: Copper
Alcohol: 5.8%
Serving temperature: 10°–13°C (50°–55.4°F)
Food: Roast pheasant or other game

Rogue Dead Guy Ale

The Rogue brewery was founded in 1988 by three beer enthusiast friends – Jack Joyce, Rob Strasser and Bob Woodell, who gave up their corporate jobs to become brewers, opening their first brewpub in Ashland, Orgegon.

The brewery is named after the Rogue River, which flows through the town of Newport, Oregon. But it also indicates the brewery's revolutionary philosophy – a desire to do things a little bit differently – which is expressed through its beers, which are carefully crafted by hand on a small scale. Its Dead Guy Ale, formerly known as Maierbock, is an example of the Maibock style, the strong, pale beer usually drunk in Germany as a celebration of the arrival of spring (*bock* being the German term for a strong beer), though this version is available all year round. Made with four types of malt and two varieties of hops, it has a fruity, malty aroma, a rich, hearty flavour and a well-balanced finish. The change of name to Dead Guy Ale came about after a one-off keg version of the Maierbock beer was brewed under that name for a local pub to celebrate the Mayan Day of the Dead (1 November). The new name proved so popular that it stuck.

SPECIFICATIONS

Brewery: Rogue Ales
Location: Newport, Oregon
Style: Maibock
Colour: Deep golden honey
Alcohol: 6.5%
Serving temperature: 13°C (55.4°F)
Food: Chicken or pork dishes with rich sauces

Rogue Hazelnut Brown Nectar

Rogue Ales' Hazelnut Brown Nectar is a twist on the classic English brown ale style.

Along with seven types of malt and two varieties of hops, this beer is brewed with the addition of hazelnut extract to give it a rich, sweet-sharp, nutty flavour and aroma. The hazelnut extract also gives the beer a slight murky haze. On the palate, malts dominate, with rich chocolate, toffee and roasted hazelnut background notes, while the subtle hops – Perle and Saaz are the varieties used – provide a balancing bitter dryness. As well as the regular bottle size, Hazelnut Brown Nectar comes in a special three-litre commemorative bottle with a ceramic flip-top lid. Rogue prides itself on the quality of ingredients used, and its publicity is keen to point out: 'Preservative, additives, chemicals: Never! Rogue does not pasteurize its products.'

SPECIFICATIONS

Brewery: Rogue Ales
Location: Newport, Oregon
Style: Brown ale
Colour: Dark mahogany brown
Alcohol: 6.2%
Serving temperature: 12°C (53.6°F)
Food: Coffee cake

Rogue Shakespeare Stout

Unlike the typically dry, bitter character of Irish stout, oatmeal stout has a much sweeter flavour.

Rogue's award-winning version is made with several different types of malt, including crystal and chocolate malts, roasted barley and rolled oats, which give it an opaquely dark black colouring and a rich, creamy head when poured. The aroma is predominantly characterised by ripe dark fruit such as plums or figs, with background hints of chocolate. The sweet maltiness continues to exert itself on the palate with dark roasted coffee and dry, hoppy bitterness coming in towards the finish. Shakespeare Stout received a welcome accreditation in 1994 when it took a score of 99 at the World Beer Championships, the top score of 309 beers in 44 categories. *Men's Journal* (June/July 1998) also placed the stout in the category of 'The 100 Best Things to Eat in America'.

SPECIFICATIONS

Brewery: Rogue Ales
Location: Newport, Oregon
Style: Oatmeal stout
Colour: Ebony black
Alcohol: 6%
Serving temperature: 13°C (55.4°F)
Food: Home-made pizza, or a fresh green salad

Rolling Rock

Ever since it was launched in 1939, Rolling Rock has always been associated with the number 33. The reasons for this are shrouded in mystery. Various theories have attempted to explain it, but no definitive answer is known – at least it provides something to think about while enjoying the beer's crisp, sweet, refreshing flavour.

The Latrobe Brewing Company was established in 1893 in the small town of Latrobe in the foothills of Pennsylvania's Allegheny Mountains, and its earliest beers were authentic German-style Pilsners. The brewery closed for a few years during prohibition, but reopened when it was purchased by the five Tito brothers, Frank, Joseph, Robert, Ralph and Anthony, who quickly set about devising a new recipe to cater for changing beer tastes, eventually coming up with Rolling Rock, which was named in honour of the tumbling streams full of pebbles that supplied the brewery with water.

SPECIFICATIONS

Brewery: Latrobe Brewing Co.
Location: Latrobe, Pennsylvania
Style: Lager
Colour: Bright, clear golden yellow
Alcohol: 4.6%
Serving temperature: 6°–8°C (42.8°–46.4°F)
Food: Pork pie

Saint Arnold Brown Ale

Saint Arnold is the oldest microbrewery in Texas, having been established in June 1994 by two local men, Brock Wagner and Kevin Bartol. Both are descended from families with German origins, so their enthusiasm for beer is fairly understandable, and Brock was already a keen home brewer.

Being beer aficionados, the two were concerned by the lack of a microbrewery in the city, so they decided to do something about it. Their brewery proved a hit, but despite its success Saint Arnold remains true to its microbrewery roots and is run by a team of eight workers who run every stage of the beer's production. The brewery produces nine different beers, of which four are made all year round, while the other five are seasonal. One of its most successful is its multiple award-winning Brown Ale, a creamy, full-bodied beer with a complex roasted malt flavour laden with chocolate, fruit and nuts. Its complexity is achieved by using a blend of five different malts in the mash, while three different hop varieties give the beer a pleasantly light hop bitterness and a subtle floral hop aroma.

SPECIFICATIONS

Brewery: Saint Arnold Brewing Company
Location: Houston, Texas
Style: Brown ale
Colour: Deep copper-brown
Alcohol: 5.3%
Serving temperature: 8°–10° C (46.4°–50°F)
Food: Herb-crusted lamb

Samuel Adams Boston Lager

Jim Koch founded the Boston Beer Company in 1984. It was the revival of a family tradition – he was the fifth generation of his family to enter brewing as a profession, although his father had quit the business some years previously due to the lack of interest in classic full-flavoured beers.

When quality, craft-brewed beers started to make a comeback in the United States in the early 1980s, Jim decided to follow in his father's footsteps, reviving a recipe that had first been brewed by his great-great-grandfather Louis Koch in 1870. He named it Samuel Adams Boston Lager after the city's famous revolutionary leader, one of the organisers of the infamous Boston Tea Party and also one of the signatories of the Declaration of Independence in 1776. Adams also happened to come from a brewing family, so the association was doubly appropriate. Koch didn't need to persuade people too hard to try his new beer – it was an instant hit and was soon picking up awards from national and international competitions. The reason for its popularity is its full, complex flavour, achieved by using a variety of malts and the time-consuming traditional decoction brewing method. Its flavour is slightly sweet with background notes of caramel and roasted malt, and the use of Tettnang and Hallertau hops gives it a floral, piney, citrussy character from the aroma through to the finish.

SPECIFICATIONS

Brewery: Boston Beer Company
Location: Boston, Massachusetts
Style: Lager
Colour: Deep amber gold
Alcohol: 4.9%
Serving temperature: 8°–10°C (46.4°–50°F)
Food: Duck or rabbit

Samuel Adams Boston Ale

Sam Adams Boston Ale is made, like the Boston Lager, according to a recipe from the Koch family archives.

It is an example of a type of beer known as a stock ale, one of the few classic beer styles to have originated in the United States, and gets its name from the cool stock cellars where the beer was stored for maturation. It produces a beer with more smoothness and body, and a rich, complex malt character with a caramel sweetness. This is balanced by a sharp, citrussy hop aroma and a dry, tannin-like bitterness in the finish that comes from the use of Goldings and Fuggles hops. The company points out that Boston Ale is 'brewed using a decoction mash, a time-consuming, traditional four vessel brewing process discarded by many contemporary brewers'.

SPECIFICATIONS

Brewery: Boston Beer Company
Location: Boston, Massachusetts
Style: Stock ale
Colour: Dark amber-brown
Alcohol: 5.1%
Serving temperature: 10°–12°C (50°–53.6°F)
Food: Braised meat dishes

Samuel Adams Triple Bock

The Boston Beer Company now brews 17 different beers under the Samuel Adams label. These include various traditional recipes, as well as a range of seasonal beers, such as the Belgian-style White Ale wheat beer, which is flavoured with 10 different spices, plus what it calls 'Extreme Beers'.

These are the beers with the most challenging flavours, such as the Triple Bock, which has the deep, complex flavours of a mature sherry, with notes of vanilla, plums, oak and toffee. It is full bodied to the point of being thick and almost syrupy, with a treacly blackness. It is also explosively alcoholic at around 18% volume, but even that level was exceeded by the Samuel Adams Utopias, the 2003 batch of which came in at a mind-blowing 25% alcohol by volume.

SPECIFICATIONS

Brewery: Boston Beer Company
Location: Boston, Massachusetts
Style: Triple bock
Colour: Very dark brown, almost black
Alcohol: 18%
Serving temperature: 13°–16°C (55.4°–60.8°F)
Food: Sticky toffee pudding

Sierra Nevada Bigfoot

Sierra Nevada is perhaps the most famous of all the new generation of craft brewers operating in the United States today.

SPECIFICATIONS

Brewery: Sierra Nevada Brewing Co.
Location: Chico, California
Style: Barley wine
Colour: Deep red-brown
Alcohol: 9.6%
Serving temperature: 14°–16°C (57.2°–60.8°F)
Food: Turkey and Christmas pudding

From a brewery established in 1979 by Ken Grosman, the beers were an instant hit. It wasn't long before this tiny brewery was struggling to keep up with demand, and in 1989 a new brewery was opened built with equipment imported from Germany, including traditional copper mash kettles. Ken's beers are justifiably renowned for the copious amounts of hops he uses in creating them, and his Bigfoot Ale is no exception. This award-winning beer is a fine example of a traditional barley wine with an intensely fruity aroma, a dense mouth-filling body and a deep, rich, complex flavour that provides a superb balance between forthright maltiness with notes of plums, chocolate, nuts and toast, and an intensely bitter, resiny, citrus hop character. Barley wines are festive beers, traditionally drunk around the Christmas season. Alternatively, the Celebration Ale is a classic winter warmer, dry hopped for a lively spicy aroma, while in summer, Sierra Nevada produces a refreshingly fruity Pilsner called Summerfest, which enjoys an extra-long lagering period to give it an extra smooth character.

Sierra Nevada Pale Ale

This pale ale was the first beer to come out of the Sierra Nevada brewery when it was launched in 1980.

It remains the most popular of the brewery's regular line-up (the others are a porter, a stout and a wheat beer) and is widely regarded as one of the foremost examples of the pale ale style available in the United States today. Hops dominate the aroma with a fragrantly spicy, floral character, while on the palate this is a remarkably full-bodied, mouth-filling beer with a lively, complex maltiness with notes of orange fruit and toffee contrasting against a citrussy hop bitterness in perfect balance. The Pale Ale is also a visually attractive beer, with a rich golden colour that truly reflects the complex flavours present during drinking.

SPECIFICATIONS

Brewery: Sierra Nevada Brewing Co.
Location: Chico, California
Style: American pale ale
Colour: Deep amber
Alcohol: 5.6%
Serving temperature: 10°–12°C (50°–53.6°F)
Food: Buffalo wings

Stone Ruination IPA

'A liquid poem to the glory of hops' proclaims the label of Stone's Ruination IPA, while the devilish figure hints at the powerful flavours that reside within the bottle.

Even by the standards of a brewery that is known for its love of hops, this is a particularly hoppy beer with an intensely bitter flavour (rated at over 100 IBUs/International Bitterness Units) that aims to have a 'ruining' effect on your palate – hence the name. The strong flavour of Stone Ruination is backed up by an equally strong 7.7% alcohol content, making it well above the more typical 5–5.5% regions of IPAs. More moderate than Stone Ruination is Stone Smoked Porter, a smooth, silky dark beer with robust chocolate and coffee-like flavours and a hint of whisky-like smokiness that comes from the use of selected malts roasted over peat.

SPECIFICATIONS

Brewery: Stone Brewing Company
Location: San Marcos, California
Style: India pale ale
Colour: Bright, pale amber-orange
Alcohol: 7.7%
Serving temperature: 10°–12°C (50°–53.6°F)
Food: Fried seafood

Stone Double Bastard Ale

Stone was founded in 1996 by brewer Steve Wagner and businessman Greg Koch, not only serious beer enthusiasts, but also idealists when it comes to brewing.

The brewery's emblem is a gargoyle, which they claim is to ward off evil spirits such as chemical preservatives, additives and adjuncts, keeping their beers pure and natural. Double Bastard Ale is a seasonal beer, released in limited quantities every November. It is a deliberately over-the-top beer, stronger and even more complex than the brewery's aggressively flavoured Arrogant Bastard Ale. As such it is not a drink for through-the-night quaffing, and should be handled with care. The initial aroma is sweet and deeply malty, while on the palate the rich, fruity malt flavours are balanced by an intense resiny, herbal hop bitterness.

SPECIFICATIONS

Brewery: Stone Brewing Company
Location: San Marcos, California
Style: Barley wine
Colour: Dark mahogany brown
Alcohol: 10%
Serving temperature: 13°C (55.4°F)
Food: Dark bitter chocolate

Stoudt's Fest

Stoudt's Fest is a medium-bodied dark amber lager with a sweet, fruity malt aroma that exhibits hints of toffee, raisins and apples. A similarly sweet caramel malt character on the palate is tempered by a subtle hint of dry hop bitterness.

Fest is made in the style of beer originating in Munich which is brewed in March for storage over the summer months when the heat made brewing difficult, and traditionally drunk at the city's annual celebrations in October. Stoudt's version is made all year round, although for the months of August, September and October the regular label is replaced with a different label which bears a traditional German motif. Stoudt's seasonal beers focus on traditional German recipes such as a light, refreshing summer wheat beer and a pale, full-flavoured double bock for spring. There is also a Holiday Reserve for the Christmas period.

SPECIFICATIONS

Brewery: Stoudt's Brewing Co.
Location: Adamstown, Pennsylvania
Style: Märzen / Oktoberfest
Colour: Clear amber-red
Alcohol: 5%
Serving temperature: 10°–12°C (50°–53.6°F)
Food: German bratwurst sausages

Stoudt's Pils

Carol and Ed Stoudt founded their brewery on the principles of traditional craft brewing on a small scale. Despite the huge popularity of their award-winning beers they staunchly resist the temptation to expand, ensuring that their business never grows too large for them to keep a hands-on role in every stage of the brewing process.

The recent addition of a bottling line has enabled them even to bottle their beers themselves (bottling was previously contracted out). At the heart of their range is an authentic European-style Pilsner with a crisp, refreshingly dry floral hop profile in both the aroma and taste, superbly well balanced with nutty, grainy malt flavours in the background. Alongside it is the fuller-bodied Gold Lager, a creamy, fruity Munich-style lager, as well as several bottle-conditioned beers. These include the spicy Belgian-style Abbey Double and Abbey Triple; a Scotch-style ale with a full-bodied flavour defined by roasted and peat-smoked malts; a complex German-style Double Bock brewed annually to celebrate the brewery's anniversary; and a rich, chocolatey imperial stout called Fat Dog.

SPECIFICATIONS

Brewery: Stoudt's Brewing Co.
Location: Adamstown, Pennsylvania
Style: Pilsner
Colour: Pale straw yellow
Alcohol: 4.8%
Serving temperature: 8°C (46.4°F)
Food: Serve by itself as an appetizing aperitif

Sudwerk Helles

The Sudwerk Restaurant and Brewery brews all of its beers to traditional German recipes, following the Reinheitsgebot purity laws dating from 1516 and still in effect in Germany today. The yeast is provided by the Weihenstephan brewery, the oldest brewery in the world, which is situated near Munich. The Hallertau and Tettnang hops are also imported from Germany. Sudwerk brews mainly bottom-fermented lagers, using a slow, cold fermentation process followed by a long period of maturation.

Helles, from the German for light (as opposed to 'dunkel', meaning dark), is a golden lager with a full-bodied creamy texture and a rich, complex malty flavour tending towards sweetness, although this is artfully balanced with subtle hop bitterness. This style, popular throughout Bavaria, is named after the dark lagers of Munich to distinguish it from the drier, hoppier character of the Pilsner style, such as the fragrantly hoppy version brewed by Sudwerk. The brewery has won many awards for its beers in national and international competitions.

SPECIFICATIONS

Brewery: Privatbrauerei Sudwerk Hubsch
Location: Davis, California
Style: Munich Helles Lager
Colour: Pale golden yellow
Alcohol: 5%
Serving temperature: 8°C (46.4°F)
Food: Spicy Mexican food such as fajitas or burritos

Victory Hopdevil Ale

The Victory brewery was launched in 1996, although the story behind its creation runs all the way back to 1976, when company owners Ron and Bill first met as ten-year-old schoolboys. The initial spark that set them on the road to opening the brewery was a trip around the brewing abbeys of Belgium in 1987 and subsequently sampling the creations of some of the new wave of American craft brewers that were significantly gaining in number by that time. Their enthusiasm for these beers eventually led them to decide on a change of career and become brewers themselves. They now produce a range of more than 20 different beers, including a number of seasonal and limited edition ales.

Hopdevil Ale is one of Victory's regular beers, available all year round, and it is a powerfully aromatic India pale ale with a bold, spicy hop flavour and a smooth, creamy, full-bodied texture. It is typical of the brewery's tendency towards heavily hopped beers, although they also produce some richly malty ales and lagers, such as St Victorious, an authentically nutty, fruity double bock made with seven varieties of German malt and aromatised with four varieties of hops. Victory also brews a series of high-gravity vintage beers designed to improve with keeping – V Grand Cru is an aromatic amber ale, brewed with plenty of whole hop flowers including East Kent, Styrians Golding and Tettnang varieties which impart spicy, herbal aromas and flavour.

SPECIFICATIONS

Brewery: Victory Brewing Company
Location: Downington, Pennsylvania
Style: India pale ale
Colour: Bright, clear copper
Alcohol: 6.7%
Serving temperature: 10°–12°C (50°–53.6°F)
Food: Crusty bread sandwiches

Above

The people of Latin America and the Caribbean are noted for their love of beer as much as for their love of life. As well as brewing quality, distinctive lagers and beers for the domestic market, the region has also become one of the largest beer exporting territories in the world, building international popularity through brands such as Sol, Corona Extra and Red Stripe.

Latin American and Caribbean Beers

Before the arrival of the Europeans in the sixteenth century, beer was unknown in Latin America. But civilisations such as the Aztecs, Incas and Mayans had traditions for drinking fermented beverages brewed from corn, while in the Caribbean the native populations brewed maize to make drinks that varied in recipe from island to island.

ABOVE

Latin America, like any other world region, has some state-of-the-art brewing facilities. It also, however, has seen the continuation of traditional brewing among many of the smaller companies.

THE AZTECS CREATED DRINKS FROM the leaves and juice of the agave plant, too, including a simple brew called *pulque*, which was drunk for medicinal and religious reasons. When the conquistadors arrived, they introduced the process of distillation, which led to the creation of mezcal, which soon became the most popular drink in Latin America and also a valuable commodity.

The conquistadors set up many small breweries across the continent, but it was not until the arrival of refrigeration in the late nineteenth century, and the introduction of golden lagers by Bavarian, Swiss and Austrian brewers, that beer became truly popular. Later on, when prohibition hit North America, the sleepy border town of Tijuana in Mexico became a popular refuge for Americans looking for a drink, which created a lasting legacy for the Mexican brewing industry, making it by far the largest brewing nation in Latin America.

The next largest brewing country in Latin America is Brazil, where a notable addition to the usual range of light, Bavarian-style golden lagers is a distinctive black beer, which is brewed using roasted barley and a blend of dark-coloured indigenous grains, as well as lupins for aroma (lupins are related to hops and have a similar bitter flavour). These black beers were first created in the very early days of colonialism, but have nevertheless endured, with several examples on the market today including Xingu, brewed by Cervejaria Cacador.

Strong, sweet lagers are also the mainstay of Caribbean drinking, but stout is also very popular throughout the region and Guinness has been brewed in Jamaica for around 150 years.

STATISTICS

Total production: 223,990,000 hectolitres (5,917,190,000 gallons) per year

Consumption per capita: 55 litres (15 gallons) per year

Famous breweries: Bucanero Cervecería; Cervecería Cuauhtémoc; Cervecería Modelo; Cervecería y Maltería Quilme; Desnoes & Geddes; Especialidad Cerveceras

Famous brands: Corona Extra; Dos Equis; Igúazu; Mayabe Calidad Extra; Quilmes; Red Stripe; Sol

Casta Bruna

This is a smooth and well-balanced English-style pale ale with a delicate floral aroma in which hints of toffee sweetness are apparent.

Four types of pale roasted malts and English hops give Casta Bruna a medium body and a complex range of flavours, including notes of chocolate, peaches and a herbal hop bitterness. The excellent range of quality ales from Especialidad Cerveceras also includes the vigorously aromatic Casta Dorada, brewed in the style of Belgium's strong golden ales with a fragrantly spicy bitterness, while Casta Milenia is a limited edition vintage ale in the tradition of the strong Belgian abbey beers, bottled with unfermented wort to create a beer that improves with extended cellaring.

SPECIFICATIONS

Brewery: Especialidad Cerveceras
Location: Apodaca, Mexico
Style: English pale ale
Colour: Copper red-brown
Alcohol: 5.4%
Serving temperature: 10°–12°C (50°–53.6°F)
Food: Pasta with tomato-based sauces

Casta Morena

Casta is the Spanish for 'purity', and the name reflects Especialidad Cerveceras' philosophy of adhering to the highest principles of beer production, namely the German Reinheitsgebot purity laws of 1516 which stipulate that beer is made with nothing but malt, water, hops and yeast, with wheat allowed under a later amendment .

Especialidad Cerverceras brews only top-fermented ales, the first brewery in Mexico to do so. The malts and hops used are imported from England, the United States and the Czech Republic, and each different beer in the range uses a distinct strain of yeast. Casta Morena is a complex and refined beer, brewed with six different types of malt, including caramel and chocolate malt, creating a dark, full-bodied ale similar to the traditional strong ales of Scotland. It is aromatised with two varieties of hops for a subtle hint of bitterness.

SPECIFICATIONS

Brewery: Especialidad Cerveceras
Location: Apodaca, Mexico
Style: Scotch ale
Colour: Dark red-brown
Alcohol: 6%
Serving temperature: 9°C (48.2°F)
Food: Red meat and game with rich sauces

Dos Equis

The name Dos Equis means simply 'two crosses', as represented in symbolic form on the label of the bottle. It comes in two varieties, the most popular of which is this simple light lager.

It is also available as a rich, dark amber Vienna style lager with a sweet, fruity malt flavour and hints of chocolate. It is currently one of the leading brands of Mexico's largest brewer, Cervecería Cuauhtémoc, which was founded in 1890 by two Spanish men, Isaac Heron and Jose Calderón. The brewery's first beer was Carta Blanca, a sparkling beer originally packaged in corked bottles.

SPECIFICATIONS

Brewery: Cervecería Cuauhtémoc Moctezuma (Femsa)
Location: Monterrey, Mexico
Style: Vienna lager
Colour: Golden amber-yellow
Alcohol: 4.8%
Serving temperature: 6°–8°C (42.8°–46.4°F)
Food: Grilled white fish

Sol

One of the most famous Mexican beer brands, Sol is a light, refreshing lager brewed for a smoother, fuller body.

SPECIFICATIONS

Brewery: Cervecería Cuauhtémoc Moctezuma (Femsa)
Location: Monterrey, Mexico
Style: Lager
Colour: Bright, clear golden yellow
Alcohol: 4.6%
Serving temperature: 5°–7°C (41°–44.6°F)
Food: Steak and sautéed potatoes

It has a fruity malt aroma and a hoppy bitterness on the palate that gives it an invigorating dryness. It is presented in a clear bottle, allowing its vibrant golden yellow colour to shine out, and this is what gives the beer its name (Sol means 'sun' in English). In the 1980s, Sol became the most popular of Mexican beers, finding widespread popularity in Europe and the United States, as well as in its domestic market of Mexico.

Other brands from the group include Tecate, launched in the city that gives the beer its name in 1944 as a light, thirst-quenching beer with a fairly low alcohol content, making it ideal for Mexico's hot climate. It was created by Alberto Aldrete, an ambitious farmer proud of his Mexican roots, and was originally served with salt and fresh lemons, which is the root of the modern fashion for drinking Sol and other Mexican beers with a wedge of lime in the neck of the bottle.

Bohemia

Between 1864 and 1867, Mexico came under the rule of Austrian Emperor Maximilian. His spell in charge may have been brief, but he left a profound mark on the nation's brewing habits, and today the Vienna lager style is probably more popular in Mexico than it is in Austria.

The original Vienna lagers were characterised by an amber-red colour, which was due to the particular way the malts were kilned, although most of the Mexican versions are more of a golden yellow colour. Bohemia is one of the better examples of the style, being strong and full flavoured, with a fruity malt profile backed up by a fragrant hop bitterness provided by imported Saaz hops.

SPECIFICATIONS

Brewery: Cervecería Cuauhtémoc Moctezuma (Femsa)
Location: Monterrey, Mexico
Style: Vienna lager
Colour: Golden yellow
Alcohol: 5.4%
Serving temperature: 8°C (46.4°F)
Food: Herb-flavoured roasted meats

Corona Pacifico Clara

Pacifico Clara is part of the extensive range of beers from the Modelo brewery of Mexico City, although it is mostly produced at the company's subsidiary Pacific Brewery in Mazatlán, Sinaloa, in the north of Mexico.

It is a subtle, refined beer with a vigorous carbonation and a light, well-balanced flavour. As well as its famous Corona and Modelo beer ranges, the brewery produces several other brands, notably including Victoria, a malty Vienna-style lager that was originally brewed by the Toluca brewery, one of Mexico's oldest breweries, founded in 1865 and acquired by Modelo in 1935.

SPECIFICATIONS

Brewery: Cervecería Modelo
Location: Mexico City, Mexico
Style: Pilsner
Colour: Golden yellow
Alcohol: 4.5%
Serving temperature: 7°C (44.6°F)
Food: Sharp, spicy dishes

Corona Extra

Corona Extra is the number one selling beer in Mexico and also the country's leading export brand, now available in more than 150 countries worldwide.

It was first brewed by Cervecería Modelo in Mexico City in 1925. The company's first brew was called simply Modelo, and Corona was introduced a month later. Modelo celebrated its tenth anniversary in 1936 with the addition of a dark lager called Moravia to its range. The brewery currently produces 10 beers, including a light version of Corona Extra with around 30% fewer calories. The original Modelo beer now comes in three versions: Modelo Especial, a straightforward Pilsner-style lager with a significant hop profile; Modelo Light; and Negro Modelo, the latter being an amber-coloured smooth, malty lager with notes of chocolate and dark fruit and a refreshingly bitter hop finish.

SPECIFICATIONS

Brewery: Cervecería Modelo
Location: Mexico City, Mexico
Style: Lager
Colour: Pale golden yellow
Alcohol: 4.6%
Serving temperature: 5°–7°C (41°–44.6°F)
Food: Baked ham and salad

Mayabe Calidad Extra

One of the largest towns in Cuba, Holguin lies close to the spot on the coast where Christopher Columbus first landed in 1492. It is also home to the Bucanero brewery, which produces Cerveza Cristal lager, the best-selling beer brand in Cuba.

Bucaneros specialises in easy-drinking lagers and Mayabe Calidad Extra is the brewery's 'premium' brand, brewed slightly stronger and with a smoother body. It has a light, uncomplicated, slightly sweet grainy flavour. Another stronger version is called Fuerte, and the range includes a clear golden Pilsner-style beer called Palma Cristal.

SPECIFICATIONS

Brewery: Bucanero Cervecería
Location: Holguin, Cuba
Style: Lager
Colour: Pale straw yellow
Alcohol: 5%
Serving temperature: 5°–7°C (41°–44.6°F)
Food: Fried fish and seafood

Red Stripe

Red Stripe is a pale golden strong lager with a full malty flavour balanced by a light hop aroma and refreshingly dry, bitter finish. It comes from the Desnoes & Geddes brewery, which was established in 1918 in Kingston, Jamaica, and is named after its two founders, Eugene Desnoes and Thomas Hargreaves Geddes.

At first the company produced only soft drinks, but turned to brewing in 1927. The first Red Stripe was a rich, flavourful ale, but it was replaced in 1938 with the golden lager that we know today. In recent years, Desnoes & Geddes has entered into business arrangements with Heineken that has seen its beers exported and in some cases brewed overseas, making it one of the few breweries in the Caribbean to enjoy a truly worldwide reputation. Outside of Jamaica, it is particularly well known in the United Kingdom, where it was made popular by the large West Indian immigrant population, and Red Stripe is now brewed under licence in the United Kingdom.

It also found popularity among Canadian and US soldiers who were stationed in the Caribbean during World War II and is currently one of the fastest-growing beer brands in the United States. The company remained in family ownership until was taken over by Guinness in 1993. The brewery's other brands include Dragon Stout, a dark, sweet, rich, malty stout with hints of licquorice and a fortifying 7.5% alcohol. Desnoes & Geddes also brews the Caribbean version of Guinness.

SPECIFICATIONS

Brewery: Desnoes & Geddes
Location: Kingston, Jamaica
Style: Lager
Colour: Pale golden yellow
Alcohol: 4.7%
Serving temperature: 6°–7°C (42.8°–44.6°F)
Food: Fried seafood and saffron rice

Igúazu

Igúazu is one of a wide range of beers originating from the Quilmes brewery of Buenos Aires.

It takes its name from a spectacular horseshoe-shaped waterfall, 80 metres high and nearly three kilometres across, that is famous outside Argentina for having featured in the Robert de Niro film *The Mission*. In local dialect, the name, unsurprisingly, means 'big water'. Igúazu is a bottom-fermented golden lager with a light grainy flavour and a subtle hop aroma. Other products in the Quilmes range include alcohol-free Liberty, and a pair of beers that reflect the brewery's German origins: Bock and a wheat beer called Andes.

SPECIFICATIONS

Brewery: Cervecería y Maltería Quilmes
Location: Buenos Aires, Argentina
Style: Lager
Colour: Golden yellow
Alcohol: 4.9%
Serving temperature: 6°–8°C (42.8°–46.4°F)
Food: Salads and cheese

Quilmes

The Quilmes brewery and maltery was founded in the Quilmes district of Buenos Aires in 1888 by German immigrant Otto Bemberg, since which time the name Quilmes has gone on to become synonymous with beer in Argentina.

Expansion throughout the early part of the twentieth century saw the brewery become one of the biggest businesses of any type in Buenos Aires, with its beers being exported far and wide, including to Europe, and Quilmes has even gone on to become the official sponsor of the Argentine national football team. The brewery's main product is this clear golden lager, which has a light malty flavour.

SPECIFICATIONS

Brewery: Cervecería y Maltería Quilmes
Location: Buenos Aires, Argentina
Style: Lager
Colour: Pale golden yellow
Alcohol: 4.9%
Serving temperature: 6°–8°C (42.8°–46.4°F)
Food: Potato chips

ABOVE

Viking is the best-selling beer in Iceland, and Icelanders are proud of the purity of the water used in the brewing process. Produced in Akureyri, in the north of the country, Viking is fast increasing its market share. However, the high taxes charged on all alcoholic drinks in Iceland mean that an evening spent sampling the local brews in Reykjavik is likely to be an expensive night out.

Scandinavian Beers

Of all the Scandinavian countries, Iceland has the shortest brewing tradition, at least in the legal sense. In the past, Iceland was only allowed to produce 2.2% abv beers, a law repealed only a decade or so ago. The two main brews are Viking and Thule. Viking is a premium golden lager beer brewed using the European Pilsen method. The pure Icelandic water and unique fusion of malt, hops, maize and sugar give the beer a distinct bitter taste.

ABOVE

Two women enjoy a refreshing beer, perhaps one brewed in the unique Finnish style, at an outdoor café in the capital of Helsinki.

IN NORWAY, BEER BREWING IS A REGIONAL AFFAIR, with few national brews. The country boasts the world's most northerly brewery, at Tromsø inside the Arctic Circle. The Norwegian brewing industry suffers from high taxation and a mass of regulations. Much of this has to do with an active anti-alcohol lobby, which exerts strong influence on the government.

From the Middle Ages until the seventeenth century beer was Sweden's national drink, but from 1700 onwards it rapidly lost its popularity to spirits. Breweries had the exclusive right to distill and, given the large sums to be earned from spirits, had little incentive to develop the brewing side of their business. Unsurprisingly, the industry went into decline. Before the mid-nineteenth century a wide range of styles were produced; the three commonest local indigenous styles (or Svensköl) were dubbelt öl (double beer), enkelt öl (single beer) and svagöl (weak beer). All of these were top fermented.

The initial stimulus which helped beer to regain popularity came from abroad. Porter was imported from Britain throughout the eighteenth century and in 1791 William Knox founded Sweden's first porter brewery in Göteborg. As in Norway, Sweden's brewing scene has also been overshadowed by the anti-alcohol movement; until recently, for example, there was a ban on the production of beer stronger than 5.6% alcohol.

In Finland, the traditional art of brewing is very old, but this ancient Finnish brewing style is hard to find. There is nothing like it commercially produced anywhere else in the world, although the Swedish island of Gotland and the Estonian island of Saaremaa have local versions known, respectively, as Gotlandsricka and Koduõlu. Brewpubs and microbreweries are a very new thing, and micros in particular have been slow to get going, but there is an excellent one in Central Finland called Palvasalmi. There are also brewpubs in many towns.

STATISTICS

Total production: 10,723,000 hectolitres (283,272,000 gallons) per year

Consumption per capita: 62 litres (16 gallons) per year

Famous breweries: Egil; Lapin Kulta; Spendrups Bryggeri

Famous brands: Lapin Kulta; Norrlands Guld; Pilsner Egil; Spendrup's Old Gold

Pilsner Egils

Until 1989, Iceland had been subject to a ban on alcohol which had first been imposed in 1915.

Through that period, the tiny country's few breweries, such as Egill of Reykjavik, concentrated on producing soft drinks, which still make up a large part of its business, and low-alcohol beers, including Egils Malt, which has only 1% alcohol. Its light version of a Pilsner-style lager is not much stronger, but is brewed with pure Icelandic water to give it a clean, refreshing flavour. Both the brewery and its beers take their names from the Egils saga, the story of a tenth-century Icelandic warrior and poet named Egill Skalagrímsson.

SPECIFICATIONS

Brewery: Egill
Location: Iceland
Style: Lager
Colour: Golden yellow
Alcohol: 2.2%
Serving temperature: 6°–7°C (42.8°–44.6°F)
Food: Salads

Norrlands Guld Export

Norrland is the most northerly part of Sweden, originally including parts of Finland until the two countries were separated in 1809, splitting Norrland in two.

It is a rural area where the people are known for their straightforward, laidback approach to life, an image that has been appropriated by Spendrups for the promotion of its Norrlands Guld (Gold) beer in a series of television advertisements that have become famous in Sweden. The beer itself is a straightforward easy-drinking pale lager with a light, slightly sweet malty flavour balanced by a gentle hop bitterness. There is also a stronger version, Norrlands Guld Dynamit, at 7.2% abv.

SPECIFICATIONS

Brewery: Spendrups Bryggeri
Location: Grangesberg, Sweden
Style: Lager
Colour: Golden yellow
Alcohol: 5.3%
Serving temperature: 6°–8°C (42.8°–46.4°F)
Food: Roasted rabbit or chicken

Spendrups Old Gold

When it was introduced in the mid-1980s, Old Gold was one of the first true Pilsner-style lagers to be made in Sweden.

It is an all-malt golden beer with a mild floral hoppy aroma and a well-balanced flavour. It comes from Spendrups, the second-largest brewer in Sweden, which was originally known as the Grangesberg Brewery, after the town where it was founded, which is in southern Sweden, about 240 km (150 miles) northwest of Stockholm, although the company now has its headquarters in the Swedish capital. It was founded in 1949 by an entrepreneur named Gunnar Spokis Andersson who wanted to help the Swedish economy recover from the effects of Nazi occupation of the country during World War II.

SPECIFICATIONS

Brewery: Spendrups Bryggeri
Location: Grangesberg, Sweden
Style: Pilsner
Colour: Deep golden yellow
Alcohol: 5%
Serving temperature: 6°–8°C (42.8°–46.4°F)
Food: Light fish and shellfish dishes

Lapin Kulta

The Finnish brew of Lapin Kulta is a strong, smooth lager with a malty flavour.

Its name translates as Lapland's Gold and reflects the heritage of the brewery, which was founded in 1873 in the far northern Finnish town of Tornio, close to the border with Sweden, when hundreds of gold prospectors descended on the area. Both ventures proved successful – the prospectors found 130 kilograms of gold, while the brewery became a thriving business, despite Finland being hit hard by prohibition of alcohol between 1919 and 1932. Following an agreement with Hartwall in the 1960s the beers began to be distributed to the rest of Finland and even exported abroad. The company also produces Lapin Kulta Talviolut – Lapin Kulta Winter – a stronger, darker beer available between November and January.

SPECIFICATIONS

Brewery: Lapin Kulta
Location: Tornio, Lapland, Finland
Style: Lager
Colour: Golden yellow
Alcohol: 7%
Serving temperature: 6°–7°C (42.8°–44.6°F)
Food: Peppered tuna steaks

ABOVE

The Carlsberg brewery in Copenhagen, the capital of Denmark, is now the seventh largest brewery in the world, and has been in operation since 1847. The copper kettles are used to cook the mash at a steady temperature as it is turned into beer. Here one of the brewers checks the progress of the latest batch of Denmark's famous brew.

Danish Beers

Danish beer-making has long been identified with the international power of Carlsberg, which holds its status as one of the world's great beer producers with numerous high-selling brands. However, Denmark produces around 2000 varieties of beer from more than 450 individual breweries, with many smaller companies specialising in traditional brewing techniques.

ABOVE

Carlsberg and Tivoli workers take a break from loading duties in July 1952 to enjoy an early morning beer – 9am to be precise!

IN DENMARK, the beer scene is dominated by Carlsberg. The business traces its origins to the 1700s, to a family farm that almost certainly had its own brewery. The son of the family went to seek his fortune in the big city, and eventually became a brewer there. He was one of the first Danish brewers to use a thermometer. His son Jacob Christian Jacobsen went south to Germany, to Bavaria, to study at the Spaten brewery. It was the moment in Europe when top-fermenting brews (in Denmark, wheat beers) were beginning to face challenges from lagers. Carlsberg produced the first bottom-fermented beer commercially made in Denmark – or anywhere in Northern Europe.

Jacob Christian Jacobsen's son Carl also became a brewer. The two men later disagreed to the extent that for a long time each had his own Carlsberg brewery. This historic feud ended shortly before the father's death, and the two breweries merged. The company produces both Carlsberg and Tuborg mainstream lagers, which are immensely popular worldwide, as well as a range of other lagers, notably the famous Special Brew.

As in many countries, the decline of the traditional brewing branch and the rise of microbreweries has provoked unrest in the trade organisation. Many newcomers resent the way the established trade body, Bryggeriforeningen, appears to be run for and by Carlsberg and Bryggerigruppen. Their response has been to establish an organisation that will better represent their interests. Danske Bryghuse was officially founded on 21 October 2003.

STATISTICS

Total production: 8,351,000 hectolitres (220,610,000 gallons) per year

Consumption per capita: 99 litres (26 gallons) per year

Famous breweries: Carlsberg; Ceres; Faxe Bryggeri; Giraf Brewery Ltd; Harboe; Tuborg

Famous brands: Bjørne Beer; Carlsberg Elephant; Carlsberg Export; Ceres Red Erik; Ceres Royal Export; Faxe Premium; Giraf Classic; Tuborg Premium

Giraf Classic

In 1962 the people of Odense in Denmark were shocked by the news that Kalle the giraffe, a resident of the local zoo, had been found dead in his pen.

The local Albani brewery had used Kalle's image in its advertising and so in his honour it launched a new beer to fund a replacement giraffe for the zoo. Thus Giraf beer was born, and in 1997 a separate brewery was established dedicated to the production of Giraf beers. The range now includes three regular beers – Gold, Strong and Classic.

The history of Albani brewery stretches back much further. It was founded in Odense in 1859 and was one of the town's first industrial businesses. At that time, the majority of beer brewed in Denmark was top-fermented mid-strength ale, but Albani was founded on the principle of creating stronger bottom-fermented beers according to the Bavarian tradition. The brewery quickly found favour with many prominent locals, including Hans Christian Andersen, who wrote of Albani beer: 'I cannot praise this beer enough. It is refreshing, tasty and strong. Try it!' His patronage helped the brewery to expand rapidly, and from the early part of the twentieth century onwards Albani started to acquire many smaller rural breweries to form the foundations of the group that is today the second-largest brewer in Denmark. It achieved that status in 1992 when it acquired Faxe Bryggeri and Jyske Bryggerier (comprising Ceres and Thor), and became the Danish Brewery Group.

SPECIFICATIONS

Brewery: Giraf Brewery Ltd
Location: Odense, Funen
Style: Lager
Colour: Pale golden yellow
Alcohol: 4.6%
Serving temperature: 7°–8°C (44.6°–46.4°F)
Food: Mild-flavoured cheeses, white meats

Carlsberg Elephant

The elephant is the symbol of the largest brewery in Denmark, Carlsberg, which was founded in 1847 by Jacob Christian Jacobsen.

He derived the name of the brewery from a combination of the name of his five-year-old son Carl and the brewery's hillside location (*berg* being Danish for 'hill'). Instead of the top-fermented ales that were prevalent, Jacobsen, like many other new Danish brewers of the time, adopted the new bottom-fermented beer styles that were being pioneered in Bavaria. He even travelled to Munich to learn from Gabriel Sedlmayer of the Spaten brewery. Jacobson was keen on the scientific aspects of brewing, and it was at his laboratories that the first single-cell lager yeast was developed in 1883, which gave brewers greater control over the fermentation process. This was given the name Carlsbergensis.

Following Jacob's death in 1887, the brewery came into the control of the Carlsberg Foundation, while his son Carl set up a rival brewery next door with four large stone elephants standing at the gates, which were inspired by a fountain he had seen in Rome. This also became part of the Carlsberg foundation in 1902, while Carl became a patron of the arts in Copenhagen. The brewery is now owned by Kronenbourg and produces a wide range of beers, its best known being its classic Pilsner-style golden lager. Carlsberg Elephant is a strong lager in the style of a German bock, with a slightly darker colour and a fairly sweet flavour.

SPECIFICATIONS

Brewery: Carlsberg
Location: Copenhagen
Style: Lager
Colour: Rich golden yellow
Alcohol: 7.2%
Serving temperature: 8°–10°C (46.4°–50°F)
Food: Fried fish

Ceres Red Erik

Ceres, which started its brewing operations in 1856, was one of the many breweries founded in Denmark in the middle of the nineteenth century.

Named after the Roman fertility goddess, it was created by a local distiller called M.C. Lottrup in cooperation with two local chemists called N.S. Aagaard and Knud Redelien, although the latter pair withdrew from the business after a year. The brewery's Red Erik beer, named after the Viking who discovered Greenland and reputedly began brewing there, gets its distinctive colour from the addition of the juices of various fruits and berries. It is a full-bodied strong beer with a refreshingly sharp and slightly sweet flavour.

SPECIFICATIONS

Brewery: Ceres
Location: Aarhus, East Jutland
Style: Fruit beer
Colour: Ruby red
Alcohol: 6.5%
Serving temperature: 7°–8°C (44.6°–46.4°F)
Food: Fruit-based desserts

Ceres Royal Export

Ceres Royal Export was launched in 1985, and in its first year was named Danish beer of the year. It is now one of the most popular premium beer brands in Denmark.

It is made with maize as well as malt, to give it crisp, clean refreshing character. It has a smooth, full body, and the flavour is characterised by a mild maltiness balanced with a light hop bitterness. Ceres Royal Export Classic is a stronger, darker, all-malt version of the same beer, made with a blend of Pilsner, Munich and dark roasted malts for a fuller flavour and a nut brown colour.

SPECIFICATIONS

Brewery: Ceres
Location: Aarhus, East Jutland
Style: Pilsner
Colour: Pale golden yellow
Alcohol: 5.8%
Serving temperature: 8°C (46.4°F)
Food: pasta with a rich tomato-based sauce

Faxe Premium

Faxe is today part of the giant Danish Brewery group, and most of its beers are exported to Germany and other countries, but it started life in 1901 on a very small scale in the scullery of Nikoline and Conrad Neilsen at their house in the small town of Faxe.

The brewery quickly established a widespread reputation for quality beers and, following Conrad's untimely death in 1914, the business was continued by Nikoline. It was renamed the Faxe Bryggeri in 1928, by which time it was supplying beer and soft drinks across the Sealand and Lolland-Falster regions of Denmark, and to Copenhagen. The problem of meeting increasing demand for water was solved in the 1930s by drilling an 80-metre deep well, which is still used by the brewery today, the water filtered by an underground coral. The brewery remained in the family into the 1960s, coming into the ownership of the 23-year-old Bent Bryde-Neilsen, Nikoline's grand-daughter, in 1963. She developed Faxe into one of Denmark's largest breweries, establishing export markets in Germany and Sweden.

Outside of Denmark, Faxe is best known for Faxe Premium, an all-malt lager with a delicate hop aroma and flavour. For the domestic market, the brewery also produces several other beers, including Faxe Amber, a darker, fuller lager which was introduced in 2001 to celebrate the brewery's centenary.

SPECIFICATIONS

Brewery: Faxe Bryggeri
Location: Faxe, Sealand
Style: Lager
Colour: Golden yellow
Alcohol: 5.5%
Serving temperature: 8°–10°C (46.4°–50°F)
Food: Rich pasta dishes

Bjørne Beer

Outside Denmark, Bjørne Beer is very commonly known by the literal translation of its name, Bear Beer, and a polar bear is depicted on the beer's label.

It has a fragrant herbal hop aroma with background bready malt notes, while on the palate the flavour is characterised by a gentle hop bitterness. Launched in 1974, it earned the name for its high alcohol content, although the name is now applied to a range of different strength beers, each with different-coloured labels (the strongest have black labels). Bear Beer comes from the Harboe brewery, which was founded in Skaelskør in 1883 by three local businessmen. The 8.3% abv of Bear Beer makes it one of the strongest of Harboe's beers, although its Argangsbryg brand even exceeds that level with a 10% abv. To balance the equation, the brewery makes a low alcohol lager which dips down to 1.9% abv.

SPECIFICATIONS

Brewery: Harboe
Location: Skaelskør, Sealand
Style: Strong golden lager
Colour: Deep golden yellow
Alcohol: 8.3%
Serving temperature: 8°–10°C (46.4°–50°F)
Food: Spicy pizzas and pasta dishes

Tuborg Premium Beer

While Carlsberg is by far Denmark's best-known beer brand internationally, its main rival on the domestic market, Tuborg, actually outsells it at home. In fact, the two breweries merged in 1970, although they retain independent control of their brewing operations and marketing. Tuborg was founded just to the north of Copenhagen in 1875, near the city's port. At first it followed the example of Carlsberg and began brewing dark Munich-style lagers, its first beer being called Rod (Danish for 'red'), after the colour of its label.

In 1880, Tuborg became the first brewery in Denmark to produce a golden Pilsner-style lager, which became known as Grøn, after its green label. This remains the leading Tuborg beer brand today. Tuborg Guld (Gold) is the brewery's premium lager brand, a gently bitter hoppy golden lager with a sharp herbal hop aroma. As well as its beers, Tuborg has made an impact on its home country of Denmark in other ways. In 1888, it created one of Denmark's most famous landmarks, a giant 26-metre tall beer bottle containing the city's first hydraulic lift. It was built for display at the industrial fair that was being held in the famous Tivoli Gardens. It now stands in the centre of Copenhagen, close to the city hall.

SPECIFICATIONS

Brewery: Tuborg
Location: Copenhagen
Style: Pilsner
Colour: Golden yellow
Alcohol: 5%
Serving temperature: 8°–10°C (46.4°–50°F)
Food: Serve as an aperitif

ABOVE

Ireland is famed for its traditional drinking establishments, but the image can mask the fact that Ireland is a major global competitor on the beer market, particularly through its most famous brand Guinness. A full one million litres of its three million litres annual beer production is exported, and the fan base for its dark ales and porters is constantly growing worldwide.

Irish Beers

For many outside the country, the perception of brewing in Ireland begins and ends with one beer style – stout – and what's more, with one particular name, that of Dublin brewer Arthur Guinness. In fact, brewing in Ireland dates back at least to the fifth century, when St Patrick arrived in Ireland, reputedly bringing his own brewer with him.

ABOVE

The Guinness brand is rightly famous the world over, and more than any other drink is identified with Ireland. Yet although Guinness does dominate Irish brewing, the country is also home to a range of other breweries which produce beers of altogether different character.

AS IN OTHER COUNTRIES, it was the monasteries (in Ireland's case founded by St Patrick) that established the tradition of ale brewing, although even before then the native Irish drank a barley-based liquor called courmi, as noted by Roman historian Dioscorides. But Guinness is by far the biggest name in Irish brewing. The firm was established in 1759 as a brewer of traditional amber ales. Around this time, the dark English beer known as porter, named after the London market porters who were its main consumers, was being imported to Ireland in vast quantities, and it wasn't long before Arthur Guinness and other brewers such as Beamish & Crawford came up with their own versions.

The first Guinness porter came out of the St James's Gate brewery in the 1770s, but it was not until 1799 that he switched to brewing exclusively porter. In 1820, his son, also called Arthur, created a new style of porter that he called extra stout porter, later shortened to stout. The style quickly caught on, and Guinness Extra Stout was soon being exported around the world. In 1936, a second brewery was opened in Park Royal, London, to cope with the huge demand. In 1962 the first Guinness brewery outside the British Isles was opened in Nigeria, and today Guinness has many breweries around the world. Guinness is now part of the international drinks giant Diageo.

The power of Guinness in Ireland, however, should not be overstated. It has major rivals such as Heineken Ireland, which incorporates Murphy's, and dynamic young competitors such as the Carlow Brewing Company, which is offering alternative beverages to the classic Guinness brands.

STATISTICS

Total production: 8,023,000 hectolitres (211,945,000 gallons) per year

Consumption per capita: 125 litres (33 gallons) per year

Famous breweries: Beamish & Crawford; Carlow Brewing Company; Guinness Ltd; Heinenken Ireland; Murphy Brewery; Smithwick's

Famous brands: Beamish Irish Stout; Guinness Draught; Guinness Extra Stout; Harp Lager; Kilkenny Irish Ale; Murphy's Irish Red; O'Hara's Celtic Stout

Beamish Irish Stout

This popular Cork beer, the only Irish stout that is brewed exclusively in Ireland, proves that there is plenty of life in the Irish brewing industry outside Dublin. It pours pitch black with a thick, creamy head that is typical of the style.

Gentle caramel and coffee aromas fill the nose, while the keynotes on the palate are of roasted malts, bittersweet chocolate and espresso coffee. Unusually, Beamish uses a proportion of malted wheat in the brew, and its flavour is slightly sweeter than some other Irish stouts. Beamish & Crawford, originally known as the Cork Porter Brewing Company, was founded in 1792. Fortunes waned throughout the twentieth century until in 1962 Beamish & Crawford was bought by Canadian brewer Carling O'Keefe. Eventually, the company came under the ownership of British brewers Scottish & Newcastle, since when Beamish Irish Stout has enjoyed a revival.

SPECIFICATIONS

Brewery: Beamish & Crawford (Scottish & Newcastle)
Location: Cork, Co. Cork
Style: Dry Irish stout
Colour: Black
Alcohol: 4.5%
Serving temperature: 8°C (46.4°F)
Food: Seafood

Moling's Traditional Celtic Beer

The Carlow Brewing company was established in 1998 in the small town of Carlow in the Barrow Valley region of southern Ireland.

This is the traditional malt- and hop-producing area of the country and once boasted a large number of breweries. All beers produced at this brewery are based on traditional Celtic recipes and use only strictly authentic ingredients – malt, hops, yeast and water. Its Moling's red ale has fruity, caramel malt aromas, starts off with nutty caramel malts on the palate and finishes with a bitter kick of hops followed by a lingering sweetness.

SPECIFICATIONS

Brewery: Carlow Brewing Company
Location: Carlow, Co. Carlow
Style: Irish red ale
Colour: Deep red-brown
Alcohol: 4.3%
Serving temperature: 8°C (46.4°F)
Food: Grilled fish such as tuna steaks

O'Hara's Celtic Stout

O'Hara's aims to be a genuine alternative to the big three of Guinness, Beamish and Murphy's.

SPECIFICATIONS

Brewery: Carlow Brewing Company
Location: Carlow, Co. Carlow
Style: Dry Irish stout
Colour: Very dark brown, almost black
Alcohol: 4.3%
Serving temperature: 9°C (48.2°F)
Food: Smoked salmon or other seafoods

O'Hara's from the Carlow Brewing Company is one of the few Irish stouts currently available in bottle-conditioned form. This part of the brewing process gives the stout a distinctly lively, fresh character that generally isn't found in its pasteurised, filtered rivals. Roasted coffee dominates the drink's aroma and it also contains underlying hints of burnt toffee. O'Hara's has a light body, feeling smooth and dry on the palate with bitter flavours of roasted barley, espresso coffee and hints of chocolate, backed up by the citrussy bitterness of hops, leading to a smooth, bitter malt finish. The Carlow Brewing Company is a recent arrival to the brewing market, but has established a solid reputation for producing quality drinks.

Guinness Extra Stout

Of the various versions of Guinness currently available, this is the one that comes closest to the original Irish extra stout porter that was created by Arthur Guinness.

This classic style is the beer that made the company's name and will for ever be associated slogans such as 'Guinness is good for you'. The beer's roasted malts give a distinctive dry, oaky flavour full of toasted malt bitterness. Note that in the United Kingdom this classic dry Irish stout is marketed as Guinness Original, while in the United States Guinness Extra Stout is the name given to a stronger 'export' version of the beer, brewed to 8% alcohol.

SPECIFICATIONS

Brewery: Guinness Ltd
Location: Dublin, Co. Dublin
Style: Dry Irish stout
Colour: Very dark ruby red, almost black
Alcohol: 4.3%
Serving temperature: 12°C (53.6°F)
Food: Classic accompaniment for oysters

Guinness Draught

In recent years, Guinness has played heavily on the mythology of how to pour a perfect pint. This is a slow process, but patience reaps its own rewards, and modern dispensing methods are relatively straightforward compared to the two-cask serving system that prevailed until the launch of Guinness Draught in 1959.

One cask would contain recently brewed stout that was still undergoing secondary fermentation, while the second cask contained an older, more mature brew. The glass was first filled with the fresher, livelier beer, which would generate a deep foaming head, and once this had settled, the glass was then topped up with the older, flatter beer. With the launch of Guinness Draught, the wooden casks were replaced with pressurised kegs injected with nitrogen, which is what gives the stout its famously smooth, creamy texture and thick, foaming head. The beer is also pasteurised and filtered to ensure consistency and extend keeping. Then in 1989, Guinness hit on the idea of trying to re-create the draught beer experience for the home consumer, so it invented the 'widget', a small plastic device inserted in the can that releases a dose of nitrogen when the can is opened. Guinness Draught has a deep, dry roasted malt flavour with a refreshing burnt caramel bitterness and a slightly sour edge, while the widget ensures that the texture is as creamy and full-bodied as that found in the Guinness served in pubs.

SPECIFICATIONS

Brewery: Guinness Ltd
Location: Dublin, Co. Dublin
Style: Dry Irish stout
Colour: Black with a thick, creamy tan-coloured head
Alcohol: 5%
Serving temperature: 5°C (41°F)
Food: Cheese, especially strong-flavoured blue cheeses

Guinness Foreign Extra Stout

Since the early nineteenth century, as well as its regular stout, Guinness has also brewed a strong version for export to Asia, Africa and the Caribbean.

As with the English India pale ale style, which was brewed to survive the journey to India, Guinness Foreign Extra Stout is brewed to a higher alcohol content and contains a far higher hop content. Both the alcohol and the hops act as preservatives, but also produce a beer with a much fuller flavour. Today, Guinness is brewed in many different countries around the world, but the export style survives due to its continuing popularity among Guinness connoisseurs.

SPECIFICATIONS

Brewery: Guinness Ltd
Location: Dublin, Co. Dublin
Style: Dry Irish stout
Colour: Black
Alcohol: 7.5%
Serving temperature: 18°C (64.4°F)
Food: Sausages and mash

Guinness Special Export

In 1912, a Belgian beer importer asked the Guinness brewery to produce a special version of its famous stout exclusively for the Belgian market.

This smooth, silky 8% alcohol stout was the result. It is still brewed at the St James's Gate brewery before being bottled and shipped over to Belgium. This is a considerably more complex beer than some other stouts. It pours opaque black with a huge, thick milk coffee-coloured head. Bitter roasted malts and dark fruit dominate the aroma, and there's a good deal of fruit in the flavour, too, notably currants and raisins, along with a hint of liquorice. The finish is clean, dry and very bitter.

SPECIFICATIONS

Brewery: Guinness Ltd
Location: Dublin, Co. Dublin
Style: Dry Irish stout
Colour: Black
Alcohol: 8%
Serving temperature: 18°C (64.4°F)
Food: Roasted meat

Harp Lager

Hard though it may be to believe, not everyone in Ireland is a stout drinker. For those who prefer a European-style lager, Guinness produces this all-malt bottom-fermented golden beer.

It has a grainy, sweet, malty aroma and a straightforwardly clean, light and refreshing flavour, with sweet malts again dominating, giving way to a lightly hoppy finish. Harp Lager was created in 1960 when Guinness acquired the Great Northern Brewery in Dundalk, which had previously been an ale brewery. To emphasise its Irishness, it was named after the Brian Boru harp, the emblem of both the Guinness company and of Ireland itself.

SPECIFICATIONS

- **Brewery:** Guinness Ltd
- **Location:** Dundalk, Co. Louth
- **Style:** Lager
- **Colour:** Pale golden
- **Alcohol:** 5%
- **Serving temperature:** 8°C (46.4°F)
- **Food:** Charcoal grilled fish

Kilkenny Irish Ale

This traditional Irish red ale was originally brewed in 1985 for export only, by Smithwick's at the St Francis Abbey Brewery in Kilkenny (which has been owned by Guinness since 1965).

A sweet, predominantly malty aroma gives way to a smooth, dry and nutty flavour on the palate, with a short, bitter, hoppy finish. Smithwick's is one of the oldest names in Irish brewing, and has been producing ales on this site since 1710, although the Franciscan friars who founded the abbey in the mid-thirteenth century would undoubtedly have been brewers themselves.

SPECIFICATIONS

- **Brewery:** Smithwick's (Guinness Ltd)
- **Location:** Kilkenny, Co. Kilkenny
- **Style:** Irish red ale
- **Colour:** Amber-red
- **Alcohol:** 5%
- **Serving temperature:** 9°–10°C (48.2°–50°F)
- **Food:** Boiled bacon and cabbage

Murphy's Irish Red

Murphy's Irish Red is brewed to an original recipe that dates back to 1856. It pours a deep burnished bronze with a frothy ivory-coloured head and gives off a lightly toasted aroma of caramel malts.

On the palate, light carbonation gives it a lively mouthfeel, while the flavour is dry with a pronounced hoppy bitterness balanced against grainy malt sweetness. A refreshingly bitter citrus-hop finish helps this beer go down well. The better known Murphy's Irish Stout has a sweeter and milder flavour than either of its main rivals, Guinness Draught and Beamish Stout, but shares the characteristic smooth, creamy texture, pitch-black colour and thick, creamy head that are key features of the Irish stout style. Both were originally brewed by James J. Murphy at the Murphy Brewery in the city of Cork in the southwestern corner of Ireland.

Although it was established in 1856 and thus predates Guinness by three years, Murphy's has always struggled to emerge from the shadow of its famous Dublin rival, but when threatened by closure in 1983 the brewery was rescued by Heineken, which set about an extensive modernisation programme. This has enabled the brewery to compete in the international market and establish itself as the second-largest brewery in Ireland.

SPECIFICATIONS

Brewery: Heineken Ireland
Location: Cork, Co. Cork
Style: Irish red ale
Colour: Clear red-bronze
Alcohol: 5%
Serving temperature: 8°C (46.4°F)
Food: Roast suckling pig

ABOVE

Scottish beer production has become steadily more prolific over recent years. The beers range from standard high-street lagers such as Tennent's through to very individual brands such as Belhaven 80/- and Orkney Dragonhead Stout. Gradually Scotland is building a reputation for beer production which is not overshadowed by the country's world-renowned spirits.

Scottish Beers

Although Scotland has a considerably smaller population than its neighbour to the south, it has just as strong a tradition for brewing, which it has always carried out in its own unique way. Scottish beers are traditionally named according to the shilling system, which was introduced in the nineteenth century and related to the price charged for a hogshead barrel.

SIMPLY PUT, the stronger the beer the more expensive it was, so a 40/- ale would be a very light beer, while the strongest beers would be rated at 80/- or higher. The terms 'light', 'heavy' and 'export' are commonly used, in that order of strength; the strongest barley wines are also known as Scotch ales or Wee Heavies.

The character of brewing in Scotland is partly determined by the climate. As in England, barley flourishes; however, while English barley growers have always turned their crops into beer, the cold, wet conditions that prevail in Scotland mean that the barley that is grown there is better suited to the production of whisky. This climate also prevents the successful growing of hops, so the Scots have always used a variety of alternative bittering agents in their beers instead of hops, such as ginger, pepper, spices and herbs. Oats also flourish in Scottish conditions, and accordingly oatmeal has often been used as an ingredient, along with barley in Scottish beer, particularly in stout.

Although it has often played second fiddle to whisky, beer has always been extremely popular in Scotland, and throughout the nineteenth century Scotland had a brewing industry to compete with anywhere else in the world. By the beginning of the twentieth century, there were no fewer than 28 breweries in Edinburgh alone. Unfortunately, the twentieth century saw a gradual concentration of the Scottish brewing industry until by the 1970s there were just two brewers left in Edinburgh – Scottish & Newcastle, now the largest brewing group in Britain, and Tennent's, which is now part of the global giant Interbrew. The situation has improved in recent years with smaller independent breweries such as Caledonian being able to gain a foothold in the market.

ABOVE

Scotland's reputation when it comes to the production of alcoholic beverages rests mainly on whisky, but beer production is currently undergoing something of a renaissance, with smaller brewers returning to traditional methods of brewing.

STATISTICS

Total production: 20,000,000 hectolitres (528,344,000 gallons) per year

Consumption per capita: 97 litres (26 gallons) per year

Famous breweries: Belhaven Brewer Company Ltd; Broughton Ales Ltd; Caledonian Brewery; Orkney Brewery; Tennent Caledonian Breweries (Interbrew); Traquair House Brewery Ltd

Famous brands: Belhaven 80/-; Broughton the Ghillie; Caledonian Golden Promise; Orkney Dragonhead Stout; Tennent's Lager; Traquair House Ale; Traquair Jacobite

Belhaven 80 Shilling

Based in the small town of Dunbar, just 48 km (30 miles) from Edinburgh, Belhaven is one of the largest regional brewers in Scotland. It is also one of the oldest, with a brewing history stretching back at least 300 years.

The first known documents that can confirm the existence of the brewery date from 1719, when the brewery was bought by John Johnstone. In fact, it is believed to be much older, as the present brewery stands on the site of a former monastery built by Benedictine monks in the twelfth century. The fame of Belhaven beers has spread far and wide. Belhaven 80 Shilling (or 80/-) was once described by the Austrian Emperor as 'the Burgundy of Scotland', and Dr Johnson's biographer James Boswell was also known to be a fan. It has a rich red-hued colour and a deeply complex, malt-led flavour, with sweet caramel, dark fruit and nutty roasted malt notes.

Other beers in the brewery's range include St Andrew's Ale, brewed to celebrate Scotland's battle for independence from the English. It has a full-bodied malty flavour with a predominantly fruity character, balanced by a gentle, mellow hop bitterness in the finish that is a result of 'dry hopping' the casks. Belhaven Best is a lighter honey-coloured ale with a well-balanced flavour and a moderate 3.2% alcohol, making it an ideal session beer.

SPECIFICATIONS

Brewery: Belhaven Brewer Company Ltd

Location: Dunbar, East Lothian

Style: Scottish strong export ale

Colour: Dark red-brown

Alcohol: 3.9%

Serving temperature: 10°–13°C (50°–55.4°F)

Food: Spicy, tangy Chinese dishes

Orkney Dragonhead Stout

Founded in 1988 by Roger White and his wife, Irene, the multiple award-winning Orkney company is the most northerly brewery in Britain, being situated on the largest of the Isles of Orkney, off the northeastern coast of the Scottish mainland.
The brewery is housed in an old schoolhouse surrounded by two-and-a-half hectares (six acres) of grassland and lakes, and offers six regular beers in its line-up, each of which has a name inspired by the historical association of the islands with the Vikings. Dragonhead Stout is a first-rate example of the style, packed with rich, sweet roasted malt flavours balanced with an astringent dry bitterness provided by a complex blend of hops.

The strongest beer in the brewery's range is the appropriately named Skullsplitter, named after Thorfin Hausakliuuf, the seventh earl of Orkney. This strong red ale has an intense wine-like aroma, a rich, deep fruity flavour and a full-bodied smoothness that makes it dangerously easy to drink despite its 8.5% alcohol. At the other end of the spectrum, Raven Ale is a golden ale with a grainy aroma, fruity flavour and lingering hop finish, with a relatively modest 3.8% alcohol. In between, along with Dragonhead Stout, are Red MacGregor, which is a floral, hoppy pale ale; Northern Light, a light fruity beer 'as clear as Orkney skies and waters'; and a ruby-red fruity Scotch ale called Dark Island.

SPECIFICATIONS

Brewery: Orkney Brewery
Location: Sandwick, Isles of Orkney
Style: Stout
Colour: Black
Alcohol: 4%
Serving temperature: 8°–10°C (46.4°–50°F)
Food: Strong cheeses

Broughton Black Douglas

Established in 1979, the Broughton brewery is situated in Biggar, which lies just north of the border with England. The company went into receivership in 1995, but was rescued by the owner of the Whim Brewery, Giles Litchfield, and its managing director Alastair Mouat.

Since then Broughton has undergone a reversal of fortunes, establishing itself as a successful exporter of beers, as well as continuing to thrive on the domestic market. The company brews a wide range of ales, mostly provided as cask beers for the 200 pubs and other outlets it supplies throughout Scotland. It also has a varied range of bottled beers. As well as its own range of beers, Broughton also produces a bottled version of Old Izaak, a traditional old English ale, under licence from Whim Ales. Black Douglas is named after Sir James Douglas, a powerful, heroic knight and a trusted friend of Robert the Bruce. He was eventually killed in a battle against the Moors while attempting to fulfil Robert the Bruce's dying wish to have his heart buried in the holy sepulchre in Jerusalem. The beer that bears his name is brewed with Maris Otter pale malts, roasted barley and maize to create a ruby-hued ale with a sweet, almost treacle-like flavour balanced by a dark chocolatey bitterness. In its cask form, this is a seasonal winter brew, while the bottled version is available all year round.

SPECIFICATIONS

Brewery: Broughton Ales Ltd
Location: Biggar, Peeblesshire
Style: Scottish ale
Colour: Dark ruby red-brown
Alcohol: 5.2%
Serving temperature: 10°–13°C (50°–55.4°F)
Food: Meat or fish in a spicy sauce

Broughton Greenmantle

The first beer to be launched by the Broughton brewery when it opened for business in 1979 was named after a short story by the famous novelist John Buchan, who happened to live nearby. That the brewery should choose such a literary name for its beer is hardly surprising, given that Broughton's original owner, David Younger, was not only a descendant of the Younger brewing clan of Alloa, but was also related to the Collins publishing dynasty. Greenmantle Original is a pale chestnut brown colour that is more characteristic of an English-style pale ale than a Scottish ale.

The flavour, however, is more typically Scottish in character, having a sweet malty flavour with hints of honey and a gentle hop bitterness in the finish. The Greenmantle name is also applied to an India pale ale that is available in cask form only. The Broughton range of bottled beers also includes two organic beers using malted organic Scottish barley and imported organic Hallertau hops from New Zealand: Border Gold Organic Ale, a light-coloured ale with a refreshing hop aroma and flavour and a fortifying 6% alcohol, and Angel Organic Lager, which is fermented at low temperatures for a full 14 days to create a smooth, clean-tasting Pilsner-style beer.

SPECIFICATIONS

Brewery: Broughton Ales Ltd
Location: Biggar, Peeblesshire
Style: Scottish ale
Colour: Pale chestnut brown
Alcohol: 3.9%
Serving temperature: 10°–13°C (50°–55.4°F)
Food: A light quaffing beer to drink by itself

Broughton Merlin's Ale

Merlin's Ale is brewed with Maris Otter malt and roasted barley, and flavoured with four varieties of hops – English Target, Fuggles and Goldings, plus Czech Styrian Goldings for aroma.

It is a light golden hoppy ale with a delicate aroma of floral hops, followed by a predominantly grainy malty character on the palate before a dry bitter hop finish. Merlin's is named after the legendary wizard who is believed to have resided in the area near the brewery following the Battle of Adderyd near Carlisle in AD 573. This battle saw the defeat of the pagan forces of Gwendoleu by the Christian Rydderch Hael.

SPECIFICATIONS

Brewery: Broughton Ales Ltd
Location: Biggar, Peeblesshire
Style: Best bitter
Colour: Pale orange-yellow
Alcohol: 4.2%
Serving temperature: 10°–12°C (50°–53.6°F)
Food: Spicy sauced Mexican dishes, such as mole poblano

Broughton Old Jock

The term 'Jock' is used as a nickname for any Scottish person, but in its original usage specifically referred to the soldiers of the Scottish Highland and Lowland regiments, renowned for their courage and determination in battle.

Old Jock Ale is designed to reflect the strength and character of these men. Brewed with Maris Otter malt and roasted barley to a potent 6.7% alcohol, it is a warming, full-bodied ale with a robustly sweet and fruity flavour. This is balanced by a forceful hop bitterness that stems from the use of three different varieties of hops in its brewing.

SPECIFICATIONS

Brewery: Broughton Ales Ltd
Location: Biggar, Peeblesshire
Style: Scottish strong ale
Colour: Dark mahogany red-brown
Alcohol: 6.7%
Serving temperature: 10°–12°C (50°–53.6°F)
Food: A beer to savour after dinner

Broughton Scottish Oatmeal Stout

The label of Broughton's traditional black stout bears a picture of Robert Younger, great-grandfather of David Younger, who founded the Broughton brewery in 1979.

Robert Younger founded the famous Younger brewery in Edinburgh in 1844, but he was not the first member of the Younger to open a brewery – Robert's great-grandfather George opened his brewery in Alloa in 1770. It is only fitting that the family should be remembered by a beer with such a particularly Scottish character. The cool, damp Scottish climate is especially suited to the growing of oats and barley, which combine to give this stout a smooth, creamy texture and dry bitter chocolate flavours, balanced by hints of spices.

SPECIFICATIONS

Brewery: Broughton Ales Ltd
Location: Biggar, Peeblesshire
Style: Oatmeal stout
Colour: Black
Alcohol: 4.2%
Serving temperature: 13°C (55.4°F)
Food: Dark chocolate-based desserts

Broughton the Ghillie

The authentic Scottish character of Broughton brewery is reflected in the choice of names it gives to its beers. The Ghillie is no exception.

Traditionally, a ghillie was a kind of bodyguard to the chief of a clan and would always follow him into battle. Later the term came to have a more general use for a servant, particularly one who supervised sporting activities such as game hunting and fishing. Broughton's Ghillie is a well-rounded beer with a smooth, rich texture, a light copper-coloured hue and a full malty flavour balanced with a refreshingly spicy, floral hop aroma. Ingredients included in the beer are Maris Otter Malt and Crystal Malt, Fuggles and Goldings, and Target hops and German Hallertau Brewers' Gold acting, according to the company, 'as a late copper aroma hop'. Appropriately for its title, Broughton the Ghillie comes with the recommendation for its drinkers to 'enjoy after a day's fishing or at any other time.'

SPECIFICATIONS

Brewery: Broughton Ales Ltd
Location: Biggar, Peeblesshire
Style: Pale ale
Colour: Copper-red
Alcohol: 4.5%
Serving temperature: 10°–12°C (50°–53.6°F)
Food: Chinese sweet-and-sour dishes

Caledonian 80 Shilling

Scottish beers are traditionally classified by two systems. The first describes the beers in order of strength from light to heavy, and export to strong. The other method of classification is also based on the alcohol content and the level of tax applied. Eighty shillings (written as 80/-) was the rate applied to export-strength beers such as this rich, malty red-brown ale. It is characterised by a deep fruity aroma with hints of berry fruit and spicy hop background notes, and rich fruity malt flavours balanced by a fragrant hop dryness.

Caledonian 80 Shilling was named official beer of the Edinburgh Festival 2004. As well as its regular range, Caledonian produces twelve different seasonal ales – one for every month of the year, each with its own distinct identity, in several cases relating to seasonal events. The August offering, for example, is Edinburgh Tattoo, named after the military display that takes place every year in that month at the world-famous Edinburgh Festival. Brewed in the style of a traditional Scottish Export beer, it is an amber-coloured ale with a toasted nutty aroma balanced with fragrant hop spiciness, while the palate is dominated by sweet, nutty malt flavours with a hint of chocolate. January's beer is Burns Ale, brewed with rye malt for a creamy malt and toffee flavour to complement the haggis that is traditionally served on Burns Night (25 January) when the Scots celebrate their national poet.

SPECIFICATIONS

Brewery: Caledonian Brewery
Location: Edinburgh
Style: Scottish strong export ale
Colour: Rust red-brown
Alcohol: 4.1%
Serving temperature: 10°C (50°F)
Food: Roast beef or game

Caledonian Deuchars IPA

At one time, Scotland's capital city had more than 30 independent breweries, although most of these have long since vanished.

Now the city's largest brewery, Caledonian was established in 1869 as Lorimer & Clark, and still uses direct-fired open coppers to brew its beers (most breweries use steam). The brewery was bought by Vaux of Sunderland in 1919, then in 1985, when Vaux was planning to close the site, it was saved at the last moment by a management buy-out and has since gone on to become one of Scotland's most successful independent breweries. It is noted principally for its wide range of robustly malty ales, but its Deuchars IPA is an award-winning exception to the rule. It is named after Robert Deuchar, a Fife brewer who bought the New Brewery in Duddingston in 1899 in order to brew Edinburgh ales for his customers in the northeast of England.

Deuchar's was bought by Newcastle Breweries in 1953, but the name eventually died out until it was revived by Caledonian. The beer it designates is a very modern version of the traditional India pale ale style, with an intensely floral hop aroma which is followed on the palate by a crisp, almost astringently dry bitterness. The cask version of Deuchars IPA has won several major national and international awards, including Champion Beer of Britain 2002.

SPECIFICATIONS

Brewery: Caledonian Brewery
Location: Edinburgh
Style: India pale ale
Colour: Golden amber
Alcohol: 4.4%
Serving temperature: 10°C (50°F)
Food: Ideal as an aperitif before dinner

Caledonian Golden Promise

Golden Promise, the third of Caledonian's three regular beer brands, stakes its claim to the title of world's first organic beer, being brewed with organically grown Scottish barley and a single variety of organic hops from Kent.

It is also suitable for vegetarians and vegans. The original recipe for Golden Promise produced a fragrant golden ale, but the current recipe is for a dark reddish brown pale ale, although the label still bears the legend 'The Original Organic Ale'. The aroma is redolent with spicy character, with hints of cinnamon and vanilla. On the palate it has a clean, clear flavour of sweet, biscuity, buttery malts and a full-bodied creamy smooth texture, finishing on a crisp, refreshingly dry note with citrus hop flavours. The quality of the beer is attested to by a string of awards, including silver medal in the organic beer class of the 2003 International Beer Competition and winner of the Best Beverage Category in the 2002 Vegetarian Society Awards.

Recent developments at Caledonian have seen the brewery take on responsibility for brewing McEwan's 80/- on behalf of Scottish & Newcastle, which now owns a 30% stake in Caledonian, although the brewery continues to operate independently, with full control over its beer production.

SPECIFICATIONS

Brewery: Caledonian Brewery
Location: Edinburgh
Style: Pale ale
Colour: Dark red-brown
Alcohol: 5%
Serving temperature: 10°C (50°F)
Food: Steak with a rich red wine sauce

Tennent's Lager

Tennent's Wellpark brewery in the centre of Glasgow, close to the cathedral, has been in continuous operation since 1885, although beer is known to have been brewed on the site since 1556, making this one of the oldest brewing locations in Britain.

The company was the first brewery in the United Kingdom to produce a lager, which it launched in 1924. It remains a distinctive brew with a clean, crisp, well-balanced taste combining sweet malty flavours with a refreshingly tangy hop bitterness. The brewery is now owned by the Belgian global giant Interbrew.

SPECIFICATIONS

Brewery: Tennent Caledonian Breweries (Interbrew)
Location: Glasgow
Style: Lager
Colour: Golden yellow
Alcohol: 5%
Serving temperature: 6°–8°C (42.8°–46.4°F)
Food: Hot spicy curries

Tennent's Super

Glasgow's Tennent's brewery takes its name from its founder Hugh Tennent, and it is a name that has gone on to become for many synonymous with beer in Scotland and it remains one of the country's biggest-selling brands.

Among the wide range of Tennent's beers, Tennent's Super is the strongest, with a massive 9% alcohol. It has a thick, syrupy texture and a rich fruity flavour that almost succumbs to the dominating effect of the alcohol. Other beers from Tennent's include the more characterful Tennent's Ember, the equally strong Tennent's Scotch Ale, and Tennent's Export Stout.

SPECIFICATIONS

Brewery: Tennent Caledonian Breweries (Interbrew)
Location: Glasgow
Style: Strong lager
Colour: Pale golden yellow
Alcohol: 9%
Serving temperature: 8°C (46.4°F)
Food: Bread and cheese

Traquair House Ale

The history of Traquair House began around AD 950 when it was a simple heather hut on the banks of a stream, situated deep in the Forest of Ettrick.

Traquair House was granted a royal charter following a visit by King Alexander I in 1107. The present-day brewery was founded by Peter Maxwell Stuart in 1965 when he discovered the perfectly preserved equipment from an eighteenth-century domestic brewhouse that had fallen into disuse in the early 1800s. All modern-day Traquair House beers are fermented in the original oak vessels, giving Traquair House Ale its characteristic lightly oaky aroma, which blends with rich, fruity malts and spicy, citrussy hops. On the palate, dark fruity, nutty malts dominate.

SPECIFICATIONS

Brewery: Traquair House Brewery Ltd
Location: Innerleithen, Peeblesshire
Style: Scottish strong ale
Colour: Dark mahogany red-brown
Alcohol: 7.2%
Serving temperature: 10°–13°C (50°–55.4°F)
Food: Fried seafood

Traquair Jacobite Ale

The Traquair House Brewery produces three strong, old-fashioned ales.

SPECIFICATIONS

Brewery: Traquair House Brewery Ltd
Location: Innerleithen, Peeblesshire
Style: Spiced Scottish ale
Colour: Very dark red, almost black
Alcohol: 8%
Serving temperature: 13°C (55.4°F)
Food: Pasta with delicate herby sauces

One of these, Bear Ale, is named after the gates to the estate, which are known as the Bear Gates. These have remained closed since 1745, when the fifth Laird of Traquair, upon bidding farewell to his departing guest, Prince Charles Edward Stuart – otherwise known as Bonnie Prince Charlie – promised that the gates would stay shut until the Stuarts were restored to the Scottish throne. Bear Ale is a strong, rich amber-coloured ale with complex malty flavours and a subtle hint of oak. In 1995, to commemorate the 250th anniversary of Bonnie Prince Charlie's visit, Traquair House launched Jacobite Ale. This extra special ale is spiced with coriander seed and roasted grain to give it a fragrant herbal aroma, followed by a rich, complex blend of spices, hops and malt on the palate. It finishes on a bittersweet note with harmonious flavours of chocolate, dark vinous fruit and coriander spiciness.

ABOVE

Desite recent decades of rationalisation, and the demise of many small independent breweries, the United Kingdom is blessed with a bewildering array of quality, distinctive beers. While light imported beers such as Foster's and Carlsberg remain the major high-street sellers, the traditional British pint glass can be filled with such individual brews as Badger Tanglefoot and Adnams Broadside.

English Beers

Brewing and drinking beer have always been a key part of the English life. Even the wine-drinking Normans couldn't replace beer with their own favourite tipple in the eleventh century, and the Domesday Book records evidence of a thriving commercial brewing industry.

Above

Britain possesses an unusually high density of public houses stretched throughout its towns, cities and villages. Many of the these pubs feature 'guest' or speciality beers which promote a broader palate among the drinking public.

ALTHOUGH THE ENGLISH ENJOY a long tradition of small-scale domestic brewing, the monasteries were by far the largest producers of beer until their dissolution in the sixteenth century. Their practices remain an influence on brewing to this day, with methods such as the Burton Union used by Marston's having their origins in medieval monastic brewing techniques. The English have a reputation around the world as lovers of warm, flat beer, but most English ales are best served at cellar temperature, while some of the stronger, fuller-flavoured beers are best served like red wine at slightly below room temperature.

English beers come in a wide variety of styles. In the first half of the twentieth century, mild was by far the most popular, quaffed in large quantities by workers. Brewed with fewer hops than bitters and pale ales, mild beer is named for its flavour rather than its alcohol content, and comes in a range of strengths. From the 1950s onwards, bitter became more popular, but by the 1960s traditional cask ales were threatened with extinction due to the increasing trend towards production of keg beers. These are pasteurised and filtered to ensure consistency and increase keeping quality, but lack the character of 'real' ale.

Despite the continued dominance of a small handful of global brewers, who produce more than 80% of beer consumed in the United Kingdom (most of which is mass-produced keg lager), this trend has been partly reversed by the work of Camra, the Campaign for Real Ale, which fights for the values supported by small brewers using traditional methods. Thanks to their work, cask and bottle-conditioned ales are more popular today than they have been for many years.

STATISTICS

Total production: 40,000,000 hectolitres (1,056,689,000 gallons) per year

Consumption per capita: 97 litres (26 gallons) per year

Famous breweries: Adnams; Bass Brewers Ltd; Fuller, Smith & Turner plc; George Gale & Co.; Marston, Scottish & Newcastle; Young & Co.

Famous brands: Adnams Broadside; Badger Tanglefoot; Bass Pale Ale; Fuller's ESB; Fuller's London Pride; Gale's HSB; Marston's Pedigree; Newcastle Brown Ale; Old Speckled Hen; Young's Special London Ale

Adnams Broadside

The charming, picturesque seaside town of Southwold, home to the Adnams brewery, stands on Sole Bay on the east coast of England, and the name of Broadside ale commemorates the naval Battle of Sole Bay between the Dutch and the British in 1672. A classic strong ale, it has powerful sweet, fruity, toffee-like malt aromas.

On the palate, the beer is smooth and comforting, with fruity, nutty maltiness predominating the flavour, giving way to a lingering dry, hop bitterness in the finish. Broadside in bottles is somewhat stronger than the draught version of the same beer, which rates at 4.7% alcohol. The quality of Broadside has won it a solid international following, plus some important awards from respected organisations. The influential British group CAMRA (Campaign for Real Ale) gave Adnams Broadside the Gold Medal position in the Strong Bitter Category at the CAMRA 2003 Champion Beer of Britain awards. Adnams also produces a bottled version of its Suffolk Strong Ale, a deliciously dry and generously hopped bitter, which despite its name has a lower alcohol content than Broadside.

Adnams brewery started life more than 650 years ago as the brewhouse for the Swan Inn, the oldest hostelry in Southwold. Its earliest mention in history was in 1345, when Johanna de Corby of the Swan Inn was fined for serving ale in unmarked measures. The Swan was rebuilt in 1660 after a fire and the Sole Bay brewery was moved to new premises nearby, where it remains to this day. It was bought by the Adnams brothers, Ernest and George, in 1872 and is currently run by the fourth generation of the Adnams family. Adnams beers are still delivered to local hostelries by carts pulled by dray horses.

SPECIFICATIONS

Brewery: Adnams
Location: Southwold, Suffolk
Style: Strong ale
Colour: Dark ruby red
Alcohol: 6.3%
Serving temperature: 12°C (53.6°F)
Food: Roast lamb

Badger Tanglefoot

According to legend, Tanglefoot acquired its name when the head brewer tripped over his own feet after having sampled several tankards of this strong but 'deceptively drinkable' ale. It is a robustly flavoured beer, full of hoppy bitterness that dominates the fruity yeast and malt flavours on the palate, and its extremely dry, lemon-scented bitter finish is due to the use of Challenger hops.

Badger is the trading name of the Hall & Woodhouse brewery, which was founded in 1777 by Charles Hall as the Ansty Brewery. It became Hall & Woodhouse when Charles's son joined forces with George Woodhouse, and the brewery moved to its present site in Blandford St Mary in 1899. The badger is a common animal locally and was adopted as the brewery's emblem to reflect the local character of its beers. Also in its range is Fursty Ferret, named after the ferrets that would gather at the door of the nearby Gribble Inn in the hope of being able to sample the house beer. Production of this immensely popular beer was taken up by Badger when the pub's small-capacity brewery could no longer keep up with demand. Another beer, Blandford Fly, is named after a biting insect that populates Dorset's river Stour. Rumour has it that the only antidote to the insect's bite is ginger, an ingredient that is used to flavour this soothing ale.

SPECIFICATIONS

Brewery: Badger (Hall & Woodhouse Ltd)
Location: Blandford St Mary, Dorset
Style: Strong pale ale
Colour: Pale golden straw
Alcohol: 5%
Serving temperature: 12°C (53.6°F)
Food: Grilled red meats, such as lamb chops

Bateman's XXXB

The name of this famous British ale is a reminder of the days before widespread literacy, when the strength of beer was indicated by a number of Xs branded on the side of the cask. In truth, this beer is not especially strong, but it certainly does have plenty of flavour.

It is a classic bitter with a complex balance of malt and hops, opening with sweet fruity malty flavours reminiscent of plums, then giving way to a dry, spicy hop bitterness in the finish. Depicted on the label is the brewery's logo, a red windmill that represents the ivy-clad windmill that still stands next to the brewery, which has been on the same site since it was founded in 1874 by George Bateman.

The brewery is currently run by his grandson, also called George, and remains independent despite a struggle in the mid-1980s, when several shareholding family members threatened to sell off their portion of the business to the highest bidder. The matter was resolved when the cask version of XXXB won Champion Beer at the 1986 Great British Beer Festival. Today, as well as its regular range, Bateman's also frequently brews small batches of special beers with unusual flavours such as strawberry, vanilla or liquorice, and produces an own-label bottle-conditioned beer called Pour With Care for the Booths supermarket chain, which has branches throughout the north-west of England.

SPECIFICATIONS

Brewery: Bateman's

Location: Wainfleet, Lincolnshire

Style: Bitter

Colour: Dark copper-red

Alcohol: 4.8%

Serving temperature: 10°–13°C (50°–55.4°F)

Food: A traditional ploughman's lunch

Charles Wells Bombardier

Bombardier Premium Bitter was originally launched to commemorate the granting to the Charles Wells brewery of the Queen's Award for Export Achievement and is a bottled version of the cask ale of the same name. A classic English best bitter, it is strong and full of flavour and character, yet not at all heavy, making it a surprisingly easy beer to drink.

It has a fruity flavour, reminiscent of raisins and sultanas, and a lingering, dry, subtle bitterness that comes from the use of Challenger hops; while crystal malt and Goldings hops help to produce its distinctive pale copper colour. The self-styled 'Patron pint of England' is now closely associated with St George's Day, following an intensive marketing campaign by the brewery. In tune with its patriotic values, Bombardier Premium Bitter is available in imperial pint measure (568ml) embossed bottles with a label that bears the cross of St George. Established in 1876, Charles Wells is one of England's largest independent regional brewers, and is still run by descendants of the founder, based at the Eagle Brewery in Bedford, just north of London. All Charles Wells beers are brewed using water from the brewery's own well, which was sunk on the site in 1902. Among the brewery's varying seasonal beers is the highly unusual Banana Bread Beer, which is brewed with whole bananas.

SPECIFICATIONS

Brewery: Charles Wells
Location: Bedford, Bedfordshire
Style: Best bitter
Colour: Dark red-brown
Alcohol: 5.5%
Serving temperature: 12°C (53.6°F)
Food: Traditional English battered fish and chips

Coniston Bluebird Bitter

Founded in 1995, the award-winning Coniston brewery is hidden away behind the Black Bull, a 400-year-old coaching inn in the village of Coniston in the heart of the picturesque Lake District region of northern England.

Its Bluebird Bitter is named after the boat used by Donald Campbell, who was tragically killed while setting a new water speed record on Coniston Water in 1967. This copper-coloured bitter is brewed with plenty of hops to give it a peppery, spicy, orange fruit aroma. Spicy, peppery flavours and a hint of citrus continue to dominate over fruity malts on the palate through to a crisp, dry and pleasantly bitter finish. The cask version of Coniston Bluebird Bitter was awarded Champion Beer of Britain at the 1998 Great British Beer Festival, with the result that the brewery could no longer keep up with escalating demand. As a result, for the bottled version of Bluebird, brewing was contracted out to the Brakspear brewery in Hendon, Oxfordshire.

Following the demise of Brakspear, production was continued by former Brakspear head brewer Peter Scholey. He also produces a bottled version of another Coniston beer, a full-bodied ruby-coloured strong ale named Old Man after the mountain that overlooks the brewery. Both Bluebird Bitter and Old Man Ale are genuine 'bottle-conditioned' real ale, filtered after fermentation (but not pasteurised) then re-seeded with fresh yeast to allow the beer to continue to develop in the bottle.

SPECIFICATIONS

Brewery: Coniston Brewing Company
Location: Coniston, Lake District, Cumbria
Style: Bitter
Colour: Pale copper
Alcohol: 4.2%
Serving temperature: 9°–10°C (48.2°–50°F)
Food: An ideal aperitif

Fuller's ESB

Originally launched in 1969 as an end-of-year seasonal beer under the name Winter Bitter, this famous beer was renamed when it became available all year round from 1971.

Its complex flavour is heavily malt accented and slightly honeyed, but balanced with a robust hop bitterness. The letters stand for 'Extra Special Bitter' and, though the name was coined by Fuller's specifically for this beer, it has been adopted by other breweries, particularly in the United States, to designate a strong bitter style of ale, darker in colour than a typical pale ale with a more malty and less hoppy flavour. Contents include Pale Ale and Crystal malts and Target, Challenger, Northdown and Goldings hops.

ESB has a touch more strength than many similar beers, offering a respectable 5.9% abv in bottle and keg form and 5.5% in cask. The beer has won a huge number of awards, even winning the title Champion Beer of Britain in 1978, 1981 and 1985. The US Beverage Tasting Institute also gave Fuller's ESB the accreditation of 'World Champion Bitter' in 1997 and 1998.

SPECIFICATIONS

Brewery: Fuller, Smith & Turner plc
Location: Chiswick, London
Style: Strong bitter
Colour: Deep copper-red
Alcohol: 5.9%
Serving temperature: 10°–13°C (50°–55.4°F)
Food: Meaty pies

Fuller's 1845

Records show that brewing has taken place on the present site of the Fuller's brewery for at least 325 years, though the Fuller, Smith and Turner brewing company was founded only in 1845. This strong traditional ale was launched in 1995 to celebrate the brewery's 150th anniversary, with Prince Charles adding the hops to the first batch brewed.

The recipe was devised specifically to replicate the kind of beers that were available in the middle of the nineteenth century. After primary fermentation, the beer spends two weeks in conditioning tanks before it is filtered, then re-seeded with fresh yeast and bottled. The bottles are then allowed to condition for two weeks before the beer goes on sale. It has a refreshingly lively, yeasty, malty aroma with an orange fruit character. On the palate it is smooth and full-bodied, with a mouth-feel almost like that of drinking a liqueur. A powerful toasty, fruity maltiness with hints of raisins, chocolate and toffee overwhelms the taste buds at first, but is soon countered by a dry, hop bitterness that lingers through to a long, well-balanced finish.

SPECIFICATIONS

Brewery: Fuller, Smith & Turner plc
Location: Chiswick, London
Style: Strong ale
Colour: Red-brown
Alcohol: 6.3%
Serving temperature: 13°C (55.4°F)
Food: Richly flavoured stews

Fuller's Golden Pride

Brewed annually in limited quantities as a seasonal treat for Christmas, Fuller's Golden Pride is a powerful and hugely complex beer, reminiscent of a Belgian abbey beer or a German double bock.

It is a weighty beer with a rich, bittersweet aroma and flavour in which toasty grainy malt is balanced by a moderate hoppiness. Although in its homeland Golden Pride's supply is limited to a short seasonal period, in Italy it is available all year round. Fuller's Vintage Ale is a bottle-conditioned version of Golden Pride, produced in an annual batch and designed for keeping, with flavours that continue to develop complexity and depth in the bottle.

SPECIFICATIONS

Brewery: Fuller, Smith & Turner plc
Location: Chiswick, London
Style: Barley wine
Colour: Deep amber-gold
Alcohol: 8.5%
Serving temperature: 12°–13°C (53.6°–55.4°F)
Food: Rich sweet fruit and cream-based desserts

Fuller's London Pride

Fuller, Smith & Turner is one of London's two largest brewers. Fuller's flagship beer, London Pride, is a drinkably smooth and satisfying best bitter with a surprisingly complex flavour. Light nutty malts and a slightly honeyed yeastiness are the primary flavour characteristics.

The brewery's location gives its name to another Fuller's beer, Chiswick Bitter, a lighter bitter designed for quaffing. Fuller's brews a wide range of regular and seasonal beers, most of which are available in bottled form. Among them is Organic Honey Dew, approved by the Soil Association as 100% organic. This light, refreshing golden ale is laced with honey to give it a sweet, floral aroma and a smooth, well-rounded body, with a sweet flavour balanced by judicious use of zesty Target hops. Fuller's also produces a bottled version of its London Porter exclusively for export.

SPECIFICATIONS

Brewery: Fuller, Smith & Turner plc
Location: Chiswick, London
Style: Best bitter
Colour: Amber
Alcohol: 4.7%
Serving temperature: 12°–13°C (53.6°–55.4°F)
Food: Hearty meat pies and stews

Gale's Festival Mild

Gale's Festival Mild ale was created in 1994 to support attempts by Camra (the Campaign for Real Ale) to revive the traditional mild style, so called for its relatively low hop content which gives it a softer flavour.

This beer, produced primarily for export, is more complex than most traditional milds. It is brewed with a high proportion of dark malts, as well as crystal and pale ale malts, to give it a fruity, grainy aroma and a chocolatey roasted malt flavour with a gentle fruity sweetness reminiscent of blackcurrants, raisins and raspberries. The finish is tempered by a citric bitterness provided by a blend of Fuggles, Golding and Challenger hops. This bottle-conditioned beer is one of several produced by a brewery that has always been among the leading advocates of traditional methods of beer production. Gale's was founded in 1847, starting as the house brewery for the Ship & Bell Inn in Horndean, run by Richard and Ann Gale. Their son George took over the business in 1853, and it was he who recognised the potential for expansion, laying the foundations for the sizeable company that Gale's has become.

SPECIFICATIONS

Brewery: George Gale & Co.
Location: Horndean, Hampshire
Style: Mild ale
Colour: Dark ruby red
Alcohol: 4.8%
Serving temperature: 8°–10°C (46.4°–50°F)
Food: A 'session' beer for sociable drinking

Gale's HSB

The initials HSB stand for 'Horndean Special Bitter', Horndean being the small town in Hampshire where Gale's brewery was founded in 1847. This distinctive best bitter brewed with a blend of maris otter pale malt, crystal malt and black malt, and flavoured with three traditional varieties of hops, was launched in 1959 as a stonger alternative to the lower strength BBB bitter and the predominantly mild beers that the brewery was producing at the time.

In the early days, the recipe used produced a beer that was even stronger in alcohol, being brewed to a higher original gravity, although this has been reduced slightly in recent years. Initially it was not a huge success, but it gradually established itself throughout the 1970s and 1980s, and eventually became Gale's flagship brand with a widespread reputation as one of the best-loved English bitters. It has a complex fruity aroma with hints of apples, bananas and toffee, while the texture is very full-bodied and smooth. Sweet fruitiness and toffeeish maltiness continue to dominate the flavour, leading to a dry, hoppy, fruity bitter finish.

SPECIFICATIONS

Brewery: George Gale & Co.
Location: Horndean, Hampshire
Style: Best bitter
Colour: Dark amber
Alcohol: 4.8%
Serving temperature: 10°–12°C (50°–53.6°F)
Food: Traditional battered fish and chips

Gale's Prize Old Ale

While most bottled beers these days are capped with metal lids, Gale's is one of the very few British breweries to cork some of its beers, perhaps the most famous of which is its Prize Old Ale. This award-winning beer, first brewed in the 1920s, is designed to improve with keeping.

It is aged in maturation tanks for up to 12 months before being bottled, then for a further three months at the brewery. Deeply complex wine-like fruit aromas show a hint of vanilla, while the palate is richly fruity with the flavour of plums and raisins, balanced by a lingering dry bitterness.

SPECIFICATIONS

Brewery: George Gale & Co.
Location: Horndean, Hampshire
Style: Old ale
Colour: Dark ruby red
Alcohol: 9%
Serving temperature: 13°–14°C (55.4°–57.2°F)
Food: Rich fruit cake

Gale's Trafalgar

This powerful seasonal ale is brewed in the autumn every year to commemorate Trafalgar Day, 21 October, which marks Nelson's victory at the naval Battle of Trafalgar in 1805.

Accordingly, it is brewed using only ingredients that were available in Nelson's day – maris otter pale malt and crystal malt, Challenger and Fuggles hops. The aroma is surprisingly delicate for a beer of this strength, with subtle notes of fruity malt and hops, while the flavour is sweet, spicy, fruity and malty with a good balance of hop bitterness. The cask version of Trafalgar is brewed to approximately half the alcohol strength.

SPECIFICATIONS

Brewery: George Gale & Co.
Location: Horndean, Hampshire
Style: Strong ale
Colour: Dark ruby red
Alcohol: 9%
Serving temperature: 13°–14°C (55.4°–57.2°F)
Food: Dark meat and game dishes

Greene King Abbot Ale

Abbot Ale, first brewed in 1955, has become firmly established as Greene King's flagship brand.

It benefits from a long secondary fermentation at relatively high temperatures, which ensures a full-flavoured beer with rich fruity malts on the palate. Two varieties of hops are used to give an appetising bitterness in a long, dry finish and perfumed floral aromas.

The beer's name is a reflection of the long tradition of brewing in this ancient town – the Domesday Book shows that brewing was already taking place at the great abbey of St Edmundsbury as early as AD 1086, and the water used by the brewery today is drawn from the same chalk beds as used by the monks for their beers. Records show that the current brewery has been going since the early 1700s, but it was taken over by the Greene family in the early nineteenth century.

In recent years it has grown considerably, acquiring several other breweries and brands, to become one of the largest independent regional brewers in England.

SPECIFICATIONS

Brewery: Greene King
Location: Bury St Edmunds, Suffolk
Style: Pale ale
Colour: Deep amber
Alcohol: 5.0%
Serving temperature: 10°–13°C (50°–55.4°F)
Food: Roast red meats

Old Speckled Hen

Old Speckled Hen was originally produced by the Morland brewery of Abingdon in Oxfordshire, which was founded in 1711. In 1998, Morland acquired the ailing Ruddles brewery of Oakham in Leicestershire, but soon after met its own demise and in 1999 was taken over by the by Suffolk brewer Greene King.

Greene King adopted Old Speckled Hen along with Ruddles County. Old Speckled Hen is a warming and very full-bodied beer. Rich, plummy aromas are laden with intense malty sweetness, while on the palate malt loaf and toffee flavours give a sweetness that is balanced by a long, dry and satisfying bitter finish. The inspiration for the name was actually a much-loved old canvas-covered saloon car – the 'awld speckled 'un' – that over the years had become speckled in paint.

SPECIFICATIONS

Brewery: Greene King
Location: Bury St Edmunds, Suffolk
Style: Pale ale
Colour: Deep golden amber
Alcohol: 5.2%
Serving temperature: 11°–13°C (51.8°–55.4°F)
Food: Cooked cured ham

Bass Pale Ale

This most famous of British ales has been brewed in Burton upon Trent since 1777.Its red triangle is trademark no. 1 in the UK.

Bass Pale Ale remains inextricably linked to its home town of Burton upon Trent due to the unique mineral properties of the local water, which gives Bass beers their characteristic sulphurous aroma – which cannot be replicated successfully anywhere else. Originally brewed to a higher alcohol and hop content to preserve it during its long sea voyage to India, Bass is an amber-coloured top-fermented beer with a sweet, fruity aroma, caramel and malt on the palate and a long, dry, bitter hoppy finish. The iconic red triangle emblem, which adorns Bass labels to this day, earned its own place in history when it became the first registered trade mark in Britain in 1875.

SPECIFICATIONS

Brewery: Bass Brewers Ltd (InBev)
Location: Burton upon Trent, Staffordshire
Style: India pale ale
Colour: Amber-red
Alcohol: 5.2%
Serving temperature: 10°C (50°F)
Food: smoked fish or sausages

Marston's Pedigree Bitter

First brewed in 1834 and still made to the same recipe, using maris otter barley with Fuggles and Goldings hops and a 150-year-old strain of yeast, Marston's Pedigree is a living reminder of the way beer used to be in the middle of the nineteenth century. It is brewed using water drawn from one of seven wells on the brewery site and is the only beer in the world that is still made using the Burton Union system, a relic of Victorian brewing that comprises a series of giant oak vats linked by copper tubes to an iron trough. During fermentation, the foaming wort rises through the tubes into the trough, where it then subsides and filters back down into the vats below.

This continuous circulation, followed by a period of conventional maturation, produces a subtle, complex beer with nutty, malty dryness balanced against sweet, fruity flavours of apples and pears. The Burton Union method also produces excess yeast that is used to start the next batch of beer. In order to maintain the system, the brewery employs its own coopers, another way in which Marston's uniquely maintains the old traditions of brewing. The brewery was taken over in 1999 by the Wolverhampton & Dudley pub and brewing group, which also produces Banks's Original and Mansfield Bitter. Several famous old Marston's beers, such as Owd Roger, are no longer in production; however, new beers are being created, including Old Empire, which is an authentically fruity, hoppy India pale ale.

SPECIFICATIONS

Brewery: Marston, Thompson & Evershed
Location: Burton upon Trent, Staffordshire
Style: Pale ale
Colour: Pale amber-red
Alcohol: 4.5%
Serving temperature: 12°C (53.6°F)
Food: Roast beef

Newcastle Brown Ale

One of the most popular ales in Britain, and one of the best-known British beers around the world, Newcastle Brown Ale was launched in 1927 after three years of development by head brewer Jim Porter.

The Newcastle Brown Ale brand is currently owned by Britain's largest brewing group, Scottish & Newcastle, which was formed in 1960 by the merger of Newcastle Breweries with Scottish Brewers and is now the third-largest brewer in Europe. The origins of the Newcastle Breweries stretch back to 1770, when John Barras & Co. founded the Gateshead Brewery. This business was bought in 1890 by the North Eastern Railway Company, and John Barras moved across the river Tyne to take over the Tyne Brewery along with several other smaller local breweries across the north-east, and thus formed The Newcastle Breweries Ltd.

Scottish & Newcastle made a break with history in the summer of 2004 when production of Newcastle Brown was moved two miles across the river to the Federation Brewery in Gateshead. It was an immediate success, winning several gold medals at the International Brewers Exhibition in London in 1928. These medals were incorporated into the bottle's label, along with the famous blue star logo that was adopted as the company's trade mark in 1913. Today, Newcastle Brown Ale is still brewed to the original recipe and has a dry, nutty flavour with a delicate floral aroma.

SPECIFICATIONS

Brewery: Scottish & Newcastle
Location: Newcastle-upon-Tyne, Tyne & Wear
Style: Brown ale
Colour: Deep mahogany brown
Alcohol: 4.7%
Serving temperature: 10°C (50°F)
Food: Sausages and mash

Young's Special London Ale

Young's Special London Ale is the bottle-conditioned version of a beer known as Young's Export that was originally brewed specially for the Belgian market. Confusingly, the draught beer now sold in the brewery's pubs under the name Young's Export is a Pilsner, brewed in accordance with German Reinheitsgebot purity laws.

Special London Ale is a deeply complex beer, fermented for a week in open tanks, then conditioned with added whole Goldings hops for a further three weeks. The beer is then allowed to mature before being filtered and bottled with added hopped wort and fresh yeast to allow further conditioning in the bottle. It pours bright and clear with a deep bronze colour and a powerful malty aroma with hints of sweet-sharp orange zest fruitiness. On the palate, it feels smooth, rich and creamy with bready malts, banana and bitter orange balanced by tangy hops. The finish is long and bitter with a fruity hop flavour.

Young's produces a wide range of interesting bottled beers, including Double Chocolate Stout, which has whole chocolate bars added during the boil, and Waggledance, named after the dance bees do to alert other bees to the location of pollen.

SPECIFICATIONS

Brewery: Young & Co. Brewery
Location: Wandsworth, London
Style: Strong pale ale
Colour: Bronze
Alcohol: 6.4%
Serving temperature: 10°C (50°F)
Food: Roast meats

ABOVE

Tapas bars like the one above in Seville, southern Spain, are a popular location for Spaniards to relax and enjoy a beer with a small snack or two. The high temperatures in Spain have encouraged lighter beers to flourish in the country, despite competition from other traditional Spanish drinks such as sherry and wine.

Spanish Beers

Spain has experienced a decline in the variety of beers produced over recent decades, mainly through the closing of many of its microbreweries. However, the country still produces a range of quality beers, either through its eight major beers producers or through some of the independent breweries still managing to make a living.

ABOVE
Beer is a refreshing accompaniment to the traditional Spanish tapas, particularly on a hot summer's day.

THE HISTORIAN PLINY MENTIONS the use of beer in Spain under the name of *celia* and *ceria*, and in Gaul under that of *cerevisia*; and remarks that: 'The natives who inhabit the west of Europe have a liquid with which they intoxicate themselves, made from corn and water. The manner of making this liquid is somewhat different in Gaul, Spain and other countries, and it is called by different names, but its nature and properties are everywhere the same. The people in Spain in particular brew this liquid so well that it will keep good a long time. So exquisite is the cunning of mankind in gratifying their vicious appetites that they have thus invented a method to make water itself produce intoxication.'

The quality of Spanish beer in the sixteenth century was apparently poor because when Charles V – who liked a tipple or two – became king, he immediately passed a law ensuring that all beer was pure. Today, Spain has nine large breweries, the oldest of which is Damm SA of Barcelona, established in 1876. Many microbreweries have closed in recent years, the effect of increased competition from the dominating local and international producers. Most of the larger concerns specialise in brewing foreign beers under licence, but there are still good-quality indigenous beers, such as Alhambra, Cruzcampo, Estrella Damm, Mahou, San Miguel, Voll Damm and Zaragozana.

STATISTICS

Total production: 30,671,000 hectolitres (810,242,000 gallons) per year

Consumption per capita: 75 litres (20 gallons) per year

Famous breweries: Damm; Grupo Cruzcampo; San Miguel

Famous brands: Cruzcampo; Estrella-Damm; Voll-Damm; San Miguel 1516

Cruzcampo

Cruzcampo is the flagship beer of Spain's largest brewing group. It has a light, dry hop character with slightly sour citrus notes balanced by a gently sweet, grainy maltiness.

The Cruzcampo brewery group was formed through the merger in 1987 of a number of smaller regional breweries, although Cruzcampo beer has a history stretching back 100 years to 1904. The brewery currently operates across five sites in the Andalucia region, with its headquarters in Seville. The group was taken over by Guinness in 1991, then again a few years later by Heineken, which merged it with El Aguila of Madrid.

SPECIFICATIONS

Brewery: Grupo Cruzcampo
Location: Seville, Andalucia
Style: Lager
Colour: Deep yellow-orange
Alcohol: 5%
Serving temperature: 6°–8°C (42.8°–46.4°F)
Food: Cured dried meats and sausages

Estrella Damm

Damm makes the most popular beers in the Catalonia region of northern Spain, and Estrella Damm is its flagship brand.

It is a smooth, easy-drinking pale lager with a creamy head, a touch of floral hops in the aroma and a clean, dry flavour with a slightly bitter hop finish. The brewery has its headquarters in Barcelona, where it was founded in 1867 by Auguste Kuentzmann Damm, a native of Alsace in northern France who emigrated to flee the war that was ravaging his homeland, and today the company has an extensive network of brewing plants across Spain. Damm was the first brewer in Spain to produce the new bottom-fermented golden beers that were becoming popular towards the end of the nineteenth century.

SPECIFICATIONS

Brewery: Damm
Location: Barcelona, Catalonia
Style: Lager
Colour: Dark blonde
Alcohol: 5.4%
Serving temperature: 5°–7°C (41°–44.6°F)
Food: Cold cooked meats and ham

Voll-Damm

Voll-Damm is a strong pale lager in the Dortmunder style, with a full body, a deep golden colour and a rich, fruity malt flavour which is reminiscent of grapes and plums.

The beer epitomises the German roots of the company, and Voll-Damm is now one of the largest brewers in Spain, with a growing export business. Most of the brewing takes place at the La Bohemia brewery in Barcelona, close to the famous Sagrada Familia cathedral, while malting is carried out at La Moravia malthouse, which is also in Barcelona. Damm has a close association with cultural and sporting life in Barcelona, having been a sponsor for the 1982 Football World Cup and of the Olympic Games in 1992. Voll-Damm is one of the company's strongest beers, with a 7.2% abv making it a serious tipple.

SPECIFICATIONS

Brewery: Damm
Location: Barcelona, Catalonia
Style: Strong lager
Colour: Deep golden yellow
Alcohol: 7.2%
Serving temperature: 8°C (46.4°F)
Food: Smoked fish

San Miguel 1516

San Miguel 1516 is a smooth, easy-drinking pale golden lager with malty cereal aromas with overtones of hops, honey, citrus fruit and apples.

On the palate, it has a slightly sweet malty character balanced by moderate hop bitterness. The name 1516 refers to the year the Spanish king Carlos V first invited German brewers to come to Spain to introduce their craft to a predominantly wine-drinking nation. But although San Miguel has a Spanish name, it is actually a branch of San Miguel company in the Philippines, which has been brewing in Manila since 1890. It entered the Spanish market in 1946, since when it has become the leading beer brand in Spain. It is now owned by Kronenbourg.

SPECIFICATIONS

Brewery: San Miguel
Location: Lerida, Catalonia
Style: Lager
Colour: Pale golden yellow
Alcohol: 5.4%
Serving temperature: 6°–8°C (42.8°–46.4°F)
Food: A rich fish stew

ABOVE

French brewing has, as in most other countries, its dominant major player, and in France's case that role belongs to the Brasseries Kronenbourg, which resides under the ownership of the huge Scottish & Newcastle group. The Kronenbourg 1664 lager is a worldwide bestseller, but it is also an example of how a mass-produced lager can still be of premium quality.

French and Luxembourg Beers

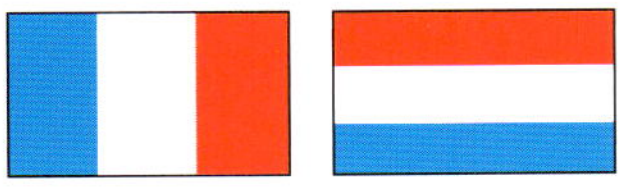

Wine is such a dominant influence on French culture that it is hard to imagine that the French have ever drunk anything else. In fact, ancient Gaul was a land of brewers, and it was only after the invasion by the Romans and their subsequent influence that wine became prevalent. Even then, northern France remained a centre of brewing excellence.

TODAY, BEER IS DRUNK WIDELY throughout the country, although it is treated principally as a thirst-quencher and receives none of the reverence that is shown by the French towards wine. The majority of France's breweries are located in the Alsace region and in the area north of Paris. The pervasive German influence on food and drink found here means that most French beers are versions of German lagers and tend to be light, uncomplicated and refreshing.

France's largest brewer is Strasbourg-based Kronenbourg, a company with a proud history dating back to 1664. In 1970, Kronenbourg was acquired by the BSN group, along with Kanterbräu. BSN later became Danone, which in 2002 sold out to the British multinational Scottish & Newcastle, now one of the largest brewing groups in Europe. The next biggest player is Dutch giant Heineken, which owns several significant brands including '33', Pelforth and Fischer. In Luxembourg, leading companies such as Brasserie de Luxembourg Mousel-Diekirch tend to produce light, easy drinking and popular lager beers.

Besides Alsace, the other area of consequence in French brewing is the Nord-Pas-de-Calais region, centred on the city of Lille, close to the Belgian border. The distinctive local style here is *bière de garde* – literally, beer for keeping – a strong, top-fermented ale traditionally made in farmhouses in the winter and spring, before the weather became too hot for brewing, then stored for drinking throughout the summer. The style is leading a revival in the popularity of brewing that in recent years has seen microbreweries opening across France.

ABOVE
France's tradition of beer production is a great one, and has generated some of the most beautiful label artwork.

STATISTICS

Total production: 18,100,000 hectolitres (478,151,000 gallons) per year
Consumption per capita: 36 litres (10 gallons) per year
Famous breweries: Brasserie Castelain; Brasserie de Luxembourg Mousel-Diekirch; Brasserie Duyck; Brasseries Kronenbourg (Scottish & Newcastle); Brasserie Pietra; Brasserie Schutzenberger; Fischer (Heineken); Les Brasseurs de Gayant
Famous brands: Jenlain; Fischer Tradition; Kronenbourg 1664; La Bio; Lutèce; Pietra; Premium Diekirch

Ch'ti Triple

Ch'ti is a word used in the local Picardy dialect for a native of the region. It is an eminently appropriate title for the range of beers made by Castelain at the Brasserie de Bénifontaine, located in a small village just north of Lens with a coal-mining heritage that is reflected in a depiction of a coal miner on the bottle label.

These are examples of the traditional local *bière de garde* style, brewed using 100% malt, matured for up to eight weeks, and available in several distinct versions. This one takes its name from the Belgian classification 'tripel', which designates the strongest beer in a brewery's range, usually a top-fermented ale. Castelain's version, like all its beers, is bottom-fermented, albeit at relatively higher temperatures than typical lagers. Its amber-gold colour is reminiscent of aged rum, the aroma is fragrantly floral, and the flavour is fruity, with hints of cherries, over an underlying dry, nutty bitterness. The finish is dry and with a pleasantly bitter aftertaste.

Ch'ti Blonde is a smooth, well-balanced lager with apricots discernible in both the aroma and flavour and a dry, nutty finish. Ch'ti Ambrée is a darker version of the Blonde, with a copper-red colour and a softer caramel flavour. Ch'ti Brune is a rich, dark, chocolate-coloured ale with a flavour of port, while Ch'ti Blanche is a wheat beer flavoured with spices. The brewery also produces several seasonal beers, including a *bière de mars* in the style of a German Märzen or Oktoberfest beer.

SPECIFICATIONS

Brewery: Brasserie Castelain
Location: Bénifontaine, Nord-Pas-de-Calais
Style: Bière de garde
Colour: Amber-gold
Alcohol: 7.5%
Serving temperature: 10°–13°C (50°–55.4°F)
Food: Sharp-flavoured fresh cheeses flavoured with herbs

Jade La Bio

The ever-increasing popularity in France of *produits de l'agriculture biologique* (organic produce) applies as much to beer as any other area of food and drink.

This example from the Castelain brewery of Bénifontaine in northern France is one of the market leaders, its organic status indicated by the green 'AB' logo on the label. It is an easy-drinking bottom-fermented lager, pale in colour, filtered but not pasteurised, with fresh herbal aromas and a refreshingly hoppy flavour. Jade is available either in a small bottle with a standard metal cap or in a larger Champagne-style bottle with a cork.

SPECIFICATIONS

Brewery: Brasserie Castelain
Location: Bénifontaine, Nord-Pas-de-Calais
Style: Lager
Colour: Pale golden yellow
Alcohol: 4.6%
Serving temperature: 7°–8°C (44.6°–46.4°F)
Food: Simple grilled fish or chicken dishes

Jenlain

The flagship beer of the Duyck brewery is an unpasteurised and bottle-conditioned top-fermented ale matured for not less than 40 days.

The aroma is dominated by fruity malt and burnt caramel with hints of spices and grassy hops. It feels smooth, creamy and slightly effervescent in the mouth and has initially sweet, malty, ripe melon flavours that give way to a dry, spicy finish with a light hoppy bite. The brewery also produces a pale version of the beer, Jenlain Blonde, and for those after something a bit more exotic, two variants with added flavourings: La J Absinthe has a lightly aniseed flavour, while La J Gingembre (ginger) is subtly spicy with a hint of lemon. Another member of the Duyck family is Torra, inspired by Corsican tradition and available in two varieties, flavoured with arbutus (strawberry tree) berries and myrtle. There is also an organic wheat beer, La Fraîche de l'Aunelle, named after the river that runs through the village, while Saint Druon is an abbey-style beer, named after the church in the nearby village of Sebourg.

SPECIFICATIONS

Brewery: Brasserie Duyck
Location: Jenlain, Nord-Pas-de-Calais
Style: Bière de garde
Colour: Amber-red
Alcohol: 6.5%
Serving temperature: 6°–8°C (42.8°–46.4°F)
Food: Rich, hearty stews

Adelscott

While the French are not especially renowned for brewing innovation, Adelscott, launched in the early 1980s, led the way for a genuinely pioneering new beer style.

At heart, it is a straightforward bottom-fermented lager, made using a combination of malts and maize, but what sets it apart is the use of whisky malt, which has been smoked over peat. This imparts a smoky, peaty flavour, which is unsurprisingly reminiscent of Scotch whisky diluted with water. The smokiness is strongest in the aroma, which has a dry, earthy character. The flavour is less dry, with a light, creamy, malty sweetness. Despite its unusual flavour, this is a light beer. There is a sister beer, Adelscott Noir, which is a far darker version of Adelscott – almost black, in fact – with a pale, creamy head and a deeper flavour, ending with a dry bitterness.

Originally brewed by the Adelshoffen brewery in Schiltigheim, Adelscott is now produced by Fischer, which is part of the Heineken group. Fischer offers several other unusual beer styles in its range, including Desperados, a Mexican-style lager flavoured with a shot of tequila, and Kriska, which has added vodka. Some of these may be closer in spirit to the ubiquitous modern 'alcopops' such as Bacardi Breezer than to the proud traditions of brewing, but they have their own merits. Adelscott's popularity has prompted the introduction of other whisky-malt beer brands such as Pelforth Amberley.

SPECIFICATIONS

Brewery: Fischer (Heineken)
Location: Schiltigheim, Alsace
Style: Smoke beer
Colour: Dark amber
Alcohol: 6.6%
Serving temperature: 9°C (48.2°F)
Food: Smoked fish, especially smoked salmon

Fischer Tradition

The flagship beer of Strasbourg's Fischer brewery, Fischer Tradition is a typical Alsace-style blonde lager which is presented in an attractive embossed bottle with a ceramic flip-top lid.

It pours with a thick, creamy head and gives off a light, malty aroma. Moderate carbonation adds a bit of weight to its light body, and the flavour is sweet and refreshingly fruity. Fischer Tradition is also available as an Amber version, and a more recent addition to the range is Pêcheur, an authentically grainy, fruity Pilsner with a crisp, clean flavour.

SPECIFICATIONS

Brewery: Fischer (Heineken)
Location: Schiltigheim, Alsace
Style: Lager
Colour: Sunny golden yellow
Alcohol: 6%
Serving temperature: 6°C (42.8°F)
Food: Goes well with simple pasta dishes

Lutèce

Lutèce (or Lutetia) was the ancient Roman name for Paris, and though it is classified as a *bière de garde*, this all-malt beer is subtitled '*bière de Paris*', its label depicting a typical Parisian scene with Notre Dame dominating the skyline.

An amber-coloured bottom-fermented beer, it is similar in style to a typical Viennese lager and has a sweet, malty aroma which is suffused with traces of whisky, butterscotch and caramel. These characteristics persist on the palate, with fruity, malty flavours dominating, reminiscent of pears, apricot and peaches. Lutèce has a hint of hoppy bitterness in the aftertaste and an alcohol warmth.

SPECIFICATIONS

Brewery: Les Brasseurs de Gayant
Location: Douai, Nord-Pas-de-Calais
Style: Bière de garde
Colour: Amber-red
Alcohol: 6.4%
Serving temperature: 6°–8°C (42.8°–46.4°F)
Food: Serve as an aperitif

Bière du Démon

First brewed in 1981, Bière du Démon was the leading contender for the title of World's Strongest Beer until the introduction of Belzebuth by local rivals Grain d'Orge, and other challengers outside France such as Samichlaus, which is produced in Switzerland by Hurlimanns.

Nonetheless, it still claims to be the strongest of all lagers and holds its own in a market for those who like their beer diabolically strong. There is a good dose of pungent maltiness to the aroma, while the flavour is dominated by the alcohol, which gives it a fiery dryness, with an underlying honey note. Founded in 1919 by the merger of four small family-owned breweries, Gayant is named after a family of giants, a popular part of local folklore who feature in a procession in honour of the town's patron saint, St Maurand, which takes place in the town of Douai every year on 16 June. The main brewery site includes a microbrewery where new beers are tested, with one new product being launched every three years. Like Fischer, Gayant produces a beer with added tequila, going by the name of Tequeiros, as well as another creation called Madison that blends a blonde lager with a shot of Grand Marnier orange liqueur. More conventional are its abbey beer, Abbaye de Saint-Landelin, and a refreshing wheat beer called Amadeus.

SPECIFICATIONS

Brewery: Les Brasseurs de Gayant
Location: Douai, Nord-Pas-de-Calais
Style: Strong lager
Colour: Pale gold
Alcohol: 12%
Serving temperature: 12°C (53.6°F)
Food: A beer to accompany desserts

Belzebuth Pur Malt

It is not without good reason that this beer is named after the devil, for Belzebuth can convincingly claim to be among the strongest beers in the world. And this is despite a reduction in the alcohol level from 15% when the beer was first launched to a slightly less intoxicating 13%. The words 'pur malt' on the label reveal that it is made entirely with malt and no added sugars or maize, which means that all the alcohol is produced by fermentation of malt sugars, and while the golden colour gives it the appearance of a lager it is in fact a top-fermented ale. Perhaps surprisingly, the result is not as thick and heavy as it might be – this is a supremely smooth beer.

Flavourwise, it offers an initial intense hit of candy sweetness, while the huge alcohol content gives a dry, spicy, peppery finish. Founded in 1898, the brewery was known as Jeanne d'Arc between 1927 and 2002, but reverted to its original name, which means 'grain of barley', when it was taken over by the former president of rival brewers Gayant. It is the oldest surviving brewery in the Lille area and now one of the largest, too. The brewery's range includes Grain d'Orge Blanche, a wheat beer, and Secret des Moines, a top-fermented ale flavoured with a secret blend of spices, including coriander.

SPECIFICATIONS

Brewery: Brasserie Grain d'Orge
Location: Ronchin, Nord-Pas-de-Calais
Style: Strong golden ale
Colour: Golden
Alcohol: 13%
Serving temperature: 10ºC (50ºF)
Food: Serve as an aperitif or with red meat dishes

Kronenbourg 1664

When a new beer was launched in 1952 to commemorate the coronation of Queen Elizabeth II, Kronenbourg decided to name it after the year in which the young Jérome Hatt was awarded his brewing diploma and set up his first brewery in the centre of Strasbourg.

This strong, traditional lager is given a lengthy period of maturation that gives it an aroma of green, leafy hops, malt and floral yeast, along with hints of ripe plums, apricots and honey. It is smooth and dense on the palate, full of well-balanced ripe fruit flavours, leading to a pleasantly bitter, floral, hop finish. Variations in the 1664 range include 1664 Brune, a mellow brown ale made with three types of malt; Fleur de Houblon, made with Alsace's highly aromatic Strisselspalt hops; and Rhum Spirit, which has an added dose of rum. The Kronenbourg name dates back to 1947, when a descendant of Jérome Hatt, also called Jérome, decided to rename the brewery's famous Tigre Bock beer after the Cronenbourg district of Strasbourg in which the Hatt brewery was then situated, albeit with a subtle change of spelling. Today, Kronenbourg is by far the largest brewer in France, producing 8.5 million hectolitres of beer a year, accounting for around 40% of the domestic market. Since July 2000, the company has been owned by Alken-Maes, part of the giant Scottish & Newcastle group.

SPECIFICATIONS

Brewery: Brasseries Kronenbourg (Scottish & Newcastle)
Location: Strasbourg, Alsace
Style: Premium lager
Colour: Dark gold
Alcohol: 5.9%
Serving temperature: 9°–10°C (48.2°–50°F)
Food: Serve as an aperitif

Tourtel

Tourtel is a non-alcoholic beer that claims to have all the qualities of a normal beer, being made with pure malt and generously hopped.

It is named after the innovative Tourtel brothers, Jules and Prosper, who owned the brewery in Tantonville, near Nancy, where Louis Pasteur first observed the role of yeast in fermentation. It has a delicate, grainy, malty, hoppy aroma with hints of lemon and honey. It feels smooth, light and slightly sparkling in the mouth, and the flavour is well balanced between sweetness and bitterness. Tourtel is also available in a brown ale version with a thick, creamy head and a rich, sweet and mildly bitter flavour.

SPECIFICATIONS

Brewery: Brasseries Kronenbourg (Scottish & Newcastle)
Location: Strasbourg, Alsace
Style: Low-alcohol lager
Colour: Straw yellow
Alcohol: 0.5%
Serving temperature: 6°C (42.8°F)
Food: Steamed fish or chicken

Pietra

Pietra has been brewed at the small brewery of the same name in the Corsican town of Furiani since 1996, and is named after the tiny mountain village of Pietraserena.

It has an intense aroma, heavy with hops, and hops also strongly dominate the palate, giving a dry, resiny flavour and lingering bitterness in the finish. The secret ingredient that firmly establishes the Corsican identity of this beer is chestnut flour, which adds a floury feel in the mouth and a subtle nuttiness to the flavour. Another beer in the brewery's small range is Colomba, a wheat beer flavoured with juniper.

SPECIFICATIONS

Brewery: Brasserie Pietra
Location: Furiani, Corsica
Style: Lager
Colour: Pale golden-amber
Alcohol: 6%
Serving temperature: 7°–8°C (44.6°–46.4°F)
Food: Game dishes, such as roast pheasant

Schutzenberger La Bio

The sole remaining independent brewery in Schiltigheim, with a history dating back to 1740, was originally known as Brasserie Royale and was the exclusive supplier of beer to the royal court.

Following the French Revolution it changed its name to Brasserie de la Patrie, and acquired its current identity in 1866 when it moved to its present site. Its organic La Bio is an unfiltered and naturally cloudy pale lager with red fruit and caramel in the aroma and a malty caramel flavour balanced with light hoppiness. The brewery's diverse and interesting range includes a rare example of a French bock beer, called Jubilator, and Bière à la Griotte, which is flavoured with cherries.

SPECIFICATIONS

Brewery: Brasserie Schutzenberger
Location: Schiltigheim, Alsace
Style: Lager
Colour: Golden and opaque
Alcohol: 5%
Serving temperature: 7°C (44.6°F)
Food: White meat dishes

Premium Diekirch

Premium Diekirch is a standard Pilsner with a softly bitter flavour and a smooth texture.

It is one of the leading beer brands produced in Luxembourg and was originally brewed by the Diekirch brewery, which was founded in 1871 by the merger of three smaller breweries in the town of the same name. In 1999, Diekirch merged with one of its main rivals, the Mousel brewery of Rheinfelden, and the Mousel brewery was closed down, with production of that brewery's beers moving to the Diekirch plant. The newly formed company now produces more than half of the beer made in Luxembourg.

SPECIFICATIONS

Brewery: Brasserie de Luxembourg Mousel-Diekirch
Location: Diekirch, Luxembourg
Style: Lager
Colour: Golden yellow
Alcohol: 4.8%
Serving temperature: 6°–8°C (42.8°–46.4°F)
Food: Grilled chicken or pork steaks

Premium Pils Mousel

Brewing reached its peak in Luxembourg in the 1860s when the Grand Duchy had around 35 breweries.

Despite being sandwiched between two of the world's major brewing nations, Germany and Belgium, it now has fewer than 10. Until it closed in 1999, Mousel (or Les Brasseries Réunies de Luxembourg Mousel et Clausen, to give it its full name) was one of the oldest, dating back to 1511, and the brewery originally stood on the site of the abbey at Altenmünster. Its beers are now brewed at Diekirch – a straightforward light-flavoured Premium Pils and an unfiltered Zwickelbier.

SPECIFICATIONS

Brewery: Brasserie de Luxembourg Mousel-Diekirch
Location: Diekirch, Luxembourg
Style: Lager
Colour: Golden yellow
Alcohol: 4.8%
Serving temperature: 6°–8°C (42.8°–46.4°F)
Food: Shellfish platters, light seafood dishes

ABOVE

Belgium is one of the homes of world beer, producing varieties of ales, porters and lagers which are a connoisseur's delight. The bars in which the beers are served can often be as distinctive as the drinks, many of them being centuries old, dimly but characterfully lit (sometimes with only candles), and containing only a few chairs for a small crowd of drinkers.

Belgian Beers

Belgium is home to more styles and varieties of beer than any other country in the world. Famously, it is where you will find the authentic Trappist beers brewed under strict conditions at one of the six monasteries – Chimay, Orval, Rochefort, Westvleteren, Westmalle and Achel – that are exclusively allowed to use the name Trappist on their labels.

ABOVE
Belgium's brewers are rightly proud of the tremendous variety of beers produced within its borders and exported across the world. Belgium is a primary destination for any beer-lover planning a vacation.

BELGIUM IS also home to perhaps the most remarkable beer style in the world, a beer that due to its very nature could not be imitated anywhere else. These are lambic beers, beers that ferment spontaneously by the action of airborne wild yeasts that exist only in the Payottenland region to the west of Brussels. These beers hark back thousands of years to the earliest days of brewing, with the wort left in open vessels overnight to be exposed to naturally occurring yeasts. The wort is then fermented in oak casks for up to two years, eventually creating a beer of incredible depth and complexity, which is blended by master brewers with other lambics and sometimes with fruit flavourings to make Gueuze.

Although in many respects the Belgian brewing industry is thriving, dynamic and healthy, it is subject to the same global market forces that have seen the bulk of world brewing consolidated into the hands of a small number of major conglomerates. By far the largest stake in the Belgian brewing industry is held by Interbrew, formed in 1988 by the merger of Artois (producers of Stella Artois) and Piedboeuf (brewers of Jupiler), which now claims to be the world's largest producer of beer by volume since it joined forces with AmBev of Brazil in 2004. The other major player in Belgium is the British Scottish & Newcastle, which acquired Belgium's second-largest brewing group, Alken-Maes, in 1988.

But there is still much to be positive about when it comes to brewing in Belgium. New brewery openings continue to outnumber the closures, and despite the power wielded by the big companies, there is a sense that as long as Belgians (and non-Belgians) remain enthusiastic about the country's many wonderful, unique beers, there will always be a place for the smaller players, and diversity will rule.

STATISTICS

Total production: 15,650,000 hectolitres (413,429,000 gallons) per year

Consumption per capita: 98 litres (26 gallons) per year

Famous breweries: Artois; Brasserie du Bocq; Brasserie de Rochefort; Brouwerij Duvel Moortgat NV; Brouwerij van Hoegaarden; Lindemans Farm Brewery; NV Brouwerijen Alken-Maes Brasseries SA

Famous brands: Duvel Verde; Grimbergen Blonde; Hoegaarden; La Gauloise Blonde; Lindemans Gueuze; Leffe Brune; Mort Subite; Satan Gold; Stella Artois

Abbaye des Rocs

Set in a small picturesque village close to the French border, this small commercial brewery takes its name from the ruins of a nearby abbey.

It began brewing in 1979, producing a range of characterful strong ales in a variety of styles, chief of which is the double-fermented ale of the same name, made using seven types of malt and aromatised with Belgian, German and Czech hop varieties. It is a rich, malty brew with complex yet subtle red wine characteristics, a sweet fruity aroma and a sharp palate with traces of burnt wood, dark fruit and bitter hops. The brewery also produces a strong unfiltered wheat beer, Blanche des Honelles, notable for its use of malted oats, as well as wheat and barley.

SPECIFICATIONS

Brewery: Brasserie de l'Abbaye des Rocs SA
Location: Montignies-sur-Roc, Hainaut
Style: Belgian abbey double
Colour: Dark red-brown
Alcohol: 9%
Serving temperature: 14°C (57.2°F)
Food: A rich, spicy fruit cake

La Chouffe Blonde

The Achouffe brewery began in 1982, as a hobby for two brothers-in-law, Pierre Gobron and Chris Bauweraerts.

Then in 1984 Pierre gave up his job to work full-time at the brewery. Chris joined him in 1988, and before long the brothers had a thriving business both domestically and in international exports. La Chouffe Blonde is an unpasteurised, bottle-conditioned strong golden ale, spiced with coriander and lightly hopped for a refreshing taste. The brewery also produces McChouffe, a strong, dark ale that may have a Scottish sounding name but bears little resemblance to the 'Scotch' ales that are popular throughout Belgium, and Esprit d'Achouffe, an eau de vie distilled from five-year-old beer.

SPECIFICATIONS

Brewery: Brasserie d'Achouffe
Location: Achouffe, Luxembourg
Style: Golden ale
Colour: Amber-gold
Alcohol: 8%
Serving temperature: 12°C (53.6°F)
Food: Hot, spicy dishes

Leffe Brune

SPECIFICATIONS

Brewery: Abbaye de Leffe SA	**Alcohol:** 6.5%
Location: Leffe, Namur	**Serving temperature:** 10°C (50°F)
Style: Belgian abbey brown ale	**Food:** A hearty beef casserole
Colour: Brown	

Leffe beers come in four distinct varieties, the most popular of which is Leffe Brune, a robustly flavoured brown ale with a rich aroma of roasted caramel and hints of chocolate and dark fruit, and a slightly sweet finish that is reminiscent of raisins, balanced by spicy hop dryness.

The Leffe brand is the best known of all the Belgian 'abbey' beers. Unlike the authentic Trappist beers, these are not genuine monastic products, but the result of a commercial arrangement whereby a brewery produces the beers under licence, with the proceeds split between brewer and abbey. The Abbaye Notre Dame de Leffe was founded in 1152 in the town of Dinant, near Namur. Brewing started on the site in the 13th century, but ceased following the French revolution.

Leffe was first produced in the 1950s by a local brewer, but though the links with the abbey remain the beers are currently brewed at the Interbrew-owned Artois in Leuven, near Brussels. Of the other three Leffe beers, the most significant is Leffe Blonde, a pale golden ale with a delicately spicy, fruity aroma, a creamy smooth body with a strong presence of orange fruit and spicy hops on the palate, and a long dry finish. Leffe Triple is a stronger beer with a full aftertaste of spicy coriander and orange, while the rarely sighted Leffe Radieuse – also known as Vieille Cuvée – is a rich, complex beer with banana, citrus fruit, coriander and cloves present in the aroma and flavour.

Stella Artois

Stella Artois, produced by the Artois brewery in Leuven, near Brussels, is one of the world's most instantly recognisable lager brands. It is an all-malt Pilsner-style bottom-fermented lager with a full-bodied, well-balanced character and a light, refreshing flavour that belies its strength.

Stella Artois can trace its roots back to 1366, with the foundation of the Den Horen brewery in Leuven, the name of which, meaning 'the Horn', is reflected in the hunting horn emblem that still forms part of the Stella Artois label. In 1708, the title of Master Brewer of Den Horen passed to Sebastien Artois, and nine years later he bought the brewery outright, renaming it after himself and subsequently passing the title of Master Brewer on to his descendants. The original brewery was destroyed by artillery fire during World War I, but was rebuilt on the same site, and in 1926 the company's most famous product was launched, named Stella from the Latin for 'star'.

Originally devised as a Christmas beer, Stella Artois is brewed using water drawn from a well deep beneath the brewery and fermented with a unique strain of yeast. A second brewing plant was built in 1948, and the company continued to grow until in 1987 it merged with the Jean-Theodore Piedboeuf brewery to form Interbrew, which has gone on to become one of the largest brewing conglomerates in the world, marketing Stella Artois in more than 80 countries.

SPECIFICATIONS

Brewery: Artois
Location: Leuven, Brabant
Style: Strong Pilsner-style lager
Colour: Pale golden
Alcohol: 5.2%
Serving temperature: 6°C (42.8°F)
Food: Fried or grilled fish

Maes Pils

The Maes brewery was founded in 1880 when the ambitious Egid Maes took over the ailing Sint Michäel de Waarloos brewery.

It was principally an ale brewer until 1946, when it first introduced Maes Pils, a light, crisp lager with a mellow flavour. The history of Maes is a litany of brewery acquisitions and mergers. In 1988, Maes merged with Alken, the brewery that had introduced Cristal Alken in 1929, the first Pilsner-style lager to be brewed in Belgium. The new company, Alken-Maes, remained in control of the Maes family until 1993, and since 2000 has been owned by Scottish & Newcastle.

SPECIFICATIONS

Brewery: Brouwerij Alken-Maes
Location: Alken, Limburg
Style: Pilsner-style lager
Colour: Pale golden yellow
Alcohol: 4.9%
Serving temperature: 6°–8°C (42.8°–46.4°F)
Food: Grilled fish and seafood

Bavik Wittekerke

This traditional golden wheat beer is named after a popular Flemish television soap opera set in a fictional village of the same name, and was launched as a promotional tie-in with the series.

Wittekerke is brewed according to the time-honoured method using a proportion of malted oats, as well as barley and wheat, to give the beer a smoother, fuller body and slightly sweeter flavour. It has a fragrantly fruity aroma with the blend of Curaçao oranges and coriander shining through, while on the palate the flavour is well balanced with fruity malts which are set off against a subtle bitterness.

SPECIFICATIONS

Brewery: Brouwerij Bavik
Location: Bavikhove, West Flanders
Style: Belgian witbier / wheat beer
Colour: Sunny golden yellow
Alcohol: 5%
Serving temperature: 9°–10°C (48.2°–50°F)
Food: Lightly flavoured pasta dishes

Bavik Petrus Winterbier

Petrus is the name given to the range of top-fermented ales from the Bavik brewery, including this seasonal version brewed throughout November. The aroma is soft and malty with a lightly roasted and slightly sweet character, while high carbonation gives it a Champagne-like mouthfeel.

The blend of spices used to flavour this beer are subtly apparent on the palate, balanced with a citrussy hop dryness and a caramel malt sweetness. As well as the seasonal beer, Bavik brews four other ales under the Petrus label, the name being taken from the famous Grand Cru wine of St Emilion near Bordeaux in France. The first Petrus was Oud Bruin, a deep, dark red beer made from a blend of brown ale and beer that has been aged in oak casks for a full two years. This gives Oud Bruin a slightly sour, vinous character, and its relatively light 5.5% alcohol make it a refreshing thirst quencher. It was introduced in 1975 to revive the fortunes of a brewery that was suffering due to competition from the mass-market brewers, and fortunately proved an instant success. Thus Bavik was able to celebrate its centenary in 1994, having remained throughout in the hands of the De Brabandere family from its foundation by farmer Adolphe de Brabandere through four generations. The Petrus range also includes a traditional amber coloured ale called Speciale, and an elegant blond Tripel. The oak-aged brown ale that forms the base of the Oud Bruin is also exported in casks to the United States, to be sold in its unblended form.

SPECIFICATIONS

Brewery: Brouwerij Bavik
Location: Bavikhove, West Flanders
Style: Strong dark ale
Colour: Copper red-brown
Alcohol: 6.5%
Serving temperature: 8°–10°C (46.4°–50°F)
Food: Hearty soups or barbecued meat

Block Satan Gold

The De Block brewing family has a long and illustrious history stretching back to the fourteenth century, when Henricus De Bloc was granted the right to brew beer for the Duke of Brabant and Burgundy. However, it was not until 1887 that one of his descendants, Louis De Block, founded the modern-day brewery in the small hamlet of Peizegem, northwest of Brussels in the Flemish-speaking part of Brabant.

The brewery currently produces four regular beers, of which the two under the Satan label are its most popular. Satan Gold is a strong blond ale brewed with a blend of pale malts to give it a soft, fruity character balanced with a touch of spicy bitterness provided by the subtle use of hops and spices. Satan Red is differentiated by the use of dark malts, along with a similar blend of spices and fragrant hops, to produce a well-balanced, creamy textured dark ale with a refreshing flavour. Triple Abbeybeer Dendermonde is brewed according to the Belgian custom for a strong, pale golden beer with a full-bodied malty profile, while Kastaar is an old-fashioned dark brown ale with a lower alcohol content and a refreshingly bitter flavour balanced with sweet fruity malts and a hint of coriander. Its name comes from an old Flemish word meaning 'strong fellow'.

SPECIFICATIONS

Brewery: Brouwerij De Block-Joostens
Location: Peizegem, Flemish Brabant
Style: Strong Belgian pale ale
Colour: Golden amber
Alcohol: 8%
Serving temperature: 8°–10°C (46.4°–50°F)
Food: Pizza or spicy Mexican food

La Binchoise Bière des Ours

The Binchoise microbrewery was founded in 1987 in the town of Binche, which lies between Mons and Charleroi. As well as two straightforward classic strong spiced ales, a Blonde and a Brune, it also produces a strong dark ale which has honey added prior to fermentation and is appropriately named 'Bears' beer'.

The honey not only gives the beer a soft, mellow smoothness, but also provides extra fermentable sugars that convert to alcohol. Bière des Ours is also known as Berenbier when translated for sale in the Flemish-speaking parts of northern Belgium and the Netherlands. Other beers in the Binchoise range include Rose, a raspberry flavoured summer ale, and the powerfully aromatic Spéciale Noël Christmas beer.

SPECIFICATIONS

- **Brewery:** Brasserie La Binchoise
- **Location:** Binche, Hainaut
- **Style:** Strong dark ale
- **Colour:** Golden amber
- **Alcohol:** 8%
- **Serving temperature:** 10°C (50°F)
- **Food:** Roasted duck or venison

Blanche de Namur

Blanche de Namur is a mild, refreshing, golden wheat beer with a smooth fruity flavour with a hint of coriander spice and bitter orange.

It is part of the regular range of the Du Bocq brewery, the origins of which date back to 1858, when farmer Martin Belot started brewing his own beer on his farm in the village of Purnode, close to Dinant. Originally a project to keep his workers occupied during the winter months, the brewing side of the business soon took over and the farm was closed down in 1960. The Du Bocq brewery remains an independent family-run concern to this day.

SPECIFICATIONS

- **Brewery:** Brasserie du Bocq
- **Location:** Purnode, Namur
- **Style:** Belgian witbier / wheat beer
- **Colour:** Hazy golden yellow
- **Alcohol:** 4.5%
- **Serving temperature:** 6°C (42.8°F)
- **Food:** Fish, white meat and poultry

La Gauloise Blonde

For many years La Gauloise Brune was the mainstay of the Du Bocq brewery, but in 1994 the brewery increased its range by introducing this blonde ale.

It has a fragrant hoppy character in the aroma which becomes subdued on the palate, giving way to a soft, mellow malt profile, finishing with a touch of refreshing hop bitterness. The third beer in the La Gauloise range, also introduced in 1994, is Ambrée, a sparkling amber-coloured bitter ale with a hint of liquorice. As well as its own extensive range, Du Bocq brews a number of other beers on commission, mainly small-scale runs of speciality beers for larger brewers.

SPECIFICATIONS

Brewery: Brasserie du Bocq
Location: Purnode, Namur
Style: Belgian pale ale
Colour: Bright golden yellow
Alcohol: 6.3%
Serving temperature: 8°–12°C (46.4°–53.6°F)
Food: Fish, white meat, poultry

La Gauloise Brune

Launched in the early 1920s, La Gauloise Brune was the first beer to be sold commercially by the Du Bocq brewery, originally distributed locally and later gaining popularity further afield.

It is a top-fermented dark beer brewed to an old-fashioned recipe and 'lagered' in cold tanks for several weeks, then bottled unfiltered and unpasteurised, just as it always has been. The resulting beer has a rich yeasty aroma with hints of coriander spice, while on the palate La Gauloise Brune is full-bodied and well balanced between malt and hops, and finishes with a slightly bitter aftertaste.

SPECIFICATIONS

Brewery: Brasserie du Bocq
Location: Purnode, Namur
Style: Belgian strong dark ale
Colour: Dark reddish brown
Alcohol: 8.1%
Serving temperature: 8°–12°C (46.4°–53.6°F)
Food: Game, red meat, or spicy white meat dishes

Triple Moine

Though designated a tripel, this is a relatively light beer with a comparatively modest alcohol content. Its aroma is full of herbal hoppiness, while on the palate a crisp refreshing hop bitterness dominates over a background of fruity malts.

Triple Moine is similar in character to the brewery's Deugniet, although the latter is a somewhat stronger beer with a hint of green apples in the aroma. Du Bocq also brews two seasonal beers under the Regal label, originally from the Marbaix-la-Tour brewery, which Du Bocq bought and eventually closed in 1983. Completing the range are two beers under the St Benoit label, a light easy-drinking Blonde and a fruitier Brune.

SPECIFICATIONS

Brewery: Brasserie du Bocq
Location: Purnode, Namur
Style: Belgian abbey tripel
Colour: Golden copper colour
Alcohol: 5.5%
Serving temperature: 8°–12°C (46.4°–53.6°F)
Food: Spicy pasta dishes, pizzas, strong cheeses

Pauwel Kwak

Every Belgian brewery traditionally markets its own distinctive shape of glass, which is supposed to be the ideal vessel for drinking its beers.

None, however, is as distinctive as the hourglass-shaped round-bottomed flagon in which Pauwel Kwak is served. It is modelled on the stirrup cup served to coach drivers on horseback, who could take a sip, then set the glass in their stirrup, and was inspired by a legendary innkeeper who was famous for a strong ale similar to the one that now bears his name. Brewed with three types of malt and sweetened with candy sugar, it is rich and warming with a caramel malt character.

SPECIFICATIONS

Brewery: Brouwerij Bosteels
Location: Buggenhout, East Flanders
Style: Strong Belgian ale
Colour: Golden amber-red
Alcohol: 8%
Serving temperature: 13°C (55.4°F)
Food: Dark chocolate

Tripel Karmeliet

Bosteels brewery, founded in 1791, has been in the family from which it takes its name for seven generations and in recent years has turned its vast wealth of brewing experience to producing some highly individual and characterful strong ales.

This particular example is inspired by a beer made in the seventeenth century at the Carmelite monastery in nearby Dendermonde. It is brewed with a blend of malted and unmalted wheat, oats and barley, and heavily spiced for an intriguingly complex flavour, starting off sweet but leading to a dry finish.

SPECIFICATIONS

Brewery: Brouwerij Bosteels
Location: Buggenhout, East Flanders
Style: Belgian abbey tripel
Colour: Dark orange
Alcohol: 8%
Serving temperature: 10°–14°C (50°–57.2°F)
Food: A sharply flavoured dessert, such as lemon tart

Chimay Rouge

Chimay Rouge (Red), also known as Première, is a copper-coloured ale with a light, fruity aroma with hints of apricot and blackcurrant. On the palate, it has a silky smooth texture.

SPECIFICATIONS

Brewery: Bières de Chimay SA
Location: Abbaye de Notre Dame de Scourmont, Chimay, Hainaut
Style: Belgian abbey dubbel (Trappist)
Colour: Copper
Alcohol: 7%
Serving temperature: 14°C (57.2°F)
Food: Fried fish or seafood

The fruity nuances are again apparent, balanced by a pleasantly bitter astringency and a dry, spicy finish. Chimay Cinq Cents (White, also known as Tripel) is a paler golden-orange colour and is dominated by its big hop aroma with muscat raisin and citrus notes. The hop character continues to dominate on the well-balanced palate, in which fruity malts are complemented by a touch of bitterness. Both Chimay Rouge and Tripel beers undergo secondary fermentation in the bottle.

Chimay Bleue

Originally brewed as a Christmas beer, Chimay Bleue is both the strongest and the most popular of the three beers produced at the most famous of Belgium's trappist breweries. A classic strong, dark, warming winter ale, top-fermented with secondary fermentation in the bottle, it keeps well in the bottle for at least five years, maturing to become smoother and drier in the style of a good port.

Hints of caramel and a fresh, light floral and yeasty aroma give way to rich fruit, spice and roasted malt flavours on the palate, but with a lightness that belies its strength. The name comes from the distinctive blue cap on the bottle (the other Chimay beers have red and white caps), but Chimay Bleue is also available in larger corked bottles, labelled as Chimay Grande Reserve. The Abbaye de Notre Dame de Scourmont was founded in 1850 when 17 monks from the Trappist abbey at Westvleteren left to build a new monastery on land donated by the Prince of Chimay, close to the village of Forges-les-Chimay in the Hainaut province of southern Belgium.

The brewery was opened in 1862 to provide sustenance for the monks and to raise funds for the abbey, and Chimay beers have been widely available commercially since 1925. Having established the commercial operation, which is now the largest employer in the region, the monks have withdrawn to their life of prayer and study, while the brewery operates as a separate enterprise.

SPECIFICATIONS

Brewery: Bières de Chimay SA
Location: Abbaye de Notre Dame de Scourmont, Chimay, Hainaut
Style: Strong dark Belgian abbey ale (Trappist)
Colour: Deep copper
Alcohol: 9%
Serving temperature: 14°C (57.2°F)
Food: An after-dinner beer to enjoy with a cigar

Mort Subite Framboise

The Payottenland region to the west of Brussels is the home of lambic beers, which are fermented by the action of naturally occurring wild airborne yeasts. Perhaps the most famous lambic beers are the ones produced by De Keersmaeker brewery under the Mort Subite label.

To make the unusual musky flavour of its beers more palatable to a wider audience, De Keersmaeker blends its lambics with conventionally fermented brews, and flavours them with fruit extracts. Principal among these are its Framboise or Frambozen (raspberry), and Kriek (cherry) versions, although it also produces lambics flavoured with *cassis* (blackcurrant) and *pêche* (peach). Mort Subite Framboise is a fragrantly sweet and fruity beer, perhaps not as complex as some other fruit lambic beers, but with a pleasantly tart, refreshing flavour. The more traditional Kriek is made with cherries grown specifically for the purpose by specially commissioned orchards and the result is a well-balanced sweet–sour beer with cherry-almond notes. Less commonly available is Mort Subite Fond Gueuze, a beer blended from unfiltered aged lambic beer with a fresh, young lambic; yielding highly complex flavours. The origins of the Mort Subite name ('sudden death') lie in a seventeenth-century dice game, and stem from the café in Brussels where the beers were first served and this game was played.

SPECIFICATIONS

Brewery: Brouwerij De Keersmaeker
Location: Kobbegem, Flemish Brabant
Style: Fruit lambic
Colour: Deep pink
Alcohol: 4.3%
Serving temperature: 8°–9°C (46.4°–48.2°F)
Food: Light fruit-based desserts, such as a fresh fruit salad

De Koninck Antoon Blond

The city of Antwerp's only brewery was founded in 1833 by the De Koninck family and provided beers for the family-run inn.

It still bears their name, although the brewery was sold to the Van Den Bogaerts in 1912 and is now owned by the fifth generation of that family. The brewery's original beer was a well-rounded amber-coloured pale ale – according to many, one of the best examples of its kind in Belgium, with a flavour somewhere between that of an English bitter and a German altbier – and this is still known simply as De Koninck. It has always been served on draught throughout Antwerp's bars and cafés, in a distinctive glass known as a 'bolleke', although it is also available worldwide in bottled form. A stronger version was launched in 1993, known as Cuvée De Koninck, and in 1998 the brewery increased its range further with a blonde version called Antoon. Despite its pale golden colour, this is an ale (top-fermented at warmer temperatures), rather than a lager. It is light-bodied, but has a full flavour and aroma, predominantly sweet and malty with subtle hops in the background. A seasonal brew, the deep amber Winterkoninck, is sold throughout the winter months in a 75cl bottle with a Champagne cork.

SPECIFICATIONS

Brewery: Brouwerij De Koninck NV

Location: Antwerp, Antwerp

Style: Belgian pale ale

Colour: Clear, bright golden yellow

Alcohol: 6%

Serving temperature: 8°–10°C (46.4°–50°F)

Food: Rich, spiced desserts

Moinette

The Moinette name, from the French for 'monk', is applied to the Dupont brewery's range of strong ales. As is typical of many Belgian breweries, Dupont's ales come in Blonde and Brune (brown) versions, both of which weigh in at 8.5% alcohol.

The Blonde version has a spicy hop aroma balanced with a sweet malty flavour, while the Brune has more of a roasted malt character with a hint of burnt caramel and natural spiciness in the flavour. Dupont is a small family brewery that came into existence in 1920 when Alfred Dupont bought the Rimaux-Deridder farmhouse brewery for his son, in order to keep him from emigrating to Canada. Rimaux-Deridder was established in 1844 and was well known for its honey-flavoured Bière de Miel, which is still produced today. It has an intensely floral hoppy flavour and a subtle touch of honey sweetness.

Dedicated to traditional methods of beer production, Dupont matures all of its beers in warm cellars for two months and bottles them unfiltered and unpasteurised, giving them a characteristic cloudiness. Since 1990, the brewery has also been leading the way in organic brewing, with several beers from its regular range brewed exclusively to organic methods, including the Bière de Miel, while a handful of others are available as organic or non-organic versions.

SPECIFICATIONS
Brewery: Brasserie Dupont sprl
Location: Tourpes-Leuze, Hainaut
Style: Strong ale
Colour: Pale golden yellow
Alcohol: 8.5%
Serving temperature: 10°–12°C (50°–53.6°F)
Food: Barbecued meats

Saison Dupont Vieille Provision

Saison, the French for 'season', is a style of beer unique to the Wallonia region of Belgium, brewed in the spring for consumption throughout the hot summer months when the effect of the heat on the yeast makes brewing an unpredictable business.

These beers typically have a high hop content (for their preservative effect) and are fully fermented to give them a refreshing character. Dupont's Vieille Provision version is one of the best and most traditional examples of the style. It has potent hop aromas and a dry herbal hop flavour on the palate, with an intensely dry, spicy finish.

SPECIFICATIONS

Brewery: Brasserie Dupont sprl
Location: Tourpes-Leuze, Hainaut
Style: Saison
Colour: Golden oak
Alcohol: 6.5%
Serving temperature: 10°C (50°F)
Food: Fresh green salad, grilled fish

Ellezelloise Quintine Blonde

Ellezelloise started as a small farmhouse brewing operation in 1993, producing a small range of highly characterful beers in distinctive flip-top bottles.

The Blonde is a strong, full-bodied ale with a zesty aroma of citrus and herbs and a yeasty hint of bananas, while on the palate a potent hoppy bitterness dominates over a sweet malty background flavour. Quintine is also available as an Ambrée (pale ale) in which a sweet maltiness dominates, balanced with a herbal hop bitterness leading to a dry bitter caramel finish. The brewery also produces a powerful, rich, black stout called Hercule, a mild, sweet wheat beer and a sweet, refreshing Saison.

SPECIFICATIONS

Brewery: Ellezelloise
Location: Ellezelles, Hainaut
Style: Belgian pale ale
Colour: Golden yellow-orange
Alcohol: 8%
Serving temperature: 10°C (50°F)
Food: Grilled sausages or burgers

Fantôme

Marketed as 'a brewery unlike any other', Fantôme was founded in 1988 by Dany Prignon, who wanted to revive the tradition of the village brewery to go alongside the baker and the butcher.

Everything is done by hand on a small scale, including bottling, and one small run of a single beer is made per week. The flagship Fantôme beer is a strong fruity ale with a flavour of apples and pears. Others products from the brewery include a Saison, which is brewed all year round, but varies in character according to the time of year, and assorted one-off brews with names such as Pissenlit and Black Ghost.

SPECIFICATIONS

Brewery: Brasserie Fantôme
Location: Soy, Luxembourg
Style: Belgian strong dark ale
Colour: Dark amber-red
Alcohol: 8%
Serving temperature: 12°C (53.6°F)
Food: Strongly flavoured cheeses

Gildenbier

Gildenbier is a strong brown ale with a fairly sweet caramel flavour made by Haacht, the largest independent brewery in Belgium. It was founded in 1898 in the small town of Boortmeerbeek, just north of Leuven, and for a period during the 1990s it was part-owned by Interbrew, but regained independence in 1998.

Most of the beers the Haacht brewery produces are straightforward mass-market lagers, including a standard Pilsner called Primus, a Dortmund-style sweet lager called Adler, and a spiced wheat beer called Witbier Haacht. These are drunk widely throughout the brewery's extensive chain of cafés. Its range of ales includes a selection of abbey-style beers under the Tongerlo brand.

SPECIFICATIONS

Brewery: Brouwerij Haacht NV
Location: Boortmeerbeek, Flemish Brabant
Style: Belgian strong brown ale
Colour: Walnut brown
Alcohol: 7%
Serving temperature: 10°C (50°F)
Food: Grilled steak with a rich sauce

Steenbrugge Dubbel

The first brewery to stand on this site was built by Jan Hugheins in 1455. Over the years it has alternated between brewing and distilling; the current brewery dates from 1872 when the 't Hamerken distillery was bought by Jules Vanneste, and it began brewing top-fermented ales.

Then in the 1930s with the growing popularity in Belgium of Pilsner it switched production to bottom-fermented beers, including a bock, a Dortmunder-style export and a Pilsner. The company underwent a major restructuring in 1983, being renamed Gouden Boom (Golden Tree) and changing back to brewing top-fermented ales, the most famous of which was its Brugs Tarwebier, although it has since sold this brand to Alken-Maes, and the majority ownership of the brewery is now held by Palm. Gouden Boom currently brews two abbey-style beers under the Steenbrugge label, a Dubbel and a Tripel, named after the abbey on the outskirts of the city. The dark reddish-brown Dubbel has a smooth, full-bodied texture and a rich, fruity, nutty, caramel malt flavour leading to a tangy bitter fruit finish. The Tripel is a golden blond colour and has a spicy, floral aroma with a sweet malt character dominating the palate. Currently most of the brewery's efforts are directed towards the Brugge Tripel and another strong ale called Brugge Blond. The 9% alcohol Tripel is the more interesting of these, with its full malty flavour and mellow, aromatic aftertaste.

SPECIFICATIONS

Brewery: Brouwerij de Gouden Boom
Location: Brugge, West Flanders
Style: Belgian abbey dubbel
Colour: Chestnut brown
Alcohol: 6.5%
Serving temperature: 10°–12°C (50°–53.6°F)
Food: Spicy pizzas or pasta in tomato sauce

Hoegaarden Blanche

To the east of Brussels is the main wheat-growing region of Belgium, and the area once boasted more than 30 breweries that all made a distinctive spiced wheat beer. By the late 1950s the breweries were all closed down and the wheat beer style had all but completely died out, having lost out in popularity to Pilsner-style lagers.

Fortunately, they were not gone for long. Pierre Celis grew up in the town of Hoegaarden next door to the Tomsin brewery, which was the last of the wheat beer breweries to close, and it was here that he learned the art of brewing as a teenager. Determined to revive his favourite beer style, he started brewing Hoegaarden in 1966, and the current popularity of wheat beers around the world is entirely to his credit. Flavoured with coriander seed and Curaçao orange peel, Hoegaarden is light and refreshing. As well as regular Hoegaarden, there is also an amber-coloured Hoegaarden Grand Cru, which is made with a higher proportion of malt. Following a fire at the brewery in 1980, Interbrew stepped in to assist with the rebuilding costs and subsequently bought the brewery outright. Pierre Celis then emigrated to the United States, where he established a new company to brew a beer very similar to the original Hoegaarden called Celis White. Thus he is one of few individuals to have enjoyed brewing success in two major beer-producing nations.

SPECIFICATIONS

Brewery: Brouwerij van Hoegaarden
Location: Hoegaarden, Flemish Brabant
Style: Belgian wheat beer
Colour: Cloudy golden orange-yellow
Alcohol: 5%
Serving temperature: 9°–10°C (48.2°–50°F)
Food: Grilled chicken with light vegetable accompaniment

Delirium Tremens

The Huyghe brewery, in the small town of Melle which lies on the outskirts of Ghent, was founded by Léon Huyghe in 1906, when he took over the Appelhoek brewery, the origins of which date back to 1654 and possibly earlier.

Until 1913, the brewery had its own maltings, but this was replaced with a bottling plant, and in 1928 the brewery was significantly rebuilt and expanded with further expansion in the 1930s and again in the 1960s. A restructuring in 1985 broke the company up into four parts, with brewing operations separated from the Huyghe chain of cafés, and it has since gone on to massive commercial success, all the while remaining under the ownership of Léon's descendants. Huyghe's vast list of beers – it names as many as 60 different brews in its portfolio – is a result of the practice of acquiring and reviving brands from defunct breweries, as well as imitations of other popular brands. Perhaps the most famous beers are the Delirium range, which are presented in stoneware bottles with pink elephants on the label – as well as Delirium Tremens these include a seasonal variation called Delirium Noel and a dark version called Delirium Nocturnum. Delirium Tremens was launched in 1989. It is a pale golden beer with a distinctive spicy character, which stems from the use of a blend of three different yeasts and plenty of hops, and finished with an intense dry hoppy bitterness.

SPECIFICATIONS

Brewery: Brasserie Léon Huyghe
Location: Melle, East Flanders
Style: Belgian strong pale ale
Colour: Cloudy golden amber
Alcohol: 9%
Serving temperature: 10°C (50°F)
Food: Mussels and French fries

Floreffe Double

Brewed for the Norbertine Floreffe Abbey near the town of Namur, Floreffe is a range of bottle-conditioned ales which are produced by the Lefèbvre family-owned brewery not too far away in the small town of Quenast, southwest of Brussels. Founded in 1876, the brewery produces a traditional dubbel and tripel, as well as a straightforward blonde ale and a strong, dark, spiced beer known variously as Meilleur or Prima Melior, which is flavoured with aniseed. Floreffe Double is a medium-strength dark brown ale with a predominantly sweet malt aroma reminiscent of candied fruits. The body is full and smooth, and malts continue to lead with sweet raisins balanced by an almost smoky, chocolatey, roasted malt flavour.

Floreffe Triple has a similarly soft, smooth-bodied texture and rich, malty flavour, although it has a much stronger hop presence, giving it a thirst-quenching bitter edge, and is a little stronger in alcohol terms, but not as strong as the classic tripels of other breweries. The best place to enjoy the beers is in the converted fourteenth-century mill at the abbey itself, but fortunately the entire range is also widely available in bottled form. Lefèbvre also brews an unfiltered spiced wheat beer, Blanche de Bruxelles, which is characterised by a citrus fruit acidity, a forthright hoppy Pilsner called La Quenast, and a honey-flavoured pale ale called Barbãr.

SPECIFICATIONS

Brewery: Brasserie Lefèbvre SA
Location: Quenast, Walloon Brabant
Style: Belgian abbey dubbel
Colour: Dark mahogany brown
Alcohol: 6.5%
Serving temperature: 10°–12°C (50°–53.6°F)
Food: Grilled beef, lamb or game

Jan van Gent

Jan van Gent is a copper-coloured pale ale with a toasty, grainy aroma with hints of dark fruit and toffee, and a mild, sweet malt flavour which is balanced by a hint of sourness.

Liefmans also produces a cherry-flavoured Kriek beer and a raspberry-flavoured Frambozen, although the brewery's home town of Oudenaarde is traditionally more famous for its Oud Bruin (Old Brown) ale, a strong, red-brown top-fermented beer made from a blend of young and old ales, and characterised by its slightly sour flavour, compared to the sweet, nutty malt flavour of brown ales from other regions. The style lives on, although it is now produced by just a handful of breweries, including Liefmans, which brews a version known as Goudenband.

Liefmans can trace its history back to 1679, the date of the earliest known written reference to a brewery in Oudenaarde. This brewery was acquired by Jacobus Liefmans in 1770 and stayed in the family until 1868 when the untimely death of Camille Liefmans, grandson of Jacobus, saw the sale of the brewery to Pierre van Geluwe de Berlaere – the Liefmans name was kept as part of the conditions of the sale. The original brewery was mostly destroyed during World War I, and it was rebuilt on its present site by the river. In 1990 Liefmans was bought by Riva and all of its brewing operations moved to Riva's plant in nearby Dentergem. However, after brewing, the wort is transported back to Oudenaarde for fermentation and maturation, which ensures that the beers retain their original character.

SPECIFICATIONS

Brewery: Brouwerijgroep Liefmans-Riva
Location: Oudenaarde, East Flanders
Style: Belgian pale ale
Colour: Copper red-brown
Alcohol: 5.5%
Serving temperature: 10°–13°C (50°–55.4°F)
Food: Simple bread and cheese

Lindemans Framboise

Southwest of Brussels, in the quiet Belgian town of Vlezenbeek, the Lindemans family has been farming and home brewing as long as anyone can remember.

Commercial brewing started in 1811 in their barn-like brewery. Lambic, or spontaneously fermented beers, are among the world's rarest. Produced more like a methode champenoise champagne than a typical beer, these products mature in oak for nearly two years prior to release. Long before hops were common in most beers, various fruits and vegetables were used to season beers. The acidity of lambic beers blends perfectly with raspberries. Framboise has a magnificent aroma, a delicate palate of raspberries with undertones of fruity acidity, and an elegant, sparkling clean natural taste.

SPECIFICATIONS

Brewery: Lindemans Farm Brewery

Location: Vlezenbeek, Flemish Brabant

Style: Raspberry lambic

Colour: Rose

Alcohol: 3.8%

Serving temperature: 7.2°C (45°F)

Food: Chocolate desserts, fresh raspberries, ice cream with a raspberry demi-glaze sauce, crème caramel, baked Alaska, Olympia oysters, caviar

Lindemans Gueuze

Possibly the oldest type of beer, Lindemans Gueuze (Geuzza) is unseasoned, wild-fermented wheat beer.

It is highly coveted by gourmands in Belgium, who lay it in their cellars like wine. Golden in colour and with a cidery, winey palate, it is reminiscent, perhaps, of bubbly dry vermouth with a more complex and natural flavour. It is traditionally served in a tall, thick tumbler with cubes of sugar to sweeten to taste, and may be served as an aperitif in place of dry sherry. The beer is of an intriguing and historically interesting flavour, but it is also of enough quality to have taken a gold medal in the World Beer Championships.

SPECIFICATIONS

Brewery: Lindemans Farm Brewery

Location: Vlezenbeek, Flemish Brabant

Style: Gueuze lambic

Colour: Golden

Alcohol: 3.8%

Serving temperature: 7.2°C (45°F)

Food: Carbonnade of beef, mussels in white wine, strong cheese

Lindemans Kriek

Lindemans Kriek is a filtered lambic beer flavoured with locally grown whole cherries and has a refreshingly sharp but not sour flavour. It comes from one of the handful of remaining breweries that produce authentic lambic beers, which are made by the action of spontaneous fermentation and have an unusual dry, wine-like flavour.

Lindemans, founded in 1809, is the most commercially successful of the independent lambic brewers (only Belle-Vue, owned by Interbrew, and De Keersmaeker, owned by Scottish & Newcastle, are bigger). Originally Lindemans was a farmhouse brewer, making beer over the winter and growing barley and wheat in the summer, but by 1930 the brewery's success meant that farming operations were discontinued. A new brewery was built in 1991 to increase capacity, and Lindemans now produces a wide range of flavoured and blended lambic beers. Their Cuvée René (named after the current owner, the eighth generation of the family to run the brewery) is a classic of the oude gueuze style, which is made from a blend of young beer with an old beer that has undergone lengthy maturation in oak casks. Although the practise of flavouring beers with cherries (Kriek) or raspberries (Framboise or Frambozen) is a time-honoured tradition, Lindemans has in recent years also experimented with new flavourings for its lambics, including peaches and even tea, the resulting beer having a refreshing sweet–sour lemon flavour.

SPECIFICATIONS

Brewery: Brouwerij Lindemans
Location: Vlezenbeek, Flemish Brabant
Style: Kriek lambic
Colour: Clear, bright red-brown
Alcohol: 4%
Serving temperature: 8°–10°C (46.4°–50°F)
Food: Roast duck with fruit-based sauce

Saison 1900

As well as its famous Trappist ales, the French-speaking southern half of Belgium is also the home of the beer style known simply as saison (French for 'season').

These light, refreshing beers were traditionally brewed in spring to be enjoyed throughout summer when brewing was not possible due to the heat, but Lefèbvre's version is available all year round. Like the brewery's other beers, it is soft and mild, and somewhat sweeter than other examples of the style. A spicy fruit aroma is followed by a predominantly fruity, toffee-ish malt character on the palate, balanced by a subtle dry hop flavour in the background.

SPECIFICATIONS

Brewery: Brasserie Lefèbvre SA
Location: Quenast, Walloon Brabant
Style: Saison
Colour: Deep golden yellow
Alcohol: 5.2%
Serving temperature: 8°–10°C (46.4°–50°F)
Food: Roast turkey and cranberry sauce

Hapkin

Hapkin is named after a Count of Flanders of the late eleventh and early twelfth century by the name of Baudouin Hapkin à la Hache ('the Axeman').

Badouin Hapkin ordered the monks of the Ter Duinen abbey to brew a strong, blonde ale for him. Legend has it that the resulting beer rendered the count and his troops invincible. No brewery would make such claims about its beers these days, but the present version of Hapkin is still a potent brew, with hoppy accents over a sharp, fruity malt background before a dry, bitter finish. The Louwaege brewery was founded in 1877 and is now owned by that most influential of British brewing groups, Scottish & Newcastle.

SPECIFICATIONS

Brewery: Brouwerij Louwaege
Location: Kortemark, West Flanders
Style: Belgian strong blonde ale
Colour: Pale golden orange-yellow
Alcohol: 8.5%
Serving temperature: 10°C (50°F)
Food: Light vegetable soups

Duvel

Duvel is famous for its potent hop aroma and despite its high alcohol content is a surprisingly refreshing, easy-drinking beer, stone dry with fragrant, zesty fruit aromas and flavour.

In 1918, Albert Moortgat decided to brew a beer similar to the pale ales brought over by the English troops during World War I. After much experimentation, the beer was launched in 1923 as Victory Ale, but upon tasting the new beer one brewery worker proclaimed, 'Da's nen echten duvel' ('That's a devil of a beer'), and so it came to be known as Duvel.

SPECIFICATIONS

Brewery: Brouwerij Duvel Moortgat NV
Location: Breendonk-Puurs, Antwerp
Style: Belgian strong blonde ale
Colour: Pale golden straw yellow
Alcohol: 8.5%
Serving temperature: 10°C (50°F)
Food: Serve on its own as a pre-dinner aperitif

Duvel Verde

The original unfiltered, bottle-conditioned Duvel comes in large (three-litre) or small (33cl) bottles with a red cap and red lettering on the label and is sometimes known as Duvel Rood.

SPECIFICATIONS

Brewery: Brouwerij Duvel Moortgat NV
Location: Breendonk-Puurs, Antwerp
Style: Belgian strong golden ale
Colour: Pale golden straw yellow
Alcohol: 8%
Serving temperature: 10°C (50°F)
Food: A crisp, green salad

Duvel Verde is a pasteurised, filtered version of the same beer, available only in the smaller size and brewed to a slightly lower alcoholic strength. Moortgat also produces a crisp, dry Belgian-style Pilsner called Vedette, as well as a stronger Bavarian-style Pilsner with a more pronounced hop character known as Bel Pils and an amber-blond ale called Passendale, launched in 2000 as a joint venture with the manufacturers of a cheese by the same name.

Orval

With its potent herbal hop aroma and intensely dry flavour with a hint of tart berry fruit, Orval is a classic of the abbey beer style.

Triple-fermented and dry-hopped with Bavarian Hallertau and Styrian Goldings hops, it is primed with liquid candy sugar before bottling to promote continued fermentation. Orval brewery's symbol of a trout with a ring in its mouth relates to the legend of Countess Matilda of Tuscany, who arrived in 1076 to visit a group of Italian monks who had settled in the area. After accidentally dropping her wedding ring in the well, she prayed for its return and immediately a trout appeared with the ring in its mouth. As an act of gratitude, she made a donation to the monks to enable them to build their abbey, and proclaimed the site a 'Val d'Or' (golden valley). The Italian monks later moved on and were replaced in 1132 by a new religious community who became affiliated to the Cistercians, later joining the stricter Trappist branch of the order.

In 1637, at the height of the Thirty Years' War, the monastery was pillaged. Although it recovered from this setback, in 1793 it was sacked again and destroyed by French Revolutionary troops. It lay in ruins until the 1930s, when the Trappist community returned and rebuilt the abbey. The brewery now operates as a separate business, but it still belongs to the religious community and follows its values with regard to quality of produce and limitation of commercial growth, with all profits going to the monastery.

SPECIFICATIONS

Brewery: Brasserie d'Orval SA

Location: Abbaye de Notre Dame d'Orval, Villers-devant-Orval, Luxembourg

Style: Belgian abbey ale (Trappist)

Colour: Golden copper-red

Alcohol: 6.2%

Serving temperature: 10°–14°C (50°–57.2°F)

Food: Bread and strong-flavoured cheese

Maredsous 6

The Maredsous abbey in Dinant commissioned the Moortgat brewery to produce its own label beers in 1963. There are three beers in the range, which are all called Maredsous, but are distinguished by a number that corresponds to their alcohol content (by volume).

Six is a blonde ale with a light floral aroma and a slightly sweet but well-rounded flavour balanced between fruity malts and spicy hops. Eight is a strong, caramel-sweet dubbel that ages well to take on the roasted malt characteristics of a stout, while Ten is a bold tripel with a malty sweetness and a warming 10% alcohol.

SPECIFICATIONS

Brewery: Brouwerij Duvel Moortgat NV
Location: Breendonk-Puurs, Antwerp
Style: Belgian abbey blonde ale
Colour: Golden yellow-orange
Alcohol: 6%
Serving temperature: 6°–8°C (42.8°–46.4°F)
Food: Chilli con carne

Steendonk

Steendonk is an unfiltered cloudy spiced wheat beer with a mild, smooth, sweet flavour. It is produced by Palm, which has been brewing in the village of Steenhuffel, near Londerzeel, north of Brussels, since 1747.

Originally it was no more than the brewhouse for the village inn, but rapidly expanded following World War I and is now one of the largest independent breweries in Belgium, and holds part or whole ownership of many smaller breweries. The brewery's regular range also includes Palm Speciale, a clean-tasting pale ale; Aerts 1900, an unusual copper-coloured ale that undergoes a double fermentation process; and Bock, which confusingly is not a bock beer, but a dry, hoppy Pilsner.

SPECIFICATIONS

Brewery: Brouwerij Palm
Location: Londerzeel, Flemish Brabant
Style: Belgian wheat beer
Colour: Cloudy golden yellow
Alcohol: 4.5%
Serving temperature: 8°C (46.4°F)
Food: Pasta in a light herby sauce

Rodenbach Grand Cru

In 1714, an Austrian nobleman named Ferdinand Rodenbach took up residence in the Austrian-ruled territories that later became part of modern-day Belgium.

The original Rodenbach brewery was founded in 1821 by one of his descendants, Ferdinand Gregoor Rodenbach, but moved to its present site in 1836 when under the direction of Maria Wauters, wife of Pedro Rodenbach. The family's association with brewing ceased in 1998 when the latest generation of Rodenbachs sold the brewery to Palm.

The traditional Rodenbach recipe, which produces a red-brown ale with a mild, lightly hopped flavour, is still brewed and fermented at the site in Roeselare, and a large proportion of it is then matured in the brewery's 300 giant oak casks for up to two years. The end product is then transported to the Palm brewery in Londerzeel for bottling. When the aged beer is bottled neat it is labelled Rodenbach Grand Cru and is widely regarded by connoisseurs as one of the world's finest beers. The extensive maturation period gives Rodenbach Grand Cru a characteristic sourness due to the natural processes of oxidation and lactic fermentation, while the oak imparts a vanilla-like flavour to complement the fruity malt character.

Rodenbach also produces a 'basic' version by blending 25% aged beer with 75% young beer that has been matured in metal tanks for no more than five weeks. Although less challenging than the Grand Cru, this is a beer with plenty of character, a perfumed fruitiness and a tart, dry finish.

SPECIFICATIONS

Brewery: Brouwerij Rodenbach NV

Location: Roeselare, West Flanders

Style: Flemish red ale

Colour: Deep, dark red-brown

Alcohol: 6%

Serving temperature: 10°C (50°F)

Food: Mussels and French fries

Lucifer

The ambitious Riva brewery, founded in 1880, has in recent years made a habit of acquiring other smaller breweries, including Liefmans in nearby Oudenaarde.

From its own range, its Dentergem Witbier is one of the biggest selling examples of a cloudy spiced wheat beer, and has a smooth, dry flavour. Lucifer is a strong, golden ale that imitates its rival Duvel in more than just its diabolical name. The aroma is spicy and fruity with hints of cloves, citrus fruit and apple, while the smooth, medium-bodied palate is well balanced between zesty hops and sweet, toasty malts.

SPECIFICATIONS

Brewery: Brouwerij Riva SA
Location: Dentergem, West Flanders province
Style: Belgian strong blonde ale
Colour: Golden yellow-orange
Alcohol: 8%
Serving temperature: 10°C (50°F)
Food: Hot, spicy food such as Indian or Chinese curries

Sloeber

Although the present brewery is relatively modern, having been built in 1930 in the small village of Mater near Oudenaarde, the Roman family dates the start of its brewing operations back to 1545.

SPECIFICATIONS

Brewery: Brouwerij Roman NV
Location: Mater-Oudenaarde, East Flanders
Style: Belgian strong pale ale
Colour: Golden amber-red
Alcohol: 7.5%
Serving temperature: 10°–12°C (50°–53.6°F)
Food: Spicy Mexican dishes

Sloeber was added to the range in 1983 when the brewery recommenced production of top-fermented ales, having brewed exclusively Pilsner-style lagers since the end of World War II. Sloeber is a mild-flavoured amber ale with a predominantly malty flavour balanced by a light hoppiness. The name of the beer is Flemish for 'Joker', another name for the devil, revealing the inspiration for this beer as being Moortgat's famous Duvel. Since 1998, Roman has also produced several beers under the John Smith's label following a licensing agreement with the Yorkshire brewery.

La Divine

The family-owned Silly brewery takes its current name from its location in the town of Silly, north of Mons. Founded in 1850 as Mynsbrugen, it adopted its current identity when it merged with the Tennstedt-Decroes brewery of nearby Enghien, and is now run by the fifth generation of the family.

Although the name may sound a little odd to English ears, its large and diverse range of beers deserves to be taken seriously, not least this powerful amber-coloured ale, which is brewed with hops from Kent, Hallertau and Saaz for a fresh citric aroma and a well-balanced palate starting with sweet raisin malt flavours before a dry, spicy hop-dominated finish.

SPECIFICATIONS

Brewery: Brasserie de Silly SA
Location: Silly, Hainaut
Style: Belgian strong pale ale
Colour: Amber
Alcohol: 9.5%
Serving temperature: 7°–10°C (44.6°–50°F)
Food: Grilled fish and shellfish

Scotch Silly

Scotch Silly is a well-rounded strong ale in the style of a Scottish 'wee heavy', with a sweet, malt-dominated flavour and a warming alcoholic strength.

It lines up in the brewery's extensive and varied range alongside Titje Blanche, a spiced wheat beer made with oatmeal, and a beer that is called Saison but is actually an oud bruin (old brown) ale of the type traditionally brewed in northern Flemish-speaking parts of Belgium. Silly also brews two double Enghien beers which it inherited from the Tennstedt-Decroes. The Brune has a creamy texture and a nutty malt flavour profile, while the Blonde has a drier, fruitier character.

SPECIFICATIONS

Brewery: Brasserie de Silly SA
Location: Silly, Hainaut
Style: Scotch ale
Colour: Chestnut brown
Alcohol: 8%
Serving temperature: 12°C (53.6°F)
Food: Roast pork with apple sauce

Sint Bernardus Prior 8

Founded in 1946, the original line-up of beers from this brewery were labelled Sint Sixtus and were licensed reproductions of the authentic Trappist beers from the Sint Sixtus abbey in Westvleteren.

After the licence expired, the abbey took control of its own brewing operations, while the Sint Sixtus brewery continued to make beers that were essentially the same, albeit with slightly modified (and some would say improved) recipes.

Although the brewery's name changed to Sint Bernardus, it maintained the practice of naming its beers in order of strength according to the monastic hierarchy, with Pater 6 at the bottom, Abbot 12 at the top and Prior 8 in between. (The numbers relate to the Belgian system of degrees used for measuring the specific gravity of the beer, a rough indication of its alcoholic strength.) Prior 8 is a classic abbey-style dubbel with a smooth body and a mellow, sweet and fruity flavour balanced with a hint of hop bitterness. Pater 6 is also a dubbel, but with more of a roasted malt character, while Abbot 12 is a dark chestnut-coloured, strong (10.5% alcohol) tripel with sweet raisin fruit aromas, a rich, full body and nutty, caramel and chocolate notes on the palate. Sint Bernardus has also been commissioned by Pierre Celis of Hoegaarden and Celis White fame to brew Grottenbier, a light brown spiced ale which is moved after fermentation to caves in Kanne, near the Dutch border, for ageing.

SPECIFICATIONS

Brewery: Brouwerij Sint-Bernardus
Location: Watou, West Flanders
Style: Belgian abbey dubbel
Colour: Dark chocolate brown
Alcohol: 8%
Serving temperature: 10°–14°C (50°–57.2°F)
Food: Grilled steaks or lamb chops

Timmermans Kriek

Although the term Kriek has come to mean any beer which is flavoured with cherries, the version from Timmermans is an authentic lambic beer, produced by the action of naturally occurring yeasts, in which whole cherries have been steeped during maturation.

It is a relatively easy-drinking example of the style, with a pleasantly sweet cherry flavour balanced with a dry sherry-like acidity that is characteristic of true lambic beers. Various other flavoured lambics are also available, including a dry, full-flavoured Framboise (raspberry), as well as a Cassis (blackcurrant) and a Pêche (peach). The brewery also produces an innovative 'white' lambic, which is a blend of lambic and wheat beers, and another beer called Bourgogne des Flandres, in the style of a traditional Belgian red ale. More conventional are its Gueuze Caveau, a blend of old and young lambic beers, and Doux Lambic, an example of the Faro style made by sweetening lambic beer with brown sugar. The brewery dates from 1832, although there is evidence that brewing has taken place on the site since much earlier. It was taken over in 1993 by the drinks distribution group John Martin, but is still run by the same family.

SPECIFICATIONS

Brewery: Brouwerij Timmermans-John Martin NV
Location: Itterbeek, Flemish Brabant
Style: Kriek (cherry) lambic
Colour: Bright cherry red
Alcohol: 5%
Serving temperature: 8°–9°C (46.4°–48.2°F)
Food: Light fruity desserts such as soufflés

Trappistes Rochefort 8

Of the six Trappist monasteries that brew commercially, the Abbaye de Notre Dame de Saint-Remy on the outskirts of Rochefort is the most traditional and secretive, and little is known to the outside world of the monks who produce the beer. What is well documented is that a convent was founded on the site in 1230, and converted to a monastery in 1464, with brewing taking place here since the late sixteenth century. The present brewhouse dates mostly from the 1960s when the business went through an expansion. As well as being mysterious, its beers are also among the most individual, being rich, dark and malty, and flavoured with a highly secret blend of spices.

Candy sugar is added to the beer before bottling to promote secondary fermentation, and each batch of beer is given up to 10 weeks of maturation. Three beers are brewed, all to the same recipe, the only difference being the strength. In practice, the percentage of alcohol by volume of each beer is slightly higher than its number: Six has 7.5% abv, Eight has 9.2% abv, while Ten has a massive 11.3% abv. Eight is the mainstay of brewing operations, a fairly sweet, fruity beer with raisins and sultanas dominating. All three beers are excellent keepers, reaching full fermentation at six months and still improving from 12 months onwards.

SPECIFICATIONS

Brewery: Brasserie de Rochefort
Location: Abbaye de Notre Dame de Saint-Rémy, Rochefort, Namur
Style: Belgian abbey tripel (Trappist)
Colour: Copper-brown
Alcohol: 9.2%
Serving temperature: 10°–14°C (50°–57.2°F)
Food: A good all-round beer, goes well with sausages

Grimbergen Blonde

Produced by Alken-Maes, this is a strong blond beer, with a yeasty softness to the palate reminiscent of Trappist beers and a tenacious, frothy head.

It has a slightly hoppy aroma, which is less pronounced in the taste. Quite sweet, but not overpoweringly so, with a strong hint of vanilla in the aftertaste, it is very drinkable, but not in quantity due to the strength. This is a complex and enjoyable Belgian ale, and well worth rooting out. According to tradition, Grimbergen Blonde is based on an ancient recipe brewed at Grimbergen Abbey in 1128. The Alken-Maes Brewery, meanwhile, dates back to 1880 and was established from two local breweries.

SPECIFICATIONS

Brewery: NV Brouwerijen Alken-Maes Brasseries SA

Location: Jumet, Hainaut

Style: Strong ale

Colour: Light blonde

Alcohol: 6.7%

Serving temperature: 7.2°C(45°F)

Food: Roast lamb, beef stews

Grimbergen Double

Grimbergen Double is a dark brown ale with a fruity malt aroma and a full-bodied malt flavour with sweet toffee, ripe dark fruit and roasted coffee notes.

The abbey at the small town of Grimbergen, in the Flemish Brabant region north of Brussels, was founded in 1128 by Saint Norbert as a refuge for pilgrims. Destroyed twice by fire, it was rebuilt for the second time in 1629, at which time it adopted the phoenix symbol, which appears in a stained-glass window in the abbey's magnificent baroque church and now graces the labels of its beers.

The abbey was dismantled after the French Revolution, but was restored in 1845. The newly established monastic community licensed the Janssens and Peeters brewery to produce a range of beers under the Grimbergen name and sell them commercially. Since then responsibility for production of Grimbergen beers has changed hands several times and currently resides with Alken-Maes, now part of the British brewing group Scottish & Newcastle.

There are currently five beers in the Grimbergen range. As well as the Blonde, Double, Triple and Optimo Bruno, there is Cuvee L'Ermitage, a 7.5% winter brew with chocolate overtones, a soft hoppy aroma and a rich malt finish.

SPECIFICATIONS

Brewery: NV Brouwerij Alken-Maes Brasseries SA

Location: Jumet, Hainaut

Style: Belgian abbey dubbel

Colour: Dark burgundy red

Alcohol: 6.5%

Serving temperature: 10°–12°C (50°–53.6°F)

Food: Rich sauce-based meat dishes such as a spicy stew

Grimbergen Triple

Brewed under licence by Alken-Maes for the Grimbergen abbey, this is a strong triple beer, with a crisp, very full bitter-sweet flavour and a long, lingering aftertaste.

This deep golden Triple has a dry, spicy hoppy aroma and a soft, well-balanced rich malt palate. It is quite sweet, but not overpoweringly so, with a strong hint of vanilla in the aftertaste. Very drinkable, but not in quantity, due to the strength. Grimbergen Triple is a complex and enjoyable Belgian ale, and one well worth investigating. More unusual is Grimbergen's Optimo Bruno, which is said to be based on an original recipe discovered at the abbey brewery. This dark amber ale is full of complex flavours with a rich vine-fruit softness balanced by peppery hops and a warming 10% alcohol.

SPECIFICATIONS

Brewery: NV Brouwerijen Alken-Maes Brasseries SA
Location: Jumet, Hainaut
Style: Strong ale
Colour: Golden
Alcohol: 9.0%
Serving temperature: 6.0°C (43°F)
Food: Oysters, most shellfish

St-Feuillien Tripel

The Friart brewery was founded in 1873 at Le Roeulx, between Charleroi and Mons, moving to more modern premises in 1920.

It closed in 1977, but reopened six years later, dispensing with most of its old lager brands and concentrating on the St-Feuillien range of abbey ales, although many of the bottles labelled St-Feuillien are actually produced under licence by Brasserie Du Bocq in Namur, the beers of which have a slightly different character. The St-Feuillien Tripel from Le Roeulx is a richly complex brew, with a fruity bouquet combined with elements of spices and hops, and a palate dominated by fruity malt flavours with a long, lingering finish.

SPECIFICATIONS

Brewery: Brasserie St-Feuillien
Location: Le Roeulx, Hainaut
Style: Belgian abbey tripel
Colour: Pale golden amber
Alcohol: 8.5%
Serving temperature: 10°–14°C (50°–57.2°F)
Food: Grilled lobster or crayfish

Judas

Judas is part of the vast range of beers from the Union brewery, which was founded in 1864 and is now part of the Alken-Maes group, which is owned by Scottish & Newcastle. Other beers in the range include the famous Grimbergen and Ciney Abbey ales, as well as several other brands.

After fermentation, Judas is matured in the brewery's cellars for a lengthy period until it develops a smooth, well-rounded body. It is then bottled with live yeast for a secondary fermentation and continues to improve. Lightly aromatised with Bohemian Saaz hops, it has a fragrant spicy sweet character with juicy, fruity malt dominating on the palate.

SPECIFICATIONS

Brewery: Brasserie de l'Union
Location: Jumet, Hainaut
Style: Belgian strong blonde ale
Colour: Pale golden yellow
Alcohol: 8.5%
Serving temperature: 10-12°C (50-53.6°F)
Food: Grilled gammon steaks

Pater Lieven Bruin

Van Den Bossche started in 1897 as a farmhouse brewery and stands next to the church on the market square of the rural community of Sint-Lievens-Esse on the outskirts of Oudenaarde. Despite the holy-sounding name of the village and the hint of a monastic connection in the name of its beer, the brewery has no abbey links.

In fact, the brewery's origins are purely commercial, the founder Arthur Van Den Bossche having married into the chocolate- and beer-producing Callebaut family, and although it has been going for more than 100 years it is currently run by only the third generation of the family. The Pater Lieven Abbey-style beers were launched in 1957 and are currently available as a Blond, a Bruin, both at 6.5% alcohol, and a stronger Tripel, as well as a seasonal special 'Kerstpater' Christmas ale that weighs in at a hefty 9% alcohol and has a rich, spicy, winter-warming flavour. The Bruin is a comparatively uncomplicated but nonetheless excellent strong brown ale made with a blend of pale Pilsner, caramel, chocolate and torrefied malts that give it a dark but fairly mild roasted coffee flavour and a lingering aftertaste. The Blonde has a much lighter flavour and aroma, with a dry hop character. The brewery also produces a dry stout-like black beer that is named Buffalo after wild west legend Buffalo Bill, whose travelling circus visited the village in 1907. Legend has it that one of the circus members was left to attend to the beer's mashing and allowed the malt to burn, which resulted in the beer having a not unpleasant slightly burnt flavour.

SPECIFICATIONS

Brewery: Brouwerij Van Den Bossche

Location: Sint-Lievens-Esse, East Flanders

Style: Belgian strong brown ale

Colour: Dark, clear chocolate brown

Alcohol: 6.5%

Serving temperature: 10°–12°C (50°–53.6°F)

Food: Roasted rack of lamb

Het Kapittel Prior

The Van Eecke family has brewed exclusively top-fermented ales since it took over the Golden Lion brewery in Watou in 1862.

This strong pale ale is flavoured with three varieties of hops for a bitter, refreshing taste. More famous are the brewery's range of Het Kapittel beers, which were introduced following the end of World War II. The name hints at monastic connections and means simply 'The Chapter', indicating the hierarchy of priests within an abbey, although the brewery is not linked with any monastic community. The beers are named after priestly ranks – Pater, Prior and Abbot – in ascending order of alcoholic strength. There is also a fourth beer, Dubbel, which is a dark, aromatic blend of Pater and Prior with additional spice flavourings. Prior is a strong dark beer with a bittersweet flavour in the traditional style of a tripel that predates the prevailing fashion for pale tripels. A malty character leads the way with hints of green apples, raisins and caramel in the aroma and a nutty, toffee-ish flavour on the palate before a spicy finish with clove, cinnamon and nutmeg notes. Abbot is only slightly stronger at 10% alcohol and is a paler brew with a potent yeasty aroma redolent of banana bread, orange fruit and spices. At the bottom of the range, with 6.5% alcohol, Pater is a dark ale with plums, cherries and raisins present in the aroma and a caramel malt character.

SPECIFICATIONS

Brewery: Brouwerij Van Eecke NV
Location: Watou, West Flanders
Style: Belgian Abbey dark tripel
Colour: Dark ruby red
Alcohol: 9%
Serving temperature: 10°–14°C (50°–57.2°F)
Food: Strong ripe cheeses

Blanche de Watou

Watou, which is close to Poperinge in West Flanders, is known historically as the brewers' town. In 1629 it became an earldom of the illustrious Yedegem family, who owned a castle and a brewery in the town.

Both were destroyed in the French Revolution and subsequently only the brewery was rebuilt. In 1862, the brewery was taken over by the Van Eecke family and was renamed the Gouden Leeuw (Golden Lion) brewery. Its Blanche de Watou, also known as Watou's Witbier, is a naturally cloudy unfiltered wheat beer with a refreshing citrus flavour. It was added to the brewery's range in 1998.

SPECIFICATIONS

Brewery: Brouwerij Van Eecke NV
Location: Watou, West Flanders
Style: Belgian wheat beer
Colour: Golden straw yellow
Alcohol: 5%
Serving temperature: 8°–10°C (46.4°–50°F)
Food: Apple tart, pie or crumble

Kasteelbier

Kasteelbier **is Flemish for 'Castle Beer', and this powerful barley wine is also known by its French name 'Bière du Château'.**

The flavour is as rich as a malt loaf laden with dried fruit, although it finishes with an intense dryness. It takes its name from a castle built in 1075 by Robrecht de Fries, Duke of Flanders, which was later destroyed and replaced with a new moated mansion in 1736. The brewery was founded in 1900, using the cellars of the castle for storing Kasteelbier during its 12-week conditioning period. The original Kasteelbier is a brown beer, but it is also available as a blond version which has hints of vanilla.

SPECIFICATIONS

Brewery: Brouwerij Van Honsebrouck
Location: Ingelmunster, West Flanders
Style: Barley wine
Colour: Deep, dark chocolate brown
Alcohol: 11%
Serving temperature: 12°C (53.6°F)
Food: Rich chocolate cake

Gentse Tripel

Van Steenberge started life in 1784, but did not become a properly commercial organisation until Paul Van Steenberge took charge in 1922.

He changed the name of the brewery to Bios and introduced modern brewing techniques to produce a beer by lactic fermentation similar to that produced by Rodenbach. Gentse Tripel, a strong, bottle-conditioned amber ale with a bittersweet honeyed flavour and a light, zesty aroma, is a more recent addition to the brewery's line-up, which now extends to more than 40 beers, most commissioned by other breweries.

SPECIFICATIONS

Brewery: Brouwerij Bios-Van Steenberge NV
Location: Ertvelde, East Flanders
Style: Belgian abbey tripel
Colour: Pale golden amber-yellow
Alcohol: 8%
Serving temperature: 10°–14°C (50°–57.2°F)
Food: Spicy Chinese food

Gulden Draak

Gulden Draak, meaning golden dragon, is named after the golden statue at the top of the clocktower in Ghent that was originally donated to the city of Constantinople (now Istanbul) by the Norse king Sigrid Magnusson in 1111 during the first crusade.

It was brought back to Belgium by Boudewijn IX, Count of Flanders, who was a later emperor of Constantinople. It is a fittingly exotic name for this highly individual beer, which comes in opaque white glass bottles. Gulden Draak has a powerful herbal hop aroma, while the palate is led by dark roasted malts with a coffee and chocolate character. Being a live bottle-conditioned beer it continues to improve with age, reaching its peak after two years.

SPECIFICATIONS

Brewery: Brouwerij Bios-Van Steenberge NV
Location: Ertvelde, East Flanders
Style: Barley wine
Colour: Dark chocolate brown
Alcohol: 10.5%
Serving temperature: 12°–14°C (53.6°–57.2°F)
Food: Beef and oyster pie

Westmalle Trappist Tripel

Westmalle Abbey is the home of the beer styles known as dubbel and tripel, the tripel being particularly unusual.

The general rule in brewing is the stronger the beer, the darker its colour, but Westmalle rewrote the rules when it created its strong, golden ale using pale Pilsner malts supplemented with other grains and candy sugar, which create a higher alcohol content without imparting colour. Westmalle Trappist Tripel has a smooth, well-balanced yet complex flavour with a floral hop aroma and tangy citrus notes on the palate complemented by spicy hop notes. The dark Dubbel (6% abv) has more of a chocolatey, fruity character with a dry, malty finish.

Known properly as the Abbey of Our Beloved Lady of the Sacred Heart, Westmalle Abbey was founded in 1794 by monks fleeing from the effects of the French Revolution, which saw several monasteries in the south of the country destroyed. In 1836, it became the first Trappist monastery since the French Revolution to recommence brewing. It began selling its beers outside the abbey in the 1860s, and business really took off in 1921 when a separate company was formed to handle brewing operations.

SPECIFICATIONS

Brewery: Brouwerij Westmalle
Location: Abdij der Trappisten van Westmalle, Malle, Antwerp
Style: Belgian abbey tripel (Trappist)
Colour: Golden orange
Alcohol: 9%
Serving temperature: 10°–14°C (50°–57.2°F)
Food: Serve as an appetising aperitif

Westmalle Trappist Dubbel

Brewed at the Trappist abbey of Westmalle, north of Antwerp, Westmalle Trappist Dubbel pours to a somewhat hazy, rich, dark, peaty colour with traces of amber and a large and foamy, pale tan head which lasts well and leaves masses of lace on the glass.

The beer has a good carbonation with lots of tiny bubbles rising to the top. Initial aromas are sweet malt and a yeasty, bready tone. There is a strong hop presence, but the overwhelming malt wins through with a fruity, ripe banana quality from the yeast backing it up. Westmalle is the largest of Belgium's six Trappist breweries and competes with Chimay for the title of most commercially oriented (although all profits go to good causes). In recent years, the brewery has undergone significant expansion and now exports its beers to 14 countries worldwide, including the United States and Japan.

SPECIFICATIONS

Brewery: Brouwerij der Trappisten van Westmalle
Location: Westmalle
Style: Trappist beer
Colour: Rich amber
Alcohol: 6.5%
Serving temperature: 6.0°C (43°F)
Food: Rabbit, hare, small game with fruit accompaniment (eg prunes)

ABOVE

Like Belgium, the Netherlands plays host to a rich tradition of beer brewing which also connects with the age-old Trappist techniques of production. The Bavaria Pilsner pictured here is one of the more popular high-street bar and bottled varieties; however, the Netherlands also has a large number of microbreweries which produce more complex, darker ales.

Dutch Beers

With Germany to the east and Belgium to the south, one might think that the brewing industry of the Netherlands would have benefited from the positive influence of its neighbours. Unfortunately, this has not always been so, and there is a case for arguing that, while Belgian brewers concentrate on quality, their Dutch counterparts prefer to direct their efforts towards quantity.

Above

The De Hooiberg ('The Haystack') brewery in Amsterdam (now a museum), where it all began for Heineken in 1863, when Gerard Adriaan Heineken bought the brewery and started the business which is now a giant in the world of brewing.

THE PRIME EXEMPLAR of this is Heineken, formerly a small family brewer, but now a giant multinational corporation and the second-largest brewing company in the world, with a presence in one form or another in just about every beer-producing country in the world. The success of the company is largely down to one man: Alfred 'Freddie' Heineken, the grandson of the brewery's founder, who brought in a visionary approach to marketing and a strong business sense when he took charge of the company in the 1950s.

There are other breweries in the Netherlands apart from Heineken, but surprisingly few for a country with such a strong tradition for beer drinking. The situation currently is not as bad as it was in the 1970s when there were just two major players – Heineken and Skol – plus a handful of small regional brewers, all producing fairly unexciting blond lagers. More recently, Dutch beer consumers have developed a taste for more interesting beers. The popularity of imports from Belgium has inspired domestic brewers to buck up their ideas and start producing a wider variety of ales, lagers and even wheat beers, including several traditional seasonal specialities that had all but died out.

Although Heineken continues to dominate both at home and abroad, there is reason to be optimistic about the future health of brewing in the Netherlands. New brands which are widening the public's palate are the La Trappe series of strong ales and Christofell's ruby red Robertus lager.

STATISTICS

Total production: 25,124,000 hectolitres (663,706,000 gallons) per year

Consumption per capita: 81 litres (21 gallons) per year

Famous breweries: Bavaria Brouwerij NV; Bierbrouwerij de Koningshoeven; Bierbrouwerij Sint Christoffel; Grolsch Bierbrouwerij NV; Heineken Brouwerij BV; Lindeboom Bierbrouwerij NV; Oranjeboom Bierbrouwerij

Famous brands: Bavaria Premium Pilsner; Christoffel Robertus; Grolsch Premium Pilsner; Gulpener Dort; Heinenken Pilsner; Lindeboom Pilsner; Oranjeboom

Bavaria Premium Pilsner

Despite the name, the Netherlands' largest independent brewery has no Bavarian connections, although it claims to brew its Pilsner according to Germany's strict purity laws.

It has a fresh, honeyed lemon aroma and a crisp, refreshing, slightly sweet grassy flavour balanced with a sharp hop bitterness leading to a dry finish. It is brewed with water from the brewery's own well and malted barley from its own maltings, and is the flagship beer of a brewery that can trace its origins back to 1719, when it was established by one Laurentius Moorees. The Swinkel family who have owned the brewery since the late nineteenth century are direct descendants of Laurentius. In recent years, Bavaria has expanded by buying up many smaller breweries and closing them down, such as the famous Kroon brewery in Oirschot.

SPECIFICATIONS

Brewery: Bavaria Brouwerij NV
Location: Lieshout, North Brabant
Style: Pilsner
Colour: Golden yellow
Alcohol: 5%
Serving temperature: 6°–8°C (42.8°–46.4°F)
Food: Roast duck

Bavaria 8.6

Taking its name from its alcohol content, Bavaria's 8.6 is the strongest beer in its range and also its most flavoursome.

Although it is a top-fermented lager, it shares many characteristics with a barley wine ale. It has a grainy, biscuity aroma with hints of vanilla and honey, and a sweet malty flavour balanced in the finish by a light hop bitterness, although it risks being overpowered by its high alcohol content. The Bavaria brewery mostly concentrates on bottom-fermented lagers, but it also produces a full-flavoured top-fermented bock beer called Hooghe Bock, with a mild bittersweet flavour. The range also includes Oud Bruin, an old-fashioned brown beer with a caramel malt flavour that is similar to the beers from the brewery's early days.

SPECIFICATIONS

Brewery: Bavaria Brouwerij NV
Location: Lieshout, North Brabant
Style: Strong lager
Colour: Golden amber-yellow
Alcohol: 8.6%
Serving temperature: 10°–12°C (50°–53.6°F)
Food: Shortcrust pies

Gulpener Dort

The town of Gulpen is in the far southeastern tip of the Netherlands, close to the city of Maastricht, sandwiched between Belgium and Germany.

Gulpen is home to the independent family-run brewery of Gulpener Bierbrouwerij. In the hands of the Rutten family since it was founded in 1825, it is currently being run by the fifth generation of Ruttens, although a large stake in the company was purchased by Grolsch in 1995. This influence has ensured that Gulpener beers now enjoy fairly widespread distribution, both domestically and in the export market. Despite the involvement of such a major commercial interest, Gulpener continues to maintain its long-standing reputation for experimentation with a wide and varied range of beer styles, bucking the national trend for not looking beyond straightforward pale Pilsner-style lagers.

Gulpener Dort, for example, is brewed in the style of the strong export lagers of Dortmund, with a fuller body than a Pilsner and a sweeter flavour. It has an aroma of dark fruit with plum and raisin notes and a similarly fruity flavour balanced by a fragrant hop bitterness. The full Gulpener beer range extends across to Oud Bruin, a traditional brown ale, and an unpasteurised, unfiltered Pilsner called Château Neubourg with a prominent hop profile. Among its more unusual offerings are a highly individual Belgian-style sour red beer called Mestreechs Aajt, made with lambic yeast, and a blond barley wine called Gladiator.

SPECIFICATIONS

Brewery: Gulpener Bierbrouwerij
Location: Gulpen, Limburg
Style: Dortmunder / export lager
Colour: Clear orange-brown
Alcohol: 6.5%
Serving temperature: 8°–10°C (46.4°–50°F)
Food: Char-grilled chicken or lamb steaks

Heineken

Heineken Pilsner is the famous flagship brand of the Dutch brewing giant. While it does have a light, uncomplicated flavour, unlike many mainstream lager brands it is brewed with all malt and no adjuncts. Other Heineken brands are the more characterful Tarwebok, a dark, sweet bottom-fermented wheat bock, and Oud Bruin, a fruity, dark lager.

Heineken is not only the largest brewer in the Netherlands, having dominated the Dutch beer market since 1968, but is also now the second-largest brewer in the world, behind American giant Anheuser-Busch, with more than 100 brewing plants producing its beers worldwide. The company was founded in 1864 by Gerard Adriaan Heineken when he bought De Hooiberg ('The Haystack') brewery in Amsterdam. By 1942 Heineken was a public company and the family had lost its controlling stake.

Alfred Henry Heineken, Gerard's grandson, was determined to buy back the family name and started by working in the brewery itself, carrying sacks of barley. He worked his way up to a position in the head office and gradually bought up enough shares to regain a controlling interest in 1954. His story is key to the present-day success of Heineken, much of which is due to the process of buying up smaller breweries, including famous old brands such as Amstel, Affligem and Brand. The original brewery in Amsterdam is now a museum and the majority of Heineken brewing in the Netherlands takes place at two massive plants in Hertogenbosch and Zoeterwoude.

SPECIFICATIONS

Brewery: Heineken Brouwerij BV
Location: Hertogenbosch, Brabant
Style: Pilsner
Colour: Pale golden yellow
Alcohol: 5%
Serving temperature: 6°–8°C (42.8°–46.4°F)
Food: Minted lamb burgers

Grolsch Premium Pilsner

The flagship beer from the Grolsch brewery of Enschede, the largest independent brewer in the Netherlands, is a full-flavoured golden Pilsner with a more bitter taste than most mainstream lagers.

The brewery claims its origins lie in the beer created by Peter Cuyper in 1615 to win the hand of the daughter of a local brewer and maintains its traditional image today with its distinctive embossed bottles with their flip-top lids. As well as its Pilsner, Grolsch also brews various other beers for the domestic market, such as Het Canon, a rich amber-coloured malty barley wine.

SPECIFICATIONS

Brewery: Grolsch Bierbrouwerij NV
Location: Enschede, Overijssel
Style: Pilsner
Colour: Deep golden yellow
Alcohol: 5%
Serving temperature: 6°–8°C (42.8°–46.4°F)
Food: Serve as a pre-dinner aperitif

La Trappe Dubbel

La Trappe Dubbel is the original beer that was brewed at the abbey when it first started in 1881.

After World War II, the abbey sold the brewery to Stella Artois, which then started to produce a 'Trappist Pils'. This venture, however, was not a success, and the monks later bought back the brewery and undertook a relaunch of their flagship ale. Whether or not it is an authentic Trappist ale, it maintains the true characteristics of a classic dubbel, with a powerful orangey fruit aroma balanced by spicy, floral hops. On the palate, complex, rich, wine-like malt flavours lead the way, finishing with a big, refreshing dose of spicy hops.

SPECIFICATIONS

Brewery: Bierbrouwerij de Koningshoeven
Location: Berkel-Enschot, North Brabant
Style: Abbey dubbel
Colour: Dark ruby red
Alcohol: 6.5%
Serving temperature: 10°–12°C (50°–53.6°F)
Food: Pork in orange sauce

La Trappe Blond

When the Trappist monks were expelled from France during the Revolution, most of them moved north to the Lowlands, settling in Belgium.

One group moved further north, building a new abbey near Tilburg. The brewery, originally called Schaapskooi (meaning 'sheep fold'), was formed in 1881, but today its status as an authentic Trappist brewery is in dispute – it is currently owned and operated by Bavaria, which label the beers Trappist despite limited involvement from the monks. In any case, its beers are highly regarded. La Trappe Blond is a top-fermented golden ale with an aromatic bitter hop aroma, which also conveys citrussy overtones, and a refreshing bitter flavour balanced by fruity malts. Distribution of La Trappe is becoming increasingly international, with export destinations (bottles and cans) including the United Kingdom, Ireland and the United States. Like many Trappist beers, La Trappe Blonde is best drunk from a large Trappist tankard or open tumbler.

SPECIFICATIONS

Brewery: Bierbrouwerij de Koningshoeven
Location: Berkel-Enschot, North Brabant
Style: Abbey blond ale
Colour: Cloudy pale straw yellow
Alcohol: 6.5%
Serving temperature: 8°–10°C (46.4°–50°F)
Food: Meatballs

La Trappe Quadrupel

La Trappe Quadrupel comes from the Bierbrouwerij de Koningshoeven brewery, and is one of the strongest of the La Trappe beers. It is an extremely powerful beer, weighing in at 10% abv. 'Quadrupel' is a label given to very strong abbey or Trappist ale, the other type of strong abbey ale being the Abt. The difference between the Abt and the Quadrupel is that the former has a darker colour and deeper, more complex aromas and palate, while the latter has a lighter colour and texture, with more flavours of peach emerging.

Despite the difference in taste and appearance, both Abt and Quadrupel share the same power, 10% abv being the typical alcohol content, and the beers are generally bottle-conditioned.

La Trappe Quadrupel is a seasonal beer, becoming available in the autumn and winter. The strong aroma of the beer has been variously described as 'leathery' and 'earthy', and it also imparts a dark sweetness to the nose. On taste, it it both malty and spicy, with a pleasant bitterness as an aftertaste. Quadrupel is one of a series of La Trappe beers produced by Koningshoeven, although none of the others approaches the strength of the Quadrupel. They include La Trappe Blonde (6.5%), La Trappe Bockbier (7%), La Trappe Dubbel (6.5%) and the La Trappe Tripel (8%).

SPECIFICATIONS

Brewery: Bierbrouwerij de Koningshoeven
Location: Berkel-Enschot, North Brabant
Style: Abbey quadrupel
Colour: Rich amber
Alcohol: 10%
Serving temperature: 10°–12°C (50°–53.6°F)
Food: Spicy sausages

Lindeboom Pilsner

The name of the small, independent, family-owned Lindeboom brewery means linden tree. It was formed by Willem Geenen in 1870. His first product was a spicy top-fermented ale that he called Geenen's.

However, it was around this time that Pilsner-style lagers were becoming popular, and in 1912 Geenen's sons, Bernard and Christien, who were now in charge of the company, christened the opening of their new brewing plant with the launch of Lindeboom Pilsner. Made with a blend of two types of pale malt and aromatised with a generous helping of whole German hops, it is a well-flavoured beer with a higher level of bitterness than most mainstream Pilsners.

The brewery's full range extends to Oud Bruin, a sweet flavoured malty brown ale, and Venloosch Alt, an authentic red-brown ale in the style of the top-fermented, cold-conditioned altbiers of Düsseldorf. Three beers called Gouverneur are also brewed – Gouverneur Bier, Blonde and Brune – which are top-fermented ales made with barley malt and rye. Each is given a lengthy period of cold storage before being bottled unfiltered to allow them to develop further character. In spite of continued interest from larger breweries, Lindeboom has managed to remain independent and is currently managed by another Willem Geenen, the grandson of the founder.

SPECIFICATIONS

Brewery: Lindeboom Bierbrouwerij NV
Location: Neer, Limburg
Style: Pilsner
Colour: Pale golden yellow
Alcohol: 5%
Serving temperature: 6°–8°C (42.8°–46.4°F)
Food: Bacon quiche

Oranjeboom Premium Pilsner

Oranjeboom was founded in 1528, originally known as the Three Horses brewery due to its location next to a blacksmith's forge, which had a sign outside depicting three horses' heads. The brewery still produces a light lager called Three Horses, with a label depicting the blacksmith's traditional sign. The current name, Oranjeboom, meaning 'orange tree', represents a close association with the Dutch royal family, whose symbol is an orange tree. It is currently owned by Belgium's global brewing giant, Interbrew, and is the largest of their three Dutch concerns, the others being Hertog Jan and Dommelsch.

Its main regular product is Oranjeboom Premium Pilsener, a refreshing, thirst-quenching golden Pilsner with an unchallenging flavour. The aroma is grassy with a hint of hops, while the palate is characterised by a dry grainy maltiness with a gently bitter hop presence in the finish. The Oranjeboom label also belongs to an Oud Bruin, bottom-fermented old brown beer with a full-bodied, sweet malty flavour, and Premium Malt, a refreshing alcohol-free beer.

Seasonal beers in the brewery's range include Herfstbock, a strong bottom-fermented spring beer with a malty, lightly hopped flavour. Although Oranjeboom has never achieved the worldwide fame of some other Dutch beer brands, the marketing power of Interbrew has seen its international profile raised considerably.

SPECIFICATIONS

Brewery: Oranjeboom Bierbrouwerij
Location: Breda, Brabant
Style: Pilsner
Colour: Pale golden yellow
Alcohol: 5%
Serving temperature: 6°C (42.8°F)
Food: Chicken roasted in olive oil

Christoffel Blond

The first beer to come from the Sint Christoffel brewery was simply called Christoffel Bier, but was renamed to Christoffel Blond when the brewery introduced Robertus to the range.

Blond is a full-bodied, pale-golden Pilsner-style lager with a well-balanced flavour characterised by a robust, fragrant hop bitterness that comes from the use of whole fresh hops in the brewing process. It is unfiltered and unpasteurised, allowing it to develop further as it matures in the bottle. Sint Christoffel was founded in the former coalmining town of Roermond in 1986 by Leo Brand, a member of the famous Brand brewing family, and is named after the town's patron saint.

Starting as a tiny operation working out of the back of a house, it quickly grew and moved to larger premises with new brewing, fermenting and lagering facilities in 1995. It is now one of the most successful of a new wave of Dutch breweries established since the start of the 1980s that adhere to traditional values for quality beer production in response to the mass-production methods of the major brewing corporations. All beers from Sint Christoffel are brewed according to German Reinheitsgebot purity laws.

In 2001, Brand sold the brewery to a leisure company called Hillebrand Beheer, which manages distribution and promotion, although brewing operations are still carried out independently.

SPECIFICATIONS

Brewery: Bierbrouwerij Sint Christoffel
Location: Roermond, Limburg
Style: Pilsner
Colour: Pale golden yellow
Alcohol: 6%
Serving temperature: 8°C (46.4°F)
Food: Lasagne

La Trappe Tripel

The strongest of the regular ales in the La Trappe range, the Tripel has a fiercely bitter hop character, with spicy Goldings hops dominating the aroma, while on the palate the flavour is balanced between hop spiciness and rich fruity malts with notes of oranges and honey.

The high alcohol content leads to an increasingly dry finish. The brewery also produces a seasonal winter beer called Quadrupel, a strong (10% abv), full-bodied barley wine with a chestnut brown colour and a rich bittersweet flavour. Completing the range is Witte Trappist, an unfiltered golden wheat beer.

SPECIFICATIONS

Brewery: Bierbrouwerij de Koningshoeven
Location: Berkel-Enschot, North Brabant
Style: Abbey tripel
Colour: Copper red-brown
Alcohol: 8%
Serving temperature: 10°–12°C (50°–53.6°F)
Food: Strong pâté and toast

Christoffel Robertus

Christoffel Robertus is a rich ruby-red beer brewed in the style of a traditional Munich dark lager.

It has a fuller, maltier character than Sint Christoffel's other beer, a Pilsner, with a rich, fruity, spicy aroma and a nutty, earthy and slightly sweet caramel flavour and only a light hop presence. Both Sint Christoffel beers are available in small bottles with old-fashioned flip-top lids held under wire tension, or alternatively in attractive two-litre flagons with handles. All brewing takes place at the single site in Roermond, but Sint Christoffel beers, which have won over a growing collection of dedicated fans, are now widely exported across Europe and North America.

SPECIFICATIONS

Brewery: Bierbrouwerij Sint Christoffel
Location: Roermond, Limburg
Style: Dark Munich lager
Colour: Dark ruby red
Alcohol: 6%
Serving temperature: 8°–10°C (46.4°–50°F)
Food: Mushroom pizza

Above

A typical street scene in Switzerland's largest city, Zurich. The most popular type of beer in eastern Switzerland is a pale, easy-drinking lager generally referred to by the German term of 'Helles', meaning in this context 'light in colour' and which other European countries might usually call a 'Pils', a term that is rarely used in Switzerland.

Swiss Beers

Swiss beer production still has a local feel, with individual areas being served by regional breweries and even by microbreweries. Generally speaking, light, lager-style beers predominate in Switzerland, although this appeal to popularity did not stop a slight decline (0.4%) in beer consumption across the nation between 1998 and 2003.

Above

A typical Swiss bar is seen here. These usually serve a mix of popular branded lager beers, but they do sometimes sell brews from in-house microbreweries.

IN GENERAL, BEER BREWED IN SWITZERLAND bears a close resemblance to that produced in neighbouring Austria and Bavaria. There are two distinct beer-producing regions in the country: the cantons (counties) of the west, where the language is predominantly French, and the German-speaking cantons of eastern Switzerland. In the west, the industry is heavily influenced by imports from Belgium and other French-speaking parts of the world, including Quebec, but rather surprisingly there is also a distinct British influence, with various British styles being produced in microbreweries. Eastern Switzerland, on the other hand, in keeping with its strong German tradition, is very much lager country, and in fact many of the breweries observe Germany's strict Reinheitsgebot purity laws. Swiss law allows the use of maize and rice, as well as up to 10% sugar and 20% starch.

Brewing in Switzerland is diversified through the proliferation of microbreweries attached to public houses. These microbreweries are becoming increasingly professional in both product and marketing, using websites to make local and even international sales of their beers. By so doing, the microbreweries have become potential big players of the future, as well as keeping alive the best traditions of Swiss beer producing. In 2003 the three biggest beer producers in Switzerland were Feldschlosschen, Heineken and Eichoff. Not surprisingly, large international brewing companies have made inroads into Switzerland, and now more than two-thirds of the Swiss beer market is held by Carlsberg and Heineken.

STATISTICS

Total production: 3,645,000 hectolitres (96,291,000 gallons) per year

Consumption per capita: 57 litres (15 gallons) per year

Famous breweries: Brauerei Eichhof; Brauerei Feldschlösschen

Famous brands: Eichhof Hubertus; Feldschlösschen Hopfenperle; Original Draft Cardinal; Original Feldschlösschen

Original Draft Cardinal

One of the first commercial breweries in Switzerland, Cardinal was founded in Freiburg in 1788, when local landlord François Piller built a brewery next to his tavern.

In 1890, Freiburg's bishop was ordained as a cardinal, and the brewery produced a special beer to commemorate the event, later renaming the brewery in its honour. By 1996, the Feldschlösschen brewing group had taken over Cardinal and threatened to close the historic brewery until local pressure stopped this. Original Draft Cardinal is a well-balanced, lightly hopped lager with a soft, mellow flavour. The brewery also produces a fuller flavoured Spéciale and seasonal beers.

SPECIFICATIONS

Brewery: Brasserie du Cardinal
Location: Fribourg
Style: Lager
Colour: Pale yellow
Alcohol: 4.9%
Serving temperature: 6°–8°C (42.8°–46.4°F)
Food: Crisp, green salad

Eichhof Barbara

Eichhof's Barbara is named after the patron saint of the artillery. It is a deep-golden strong lager with a smooth texture and a well-rounded malt flavour with a hint of sweetness balanced by a touch of hop bitterness.

It comes from the largest independent brewery in Switzerland, which was founded in Lucerne in 1834 as the Brauerei zum Löwengarten (Lion Garden Brewery) by Johann Guggenbühler. It was taken over in 1878 by Traugott Spiess and soon became the largest brewery in the city; in 1922 it merged with the smaller Luzerner Brauhaus, which had been founded in 1889 on the Eichhof estate. The new business adopted the name Eichhof in 1937.

SPECIFICATIONS

Brewery: Brauerei Eichhof
Location: Lucerne
Style: Premium lager
Colour: Deep golden yellow
Alcohol: 5.9%
Serving temperature: 8°–10°C (46.4°–50°F)
Food: Grilled fish, such as salmon or trout

Eichhof Hubertus

Hubertus is a strong dark lager from Lucerne's Eichhof brewery, one of Switzerland's growing beer production companies. Its golden brown colour, which also has reddish tints, comes from the fact that it is made with roasted malts, which are also apparent in the full, rich roasted malt aroma.

For a popular lager the beer has a good deal of alcoholic power, coming in at 5.7% abv, whereas most bottled light beers tend to cluster around the 4.5–5% mark. Nevertheless, the alcohol content of Hubertus does not mask the beer's flavours and aromas. Eichhof produces a wide range of beers of varying styles and strengths. Braugold is a bright golden lager with a herbal hop aroma and flavour, balanced on the palate by a soft, smooth maltiness before an appetizingly bitter hop-dominated finish. Another popular beer is the Pilsner-style Pony, which has an even more pronounced hop character, with fresh, herbal notes in the aroma and a complex flavour characterised by a refreshing bitterness. Other popular Eichhof brands include Braugold (pale lager), Spiess Edelhell (pale lager) and Barbara (premium lager).

Bizarrely, Eichhof is perhaps the world's only brewery to have a computer game created in its honour. The aim of this freeware game is to fight off invading 'corporate beers' from the Eichhof brewery, literally shooting down bottles of 'enemy' lagers and eventually targeting all manner of popular spirits and beverages. The game is available as a free download.

SPECIFICATIONS

Brewery: Brauerei Eichhof
Location: Lucerne
Style: Dark lager
Colour: Golden brown
Alcohol: 5.7%
Serving temperature: 8°–10°C (46.4°–50°F)
Food: Cold cooked meats

Eichhof Klosterbräu Edeltrüb

Eichhof is a brewery with a strong sense of tradition and still brews a well-balanced golden lager called Spiess Draft to the original recipe first introduced by Traugott Spiess in 1888.

Eichhof's Klosterbräu Edeltrüb is a more recent addition to the range, but has a more venerable pedigree. Its name approximately means 'noble cloudy abbey beer', indicating the fact that it is brewed according to a traditional recipe used by monks in the Middle Ages (although neither the brewery nor the beer have any formal connections to any monastic brewing). It is an unfiltered and unpasteurised dark golden lager with a natural cloudiness and a spicy yeast character in the aroma and flavour, balanced by a soft hop bitterness.

SPECIFICATIONS

Brewery: Brauerei Eichhof
Location: Lucerne
Style: Unfiltered lager
Colour: Dark golden yellow-brown
Alcohol: 4.8%
Serving temperature: 8°–10°C (46.4°–50°F)
Food: Grilled or roasted chicken

Feldschlösschen Hopfenperle

Hopfenperle was launched in 1920 and today is the second most popular beer in Switzerland after Original Feldschlösschen, from the same brewery.

It is an all-malt lager with a fuller flavour than Original Feldschlösschen and a higher hop content, giving it a refreshing bitter edge, while the fine carbonation gives it a soft feel in the mouth. Feldschlösschen brews a range of light, refreshing, predominantly malty flavoured beers in the Swiss tradition. One of its oldest is a strong, dark brown lager with a fruity flavour, which was first launched in 1882 and has been known since 1981 as Dunkle Perle. One of its newest products, launched in 2004, is called Urtrüb, a golden brown unfiltered lager made with a blend of malted barley, wheat and rye.

SPECIFICATIONS

Brewery: Brauerei Feldschlösschen
Location: Rheinfelden
Style: Premium lager
Colour: Golden yellow
Alcohol: 5.2%
Serving temperature: 8°C (46.4°F)
Food: Bread and cheese

Original Feldschlösschen

Original Feldschlösschen is a classic bottom-fermented lager, well balanced and thirst-quenching, with a refreshing malty flavour and a slight touch of hop bitterness.

Feldschlösschen was founded in 1877 in Rheinfelden, near Basel, by two local men, Mathias Wütrich and Theophil Roniger, and remained in the ownership of Wütrich's descendants until the 1990s. By 1898, Feldschlösschen had become Switzerland's largest brewer. It enhanced that status by merging with its main rivals Cardinal, in 1992, and Hürlimann, in 1996. The Feldschlösschen group has also absorbed several smaller brands, including Warteck and Gurten, and produces several foreign beers under licence in Switzerland, such as Denmark's Carslberg and Germany's Schneider Weisse.

SPECIFICATIONS

Brewery: Brauerei Feldschlösschen
Location: Rheinfelden
Style: Lager
Colour: Pale yellow
Alcohol: 4.8%
Serving temperature: 6°–8°C (42.8°–46.4°F)
Food: Sausages and pretzels

Above

German brewers were lucky. Their natural surroundings provided them with the perfect spot for storing their beers – the cold, icy caves at the foothills of the Alps – so when they brewed their last beer in March, they brewed enough for all the months leading into October. They stored the excess in the caves and celebrated with a party at the end of the summer. Over time, these parties became larger and larger, and eventually became known as Oktoberfests.

German Beers

No country takes more pride in the quality of its beers than Germany, a pride that is embodied in the Reinheitsgebot purity laws. First introduced in Bavaria in 1516 by Duke William IV, the law stipulated that beer could be made with only three ingredients: water, barley and hops. The ruling had to be amended later when the discovery was made of the importance of yeast in brewing, and was further amended to permit the use of wheat.

THE REINHEITSGEBOT has in recent years come under fire, in particular from the French who in 1987 forced the European Parliament to rule that it was a barrier to trade. Despite this, many German brewers continue to abide by the principle, enabling them to distinguish their beers from mass-market cheap lagers, even if it does mean that German beers tend to show a conservative character, lacking the innovation of modern beers brewed in Belgium, the United Kingdom and the United States.

This conservatism is further reinforced by the German habit of preferring the local beer style, which has led to different beers being closely associated with their city of origin – the strong, malty export beers of Dortmund, the altbiers of Düsseldorf, the top-fermented Kölsch ales of Cologne and the dark lager of Munich. Despite this, Germany can proudly boast some of the most distinctive beers in the world, among them Rauchbier (smoke beer), a speciality of the town of Bamberg in the Franconia region of upper Bavaria, and the Schwarzbier (black beer) of eastern Germany, newly rediscovered in the west since reunification.

Germany is also famous for the Munich Oktoberfest. This annual festival takes place for 16 days every year, finishing on the first weekend in October, and commemorates the marriage of the Bavarian Prince Ludwig to Princess Theresa in 1810. Only the six main breweries in Munich are allowed to sell their beers at the Oktoberfest, and one of these, Spaten, created a special beer for the festival in 1882, which has since become a classic, imitated by many other breweries.

As in many other countries, in recent years much German brewing has been concentrated into the hands of a few major international companies. But the consumers' loyalty to local beers has enabled many smaller breweries to survive.

ABOVE

German beer has an almost unrivalled range of brands and speciality brews, some of which have centuries of history behind them.

STATISTICS

Total production: 106,304,000 hectolitres (2,808,255,000 gallons) per year

Consumption per capita: 122 litres (32 gallons) per year

Famous breweries: Brauerei Beck; Brauerei Weihenstephan; Dortmunder Hansa Brauerei; Brauerei Gebrüder Maisel; Löwenbräu AG; Paulaner GmbH;

Famous brands: Beck's; Bitburger Premium; Dortmunder Export; Edeldstoff Augustiner; EKU Pils; Erdinger; Löwenbräu; Maissel's Weisse; Oberdorffer Weissebier; Schneider Weisse; Wernesgrüner

Andechser Bergbock Hell

Beer has been brewed at the small town of Andechs in Upper Bavaria's Five Lakes region since 1455, when the Benedictine monastery was founded by Duke Albrecht III on Andechs mountain, overlooking Lake Ammersee.

The 'Klosterbräu' designation indicates the continuing links between holy life and brewing, and beer production took place at the monastery itself until 1972, when a dedicated modern brewery was built at the foot of the mountain. It has since gone from strength to strength, supporting not only the monastery, but also the whole of the local economy. There are seven beers in the brewery's range, all of which can be sampled on tap in the Bräustüberl (brewery pub) or Klostergasthof (monastery restaurant), which is even older than the monastery itself. The full range is also widely available in bottled form.

Bergbock Hell displays all the typical characteristics of a light-coloured bock (strong) beer. It pours with a large, frothy, creamy white head and has clean, floral and herby aroma with hints of citrus fruit. This is a beer with plenty of body, giving a rich, grainy mouthfeel, while the flavour shows a good balance between sweet, fruity malt and hoppy bitterness. The high alcohol content gives a peppery finish and ensures that the beer leaves a pleasant aftertaste to be savoured. Other Andechs beers include standard dark and light lagers, a top-fermented dark wheat beer and a 'Spezial' Hell in the classic Oktoberfest style.

SPECIFICATIONS

Brewery: Andechs Klosterbrauerei
Location: Andechs, Bavaria
Style: Bock
Colour: Brilliantly clear, deep golden yellow
Alcohol: 6.9%
Serving temperature: 9°–10° C (48.2°–50°F)
Food: The meatloaf produced by the monastery's butchery

Andechser Doppelbock Dunkel

A 'doppel' (double) bock is stronger than a regular bock, brewed using a triple mash process to give it a fuller body and a higher alcohol content (although it is not twice as strong as a regular bock, as the name might suggest).

The style is particularly popular in southern Germany, and it is usually drunk in the spring, although this classic example is available all year round. It is a sensuous beer with dark fruit, herbs and spices on the nose and a smooth, silky texture that fills the mouth with caramel, chocolate, raisins and cherries.

SPECIFICATIONS

Brewery: Andechs Klosterbrauerei
Location: Andechs, Bavaria
Style: Doppelbock
Colour: Clear, deep auburn, with a lush, frothy tan-coloured head
Alcohol: 7%
Serving temperature: 9°–10°C (48.2°–50°F)
Food: A meal in itself

Edelstoff Augustiner

This crisp lager comes from the historic Augustiner brewery of Munich. The city's Augustinian monastery was founded in 1294 and records show that its brewery was in existence by 1328.

SPECIFICATIONS

Brewery: Augustiner Bräu
Location: Munich, Bavaria
Style: Dortmunder / export
Colour: Pale amber-gold
Alcohol: 5.6%
Serving temperature: 8°–9°C (46.4°–48.2°F)
Food: Grilled or fried chicken or rabbit

In 1803 the monastery was dissolved, along with many others, by Napoleon, although brewing and selling of beer in the monastery tavern continued, with the brewery moving to its present site in 1817. Augustiner is one of six breweries allowed to brew a beer for the famous Oktoberfest celebrations that take place in Munich every year. The origin of this festival was the marriage of King Ludwig I of Bavaria to Princess Theresa, and due to the strict rules surrounding the official festival not even Prince Luitpold, a direct descendant of King Ludwig, is allowed to sell his beers at the Oktoberfest. Fortunately, there are always many other unofficial celebrations outside the main event where no such restrictions apply.

As well as the Edelstoff and the Oktoberfest beers, Augustiner produces a refreshing light lager with a smooth, malty character; a dark Munich-style lager with a spicy, aromatic flavour; and in the winter months a rich, warming abbey-style double bock called Maximator.

Ayinger Bräu-Weisse

This unfiltered wheat beer is a first-class example of the style, characteristically cloudy with yeast sediment and pouring with a deep, billowing head. It has a potent aroma of bananas and lemon with underlying hints of cloves, and a refreshingly crisp, tart flavour reminiscent of green apples.

The Aying brewery also produces a rich, malty dark lager in the classic Bavarian style, and a popular doppelbock called Celebrator, as well as several other styles. The brewery was established in 1877. Although it started off small, production soon increased and, when the rail link to nearby Munich was built it brought tourists to Aying, many of whom stayed at the Brauereigasthof (brewery guesthouse).

SPECIFICATIONS

- **Brewery:** Aying Brauerei
- **Location:** Aying, Bavaria
- **Style:** Hefe-Weizen / Weissbier
- **Colour:** Cloudy, pale straw colour
- **Alcohol:** 5.1%
- **Serving temperature:** 8°–10° C (46.4°–50°F)
- **Food:** The regional speciality, weisswurst sausage

Unser Bürgerbräu Hefe-Weizen

Bad Reichenhall is a famous royal spa town in the Bayerisch Gmain region of Bavaria, situated in the Alps close to Lake Constance, halfway between the cities of Munich and Salzburg.

It is a very popular resort with tourists and has many attractions, as well as its own philharmonic orchestra. It also has the Unser Bürgerbräu, founded in 1633, the name of which simply means 'Our town brewery'. It produces a wide range of beers, including this unfiltered golden wheat ale, which has a fruity aroma and a palate characterised by a fresh wheaty sourness.

SPECIFICATIONS

- **Brewery:** Bürgerbräu Bad Reichenhall
- **Location:** Bad Reichenhall, Bavaria
- **Style:** Hefe-Weizen / Weissbier
- **Colour:** Cloudy golden yellow
- **Alcohol:** 5.2%
- **Serving temperature:** 7°–8°C (44.6°–46.4°F)
- **Food:** Salami and bread

Unser Bürgerbräu Hefe-Weizen Dunkel

Although it is designated as a dark beer, this top-fermented wheat ale from Unser Bürgerbräu has a somewhat paler colour than other examples of the style.

Nonetheless, it has an authentically fruity malt aroma and well-balanced flavour of sour wheat, sweet malt and dry, bitter hops. The brewery prides itself on its wide range of classic Bavarian beers, produced according to time-honoured methods and traditional recipes since 1633. With this beer, it advises pouring three-quarters of the bottle's contents into the glass, then gently shaking the bottle to ensure that the final pour brings the yeast sediment that gives the beer its character.

SPECIFICATIONS

Brewery: Bürgerbräu Bad Reichenhall
Location: Bad Reichenhall, Bavaria
Style: Dunkel Hefe-Weizen / dark wheat beer
Colour: Cloudy deep golden amber
Alcohol: 5.2%
Serving temperature: 7°–8°C (44.6°–46.4°F)
Food: Thick winter casseroles

Unser Bürgerbräu Suffikator

The tradition of giving doppelbock beers names ending in '-ator' stems from the original doppelbock, which was brewed by Paulaner and called Salvator, meaning 'saviour' in Latin.

Many other breweries produced beers in a similar style and named them Salvator, as if it were a generic term, but Paulaner put a stop to this in 1894 when it protected the name by trade mark. Since then the style has become known as doppelbock because it is similar to a regular bock, but brewed with double the amount of fermentable material to produce a much stronger beer. It may not be the original, but Unser Bürgerbräu's contribution is a fine example of the style, with a fresh grainy aroma and a full, malty flavour balanced by a strong hop presence, giving a dry, bitter finish.

SPECIFICATIONS

Brewery: Bürgerbräu Bad Reichenhall
Location: Bad Reichenhall, Bavaria
Style: Doppelbock
Colour: Deep golden amber
Alcohol: 6.8%
Serving temperature: 9°–10°C (48.2°–50°F)
Food: Dumplings and stewed steak

Beck's

Established in 1873 in the northern port of Bremen, Beck's has always been one of Germany's most forward-thinking breweries.

Originally known as Beck & May, the brewery was named after two of its three owners, Heinrich Beck, a brewer, and Thomas May, a businessman. Early innovations included the installation of a laboratory to develop pure cultures of the highest quality yeast, in order to ensure consistency in the finished product. Another vital component in the Beck's success story was the fact that its light, bottom-fermented beers were designed to travel well, opening the doors to a vast international export market – today, Beck's is the most exported German beer, with 34 million cases travelling to more than 100 countries worldwide annually. Beck's beers account for 85% of German beers exported to the United States. And while many other breweries allow their beers to be brewed under licence in other countries, every bottle of Beck's consumed around the world is produced at the Bremen brewery in accordance with the Reinheitsgebot purity laws.

The standard Pilsner, the original Beck's beer, is a crisp, dry beer with a clean aroma of hops and hay. Bitterness dominates the palate, with underlying hints of malt sweetness, and the finish is dry and hoppy – very much a thirst-quenching type of beer. The brewery also produces a dark Munich-style lager and a strong, dry, malty Oktoberfest beer, as well as alcohol-free and light versions of its Pilsner.

SPECIFICATIONS

Brewery: Brauerei Beck
Location: Bremen
Style: Pilsner
Colour: Pale golden yellow
Alcohol: 5%
Serving temperature: 8°C (46.4°F)
Food: All kinds of fish

Berliner Kindl Weisse

When Berlin became capital of Germany in the late nineteenth century it went through a period of massive growth in both population and industry.

It was during this period, in 1870, that the Berliner Kindl brewery was established. The brewery started producing its Pilsner in 1896, after it acquired the Potsdam brewery which specialised in the new style of bottom-fermented beer. Its wheat beer is a characteristically northern style, which unlike the wheat beers of the south is brewed with lactic acid, which gives it a sour lemony flavour reminiscent of Champagne. The low alcohol content makes it a refreshing summer drink.

SPECIFICATIONS

Brewery: Berliner Kindl Brauerei
Location: Berlin, Brandenburg, eastern Germany
Style: Berliner Weissbier
Colour: Pale yellow
Alcohol: 2.7%
Serving temperature: 8°–10°C (46.4°–50°F)
Food: Roast pork or chicken

Clausthaler Non-alcoholic

The strict Reinheitsgebot purity laws of Germany mean that no beer may be made with any ingredients other than water, malt, hops and yeast.

However, while it specifies what may go into a beer, it makes no restriction on what may be taken out. Launched in 1979, Clausthaler was developed by the Binding brewery of Frankfurt using a pioneering technique called 'arrested fermentation' to brew an authentic beer, but without the alcohol (the 0.5% alcohol is within the permitted definition for non-alcoholic beer and is lower than the alcohol content of some breads). And although it lacks alcohol, it doesn't lack flavour, having a light but pleasantly floral hoppy character.

SPECIFICATIONS

Brewery: Binding Brauerei
Location: Frankfurt
Style: Lager
Colour: Pale golden yellow
Alcohol: 0.5%
Serving temperature: 8°C (46.4°F)
Food: Light flavoured soups and pasta dishes

Römer Pils

This full-flavoured Pilsner beer was launched in 1939 by the Binding brewery of Frankfurt and is named after the ancient city hall. It is an authentic classic Pilsner and has a crisp, refreshing flavour with a herby, spicy hop character, leading to a dry, bitter hop finish.

Römer is also available in a premium version called Römer Pilsener Spezial. The extensive Binding range also includes a full-flavoured malty Export, a dark, fruity altbier called Kutscher Alt, and a strong, dark double bock with a complex fruity flavour, called Carolus der Starke, named after Karl the Great, one of the founders of Frankfurt. The Binding label bears the classic eagle emblem of the city of Frankfurt, and the beer is the defining Pilsner of both the city and the region. Other Binding products include BBK Marzen, Binding Black Lager, Binding Export and Binding Ice.

SPECIFICATIONS

Brewery: Binding Brauerei
Location: Frankfurt
Style: Pilsner
Colour: Golden yellow
Alcohol: 4.9%
Serving temperature: 8°C (46.4°F)
Food: An appetising beer to drink by itself as an aperitif

Schöfferhofer Hefeweizen

Binding is one of the largest brewing groups in Germany, based in Frankfurt where it was founded in 1870.

In 1921 it merged with two other breweries, the Frankfurter Bürgerbrauerei and the Hofbierbrauerei Schöfferhof to form Schöfferhof-Binding-Bürgerbräu AG. The Schöfferhofer label is now used as the brand for the brewery's range of Bavarian-style wheat beers, the principal of which is Hefeweizen. This vibrantly sparkling unfiltered wheat beer has a potently fruity aroma and flavour, characterised by apples, orange zest and hints of bananas, with underlying spiciness reminiscent of cloves, and a touch of hoppy bite in the finish. Others in the range include a Dunkelweizen (dark wheat beer) and a filtered Kristallweizen.

SPECIFICATIONS

Brewery: Binding Brauerei
Location: Frankfurt
Style: Hefe-Weizen
Colour: Cloudy golden yellow
Alcohol: 5%
Serving temperature: 8°–10° C (46.4°–50°F)
Food: A crisp green salad

Bitburger Premium

This dry, aromatic and hoppy Pilsner, matured in cellars for three months, is not only a classic example of the style, but also claims to have been the first beer in Germany to have been described as such, having adopted the term in 1883.

The brewery itself was established in 1817 by local brewer and landlord Johan Peter Wallenborn, but it was the construction by one of his descendants, Theobald Simon, of appropriate 'lagering' cellars that allowed the brewery to start producing bottom-fermented beers that would keep well throughout the warm summer months, such as dark Bavarian-style beers and light Vienna lagers, as well as the Pilsner style, which was still a relatively new invention at the time.

Today, Bitburger Premium Pils is one of the best-selling Pilsners in Germany and is the flagship of a product range that includes alchol-free and light beers. Since German reuinification, the Bitburger group has also encompassed one of the most famous beers of the former East Germany, namely Köstritzer Schwarzbier, which is brewed in the spa town of Bad Köstritz in Thuringia. This is a classic black beer in the popular style of the region that dates back to the sixteenth century. It is full of spicy, chocolatey aromas, which also feature prominently in its rich, dry and well-balanced flavours and smooth body.

SPECIFICATIONS

Brewery: Bitburger Brauerei
Location: Bitburg, Rhineland-Palatinate
Style: Pilsner
Colour: Golden
Alcohol: 4.8%
Serving temperature: 8°–9°C (46.4°–48.2°F)
Food: A fine aperitif to stimulate the appetite

DAB Original

In the nineteenth century, the city of Dortmund had a large coal and steel industry, and all the local breweries produced a full-flavoured malty style of bottom-fermenting beer to quench the thirst of the workers.

These beers were slightly darker and slightly less hoppy than a typical Pilsner. Dortmund rapidly became one of the leading brewing towns in Germany, and its beers were soon popular well outside the local area. It was not long before they were finding their way as far afield as Japan. It is for this reason that the style came to be known as 'export', although it is also referred to as Dortmunder – not that all beers called Dortmunder are faithful to the style of the original Dortmund beers. Founded in 1868, Dortmunder Aktien Brauerei was one of the city's original producers of the style, winning prizes for its beers at the Paris International Fair of 1900, and remains a leading exponent to this day. Still brewed to the original recipe, DAB Original is a fine-textured pale lager with a fragrant aroma of fresh-cut hay and a lingering hop bitterness.

SPECIFICATIONS

Brewery: Dortmunder Actien Brauerei

Location: Dortmund, North Rhine-Westphalia

Style: Dortmunder / export

Colour: Crystal-clear golden yellow

Alcohol: 4.8%

Serving temperature: 6°–8°C (42.8°–46.4°F)

Food: Cold meat and cheese platters

DAB Pilsener

The Dortmunder Actien Brauerei was awarded the 'Grand Prix' for its Pilsener at the Paris International Fair as early as 1937. The refreshingly bitter Pilsener has an original gravity of 11.3%.

It is part of the extensive range of beers from the Dortmunder Actien Brauerei (DAB), which is not to be confused with its main rival in the city, the Dortmunder Union Brewery (DUB). The latter was formed from the merger of several smaller breweries in the city towards the end of the nineteenth century. DAB now forms part of the giant Binding group, although it continues to operate as an independent brewery.

SPECIFICATIONS

Brewery: Dortmunder Actien Brauerei
Location: Dortmund, North Rhine-Westphalia
Style: Pilsener
Colour: Golden yellow
Alcohol: 4.8%
Serving temperature: 8°–10°C (46.4°–50°F)
Food: Meat dishes

Kronen Classic

Kronen is the oldest brewery in Dortmund, with evidence suggesting that it has been in operation since 1430, originally providing beers for the Kronen (Crown) tavern on the market square.

For many years a brewer of top-fermented ales, it started to produce bottom-fermented lagers from the late nineteenth century onwards. But rather than simply re-create the fashionable Pilsener style, Heinrich Wenker, then owner of the Kronen brewery, developed his own softer, maltier style, which quickly caught on and was imitated by other Dortmund breweries, becoming known as Dortmunder, or export. Kronen Classic is brewed to the same recipe.

SPECIFICATIONS

Brewery: Dortmunder Actien Brauerei
Location: Dortmund, North Rhine-Westphalia
Style: Dortmunder / export
Colour: Golden yellow
Alcohol: 5.3%
Serving temperature: 6°–8°C (42.8°–46.4°F)
Food: Rabbit or pheasant

Diebels Alt

The deep copper hues and rich malty, hoppy aromas of this top-fermented ale mark Diebels Alt out as a classic of the altbier ('old beer') style.

It is a beer with plenty of body, filling the mouth satisfyingly and yet feeling light and effervescent. The flavour is refreshingly dry and bitter, with aggressive Perle and Hallertau hops dominating the gentle sweetness of dark malt that gives an underlying taste of brown sugar (the husks of the malt are removed to reduce the characteristic 'burnt' taste). The brewery was founded in 1878 by Josef Diebels, in the picturesque village of Issum in the Niederrhein region, close to the Dutch border and not far from Düsseldorf, an area that is strongly associated with altbiers and home to most of its finest examples.

Diebels was already from a brewing family when he decided to set up on his own, and the brewery remains in the hands of his descendants, currently run by his great-grandson Peter. In its early years, Diebels produced a variety of beer styles, but by the 1960s it had decided to concentrate specifically on its altbier. Since then, the brewery has gone from strength to strength, becoming the sixth-biggest beer producer in Germany, although it is now owned by InBev (Interbrew) of Belgium.

SPECIFICATIONS

Brewery: Privatbrauerei Diebel

Location: Issum am Niederrhein, Rhineland

Style: Altbier

Colour: Bright, clear copper colour, with a fluffy white head

Alcohol: 4.8%

Serving temperature: 9°–10°C (48.2°–50°F)

Food: Weisswurst and sauerkraut

Hansa Export

In Germany, the term 'export' refers to a strong, pale, bottom-fermented beer that usually has more body and a fuller, slightly sweeter flavour than a typical Pilsner.

Due to the traditional popularity of the style in Dortmund, such beers are usually referred to as Dortmunder when applied to examples from that city. Hansa is a classic example of the style, with a bright golden colour, a rich, creamy texture with moderate carbonation, and a malty flavour balanced by gentle hop bitterness. Hansa brewery used to be one of the big three breweries in Dortmund, but is now owned by its former rival, DAB.

SPECIFICATIONS

Brewery: Dortmunder Hansa Brauerei
Location: Dortmund, North Rhine-Westphalia
Style: Dortmunder / export
Colour: Golden yellow
Alcohol: 5%
Serving temperature: 7°–10°C (44.6°–50°F)
Food: Hungarian goulash

St Bernhard Bräu

Not to be confused with the small family brewery and guesthouse of the same name in Waldstetten, this Engel Brewery is a large commercial organisation that produces a wide range of beers.

Many of them are presented in distinctively unusual bottles or cans, such as this Pilsner, which comes in a bottle shaped like a praying monk. It has a herbal hop aroma and a well-balanced grainy malt flavour with a refreshingly dry hop finish. Other beers in the brewery's ever-changing range have included Bomber's Pin-up, presented in a tin flask adorned with World War II imagery.

SPECIFICATIONS

Brewery: Engel Brauerei
Location: Schwäbisch Gmünd, Baden-Württemburg
Style: Pilsner
Colour: Deep golden yellow
Alcohol: 5%
Serving temperature: 8°–10°C (46.4°–50°F)
Food: Venison casserole

Trompe La Mort

Trompe La Mort is the doppelbock which comes from the Engel brewery.

Although many breweries choose to give their doppelbocks a name ending in '-ator', following the example of Paulaner's Salvator, the unusual name of this example of the style comes from the French meaning 'cheating death', and the opaque dark bottle's label accordingly bears the image of a ghostly grim reaper figure with a scythe. Despite the high alcohol content, the flavour and aroma are relatively light for a beer of this style, predominantly characterised by malty notes of apples and pears, leading to a fragrantly hoppy finish.

SPECIFICATIONS

Brewery: Engel Brauerei
Location: Schwäbisch Gmünd, Baden-Württemburg
Style: Doppelbock
Colour: Deep golden yellow-orange
Alcohol: 7.4%
Serving temperature: 8°–10°C (46.4°–50°F)
Food: Veal

Tyrolian Bräu

Tyrolian Bräu is another distinctively packaged beer from the Engel brewery in the town of Schwäbisch Gmünd, which was founded in the mid-twelfth century and has a history as a centre for gold and silver products.

It was a free imperial city until 1803, when it became part of Württemburg. The name of this beer, however, is inspired by the Austrian Tirol department, which is just across the border from Baden-Württemburg. The beer inside is perhaps not as distinctive as the packaging, being a straightforward Pilsner.

SPECIFICATIONS

Brewery: Engel Brauerei
Location: Schwäbisch Gmünd, Baden-Württemburg, southern Germany
Style: Pilsner
Colour: Deep golden yellow
Alcohol: 5%
Serving temperature: 8-9°C (46.4-48.2°F)
Food: Steak

Vamp' Beer

The Engel Brewery produces an extensive range of beers distinguished principally by their characterful individual themed packaging.

As the beers are brewed largely by commission, several of them are simply repackaged versions of the same beer, although the brewery does produce a range of different styles with names such as La Cervoise des Ancestres, which comes in a stoneware bottle, a dark amber beer called Queen Molly Pale Ale, Nova Scotia Stout, and a dark malty lager called Voodoo Dark. Vamp' Beer is a straightforward, uncomplicated Pilsner presented in a tin flask with a label depicting a sexy vampiress in a revealing black dress.

SPECIFICATIONS

Brewery: Engel Brauerei
Location: Schwäbisch Gmünd, Baden-Württemburg
Style: Pilsner
Colour: Golden yellow
Alcohol: 5%
Serving temperature: 7°–8°C (44.6°–46.4°F)
Food: Sausage and mashed potato

Erdinger Weissbier

Erdinger proudly claims to be the world's biggest wheat beer brewer and is also one of the oldest. Founded in 1886 by a local man, Johann Kienle, it was taken over by Franz Brombach in 1935 and has been run by his son Werner since 1975.

Unfiltered, bottle-conditioned Erdinger Weissbier remains the brewery's flagship product and is a classic Bavarian wheat beer, with a sweet, malty flavour and a slight hop bitterness. The brewery's range takes in seven other varieties, including a clear, fine-filtered Kristallweiss, a traditional dark version with a rich, smooth and slightly spicy flavour, and a strong, dark bock beer which has an extra-long maturing period.

SPECIFICATIONS

Brewery: Erdinger Weissbräu
Location: Erding, Bavaria
Style: Hefe-Weizen / Weissbier
Colour: Cloudy pale yellow
Alcohol: 5.3%
Serving temperature: 10°–12°C (50°–53.6°F)
Food: An appetising aperitif

Hacker-Pschorr Weisse

The Hacker Brewery was founded in 1417 as a family business and remained so for almost four centuries. It became Hacker-Pschorr in 1813 when Joseph Pschorr married Therese Hacker. Pschorr was an astute businessman, and he quickly saw to it that the brewery became a much larger operation.

In 1820, he supervised the building of large underground cellars where the beer could be kept in cool conditions, making it possible to brew consistently good beer all year round, and by the 1840s his was the largest brewery in Munich. The site of the original brewhouse is today a popular bar known as the Alte Hackerhaus. Hacker-Pschorr is still one of the city's largest brewers and today produces a wide range of beers, including this fruity, medium-bodied unfiltered wheat beer.

There is also a clear, filtered Kristall Weiss and a dark Dunkle Weiss, which has a smooth malty flavour. Hacker-Pschorr also produces its own examples of the classic Munich style – a creamy, smooth dark lager with a spicy flavour, and a sweet, malty light lager – and a Märzen for the city's famous Oktoberfest.

The Pschorr family's cultural influence spreads beyond beer – in 1864, Josephine Pschorr married Franz Strauss, and their son was Richard Strauss, the famous composer. He dedicated his opera *Der Rosenkavalier* to the brewery as a mark of gratitude for the financial support it gave him during his early career in music.

SPECIFICATIONS

Brewery: Hacker-Pschorr Bräu
Location: Munich, Bavaria
Style: Hefe-Weizen / Weissbier
Colour: Cloudy golden yellow
Alcohol: 5.5%
Serving temperature: 10°–12°C (50°–53.6°F)
Food: Munich white veal sausages with mustard and pretzels

Früh Kölsch

This beer pours a nice light golden amber with a small white head.

The aromas are a blend of malt and bread, with a slight hoplike spice, and perhaps a hint of berries. The taste is very refreshing, perfectly balanced with the nice crisp malts dominating the flavour. A slight fruit and hop bitterness is barely noticeable, but complements the style perfectly. The beer has a nice light body and is very drinkable. Kölsch is an appellation applied to top-fermented beers brewed only in Cologne.

SPECIFICATIONS

Brewery: Brauerei P.J. Früh
Location: Cologne, North Rhine-Westphalia
Style: Kölsch
Colour: Pale lemon gold
Alcohol: 4.8%
Serving temperature: 5°C (41°F)
Food: Wurst, rye bread

Hannen Alt

Part of the Danish brewing group Carlsberg since 1988, Hannen was founded in 1725 and its classic Altbier (old beer) is still brewed at the original site in Mönchengladbach, near Düsseldorf.

Altbier is a particular speciality of this region. It is a copper-coloured top-fermenting ale that spends a long period maturing in cold storage and gets its name from the fact that the style pre-dates the more modern Pilsner. Hannen's version has a smooth, creamy body and an earthy, dark fruit character in the aroma and on the palate, with moderate herbal hop bitterness in the finish. Hannen also brews Carlsberg beers in Germany.

SPECIFICATIONS

Brewery: Hannen Brauerei GmBH
Location: Mönchengladbach, North Rhine-Westphalia,
Style: Altbier
Colour: Dark copper-red
Alcohol: 4.8%
Serving temperature: 6°–8°C (42.8°–46.4°F)
Food: Hamburgers or sausages

Hasseröder Premium Pils

Hasseröder brewery was founded in 1872 in the ancient town of Wernigerode, a popular tourist spot which still has many half-timbered medieval houses and parts of the old city walls intact.

It was taken over by Ernst Schreyer in 1882, soon becoming one of Germany's major breweries. After many years hidden away behind the Iron Curtain, Hasseröder once again came to prominence following German reunification in 1990 and is one of the top five best-selling Pilsners in the domestic market. The brewery produces just one beer, the same beer that it has always made, a rich, golden Pilsner with a sweet, refreshing flavour.

SPECIFICATIONS

Brewery: Hasseröder Brauerei
Location: Wernigerode, Saxony-Anhalt
Style: Pilsner
Colour: Clear golden yellow
Alcohol: 4.8%
Serving temperature: 6°–8°C (42.8°–46.4°F)
Food: Fresh green salad

Aecht Schlenkerla Rauchbier

The historical Schlenkerla brewery tavern, founded in 1678, is located in the heart of ancient Bamberg, one of the most remarkably individual brewing towns in Germany, with nine breweries serving around 70,000 people (although at its peak in the early nineteenth century there were around 60 breweries). Aecht Schlenkerla Rauchbier is the town's most famous beer, originally brewed in the tavern, but since the nineteenth century produced at a separate site on the Stephansberg hill outside the town, also the site of the sandstone caves where the beer was – and still is – matured for several months. In the tavern, the beer is tapped directly from oak casks, but it is also available in bottled form.

The brewery produces its own malt, which is smoked over beechwood fires. This imparts a distinctly smoky aroma and flavour to the beer, which lasts all the way through to the long, dry finish. Three versions of the beer are brewed – as well as the regular Märzen, there is also a lighter flavoured wheat beer and a strong Urbock for the winter months. Officially named Heller-Bräu, the brewery and tavern were originally owned by the Heller family and are now owned by the Trum family, but have had several other owners in between. One of these was Andreas Graser, who took over in 1877. A handicap meant that he walked with a swaying motion, the German word for which is *schlenkern*, and since then the brewery has been known as Schlenkerla.

SPECIFICATIONS

Brewery: Heller-Bräu
Location: Bamberg, Franconia, Bavaria
Style: Smoke beer
Colour: Dark chocolate brown
Alcohol: 4.8%
Serving temperature: 9°C (48.2°F)
Food: Smoked ham or sausages

HAB Henninger Export Classic

The origins of Henninger date back to 1655, when the Stein brewery was founded in Frankfurt.

It remained in the same family for 200 years, but was taken over by Heinrich Christian Henninger in 1873, following the death of Johannes Stein, and has since gone on to become one of the five largest breweries in Germany.

Henninger specialises in bottom-fermented lagers. The brewery's leading brand is Kaiser Pilsner, a characteristically dry, hoppy beer, but the range also includes a full-bodied Pilsener style Export, shown here, and a smoky-flavoured beer called Highlander, which is made with malt roasted over peat.

Henninger Premium Lager is one of the most widely available German beers in the United States, and can be found both in cans and on draught.

SPECIFICATIONS

Brewery: Henninger Bräu AG
Location: Frankfurt am Main, Hesse
Style: Pilsner
Colour: Bright, clear golden yellow
Alcohol: 4.8%
Serving temperature: 6°–7°C (42.8°–44.6°F)
Food: A fresh green salad

Hopf Helle Weisse

The town of Miesbach lies 50km to the south of Munich in the foothills of the Alps. It is home to the Hopf brewery, which was founded in 1910 and is currently run by the third generation of the Hopf family.

The family produces eight varieties of wheat beer, mostly using strictly traditional methods but with an innovative approach, its flagship brew being a top-fermented cloudy golden wheat beer with a fruity flavour and a stronger hop presence than many other examples of the style. Likewise, the dark wheat beer has a distinct hop profile in the aroma, along with fresh yeasty hints of pears and bananas, and a refreshingly fruity malt character on the palate, while the seasonal Weisser Bock is a strong dark beer brewed for the winter months with a warming 7% alcohol content.

SPECIFICATIONS

Brewery: Hopf Weissbierbrauerei
Location: Miesbach, Bavaria
Style: Hefe-Weizen / Weissbier
Colour: Golden yellow
Alcohol: 5.3%
Serving temperature: 6°–7°C (42.8°–44.6°F)
Food: Light flavoured risotto or pasta dishes

Jever Pilsener

The Friesisches Brauhaus at Jever, in northern Germany, produces this famous lager, and has a tradition going back 150 years.

This is probably the most bitter of the Nothern German Pilsners. It has an aroma of resiny hops and booming malt leading to a beer with a typical pure white head and just the right amount of carbonation. The taste is of grassy, resiny hops held up well by a very supportive malt base. The label says 'Friesisch Herb', which means 'fresh, dry', and this is so. (The word 'herb' can also mean 'bitter', which is also applicable in this case.) The beer is bouncingly fresh, but dry from the high hop rate – although still with plenty of mouthfeel. It continues through in the same way to a refreshing, lasting, hop-filled finish.

SPECIFICATIONS

Brewery: Friesisches Bauhaus
Location: Jever, Friesland
Style: Pilsner
Colour: Golden
Alcohol: 4.9%
Serving temperature: 5°C (41°F)
Food: Any cheese and dark bread

Prinzregent Luitpold

The name Prinzregent Luitpold designates a range of wheat beers from the Kaltenburg brewery.

These include a light-flavoured golden beer, a richer dark beer with clove and chocolate notes, and a kristall (filtered) version. They are named after Prince Luitpold, who is not some historical figure, but the present-day patron of the brewery, which is housed in his idyllic castle in Herzen von Bayern, 40km west of Munich. The original castle was built by Duke Rudolph of Bavaria in 1292, although the present building dates from the late seventeenth century.

SPECIFICATIONS

Brewery: Kaltenberg
Location: Herzen von Bayern, Bavaria
Style: Hefe-Weizen / Weissbier
Colour: Golden orange-yellow
Alcohol: 5.5%
Serving temperature: 9°–12°C (48.2°–53.6°F)
Food: Liver and onions

Edel Premium

The publicly owned Kaufbeuren brewery was already well established by the year 1618, and is believed to have its origins as far back as 1308, when documents reveal that a local man left his property to the hospital, including his brewhouse.

The brewery began to expand in 1799, when it was acquired by Jonas Daniel Walch, moving to new premises in 1807. Today, it produces a wide range of beers, including this classic Pilsner, which has a fresh floral hop aroma with hints of apples and hay, and a flavour that balances light bready malts with dry, bitter hops, leading to a slightly sweet, malty finish.

SPECIFICATIONS

Brewery: Aktienbrauerei Kaufbeuren
Location: Kaufbeuren, Bavaria
Style: Pilsner
Colour: Pale straw yellow
Alcohol: 5%
Serving temperature: 6°–8°C (42.8°–46.4°F)
Food: Delicately flavoured salads

Jubiläums Pils

Tettnanger hops are responsible for the characteristically dry, floral aroma and flavour of this classic Pilsner-style beer from Bavaria's Kaufbeuren brewery.

The label bears the date 1907, the year the beer was first brewed. It was around this time that the Kaufbeuren brewery earned the royal patronage of Prince Ludwig, and was also the year that it acquired ownership of the Löwen (Lion) brewery, making it the major beer producer in the area. Despite several setbacks over the twentieth century, the Kaufbeuren brewery eventually achieved dominance to become the sole brewery in the town.

SPECIFICATIONS

Brewery: Aktienbrauerei Kaufbeuren
Location: Kaufbeuren, Bavaria
Style: Pilsner
Colour: Pale straw yellow
Alcohol: 5%
Serving temperature: 8°–10° C (46.4°–50°F)
Food: A thirst-quenching beer to drink by itself on a hot day

St. Martin Doppelbock

Allowing a long period of maturation gives this classic double bock a smooth, well-rounded body and richly complex malt flavours, all held together in a dark mahogany-red colour.

The aroma of this quality beer is sweet and earthy with a warming roasted malt character and dark fruity scents of figs, plums and caramel. Roasted malts appear again on the palate, with chocolate, dark treacle and a hint of smoke all in evidence before a refreshingly dry, spicy hop finish emerges. It is a very full-bodied beer with a thick, almost physically chewy mouthfeel, although it is not too heavy and goes down easily despite its fairly high alcohol content of 7.5% abv.

SPECIFICATIONS

Brewery: Aktienbrauerei Kaufbeuren
Location: Kaufbeuren, Bavaria
Style: Dark double bock
Colour: Dark mahogany red-brown
Alcohol: 7.5%
Serving temperature: 10°–13°C (50°–55.4°F)
Food: Rich fruity desserts

Steingadener Dunkel Weisse

Steingadener Dunkel Weisser is an unfiltered, bottle-conditioned dark abbey-style wheat beer, a companion to the Weizen Anno 25 pale wheat beer from the same brewery.

It is characterised by a fruity, nutty, bready malt aroma with underlying notes of sweet caramel. The caramel and soft dark fruit return in the palate to give the beer an overriding sweet flavour, although the light body and spritzy carbonation make this a refreshing beer for a summer's day. Steingadener is one of the Kaufbeuren brewery's regular standard wheat beers, but the brewery also produces a range of premium beers presented in bottles with traditional ceramic flip-top lids.

Among these is the Hefetrübes Weissbier, which was first brewed in 1885, the year that the Kaufbeuren brewery became a publicly owned company. The name comes from the German *hefe*, meaning 'yeast', indicating that the beer is unfiltered, and *trüb*, meaning 'cloudy'. Another beer in the range, Naturtrubes Kellerbier, aims to re-create the style of lager that would have been brewed in the early days of the brewery and accordingly bears the date 1308 on its label.

Similarly, the brewery's Urbayrisch Dunkel (Original Bavarian Dark) aims to re-create the authentic character of beers drank in years gone by, while Edles Radler is a blend of lager and lemonade designed to be a refreshing, energising drink with a lower alcohol content to be enjoyed by cyclists (*radler* is a southern German dialect word for cyclist, and a cyclist is depicted on the bottle's label).

SPECIFICATIONS

Brewery: Aktienbrauerei Kaufbeuren

Location: Kaufbeuren, Bavaria

Style: Dark wheat beer / Dunkle weizen

Colour: Cloudy golden chestnut brown

Alcohol: 5.1%

Serving temperature: 10°C (50°F)

Food: Spicy pizza or pasta dishes

Weizen Anno 25

This traditional Bavarian speciality wheat beer is a lively, fresh-flavoured example of the style and gets its name from the year it was first brewed, 1925.

Weizen Anno 25 has a fine yeasty flavour with hints of bananas, apples and cloves coming through in the fruity, grainy malt aroma. Its full natural carbonation gives it a spritzy, tingly mouthfeel and a full body, while the overall flavour has a rounded fruity complexity with a dry, spicy finish. The beer comes from the oldest brewery in Kaufbeuren, which produces a wide range of beers including various wheat beers, one of which is a low-calorie, low-alcohol beer named after the Kaiser Maximilian I.

SPECIFICATIONS

Brewery: Aktienbrauerei Kaufbeuren
Location: Kaufbeuren, Bavaria
Style: Hefe-Weizen
Colour: Cloudy golden yellow
Alcohol: 5.8%
Serving temperature: 8°C (46.4°F)
Food: Pasta with cheese sauce

EKU Pils

The flagship beer in the EKU range is its classic Pilsner, presented in the long, slender-necked bottles that are a traditional part of the EKU image.

It pours a brilliant clear golden yellow and has an invigorating scent of freshly cut hay with an underlying hint of malty sweetness. The flavour is crisp and refreshingly bitter, leading to a long dry finish with subtle bitter hoppiness. The EKU range also includes a light-coloured malty lager, a full-bodied strong golden export beer and a seasonal Festbier with a fragrant hop aroma. Less conventional is its blend of cola and beer, which provides a sweet-flavoured, low-alcohol alternative.

SPECIFICATIONS

Brewery: Kulmbacher Brauerei
Location: Kulmbach, Franconia, Bavaria
Style: Pilsner
Colour: Clear golden straw yellow
Alcohol: 4.9%
Serving temperature: 6°–8°C (42.8°–46.4°F)
Food: Herby vegetarian dishes

EKU 28

Since the mid-nineteenth century, the small town of Kulmbach in the Franconia region of Bavaria has been known for its strong, dark beers and its annual beer festival at the end of July that rivals the one held in October in Munich.

Alas, the once-thriving local brewing industry has undergone some major recent upheavals, with the result that the remaining breweries have merged under the banner of the Kulmbacher Brauerei group. With the merger, the beer ranges of the group's component parts have been rationalised, although several of the former individual styles remain part of the Kulmbacher repertoire, including the famous Eisbock from the Reichelsbrau brewery. Another brewery that was absorbed in the merger was EKU, which stands for Erste Kulmbacher Unionbrauerei, meaning First United Breweries of Kulmbach. Several of its beers are still produced, including EKU 28, which proclaims itself to be the strongest beer in the world, although since it first made that claim it has undoubtedly been overtaken by other stronger beers.

Nonetheless, EKU 28 remains a potent brew, and the number 28 in its name refers to the original gravity, which according to the German system of measurement means it is brewed with roughly double the amount of fermentable sugars as a typical strong beer. The exceptionally high original gravity means that the end product has a thick, heavy, almost syrupy consistency, but despite this EKU 28 is a surprisingly easy beer to drink, with complex, zesty orange fruit flavours and a fresh, clean, dry finish.

SPECIFICATIONS

Brewery: Kulmbacher Brauerei
Location: Kulmbach, Franconia, Bavaria
Style: Doppelbock
Colour: Dark ruby red
Alcohol: 13.5%
Serving temperature: 9°C (48.2°F)
Food: Fruity desserts such as apple tart

Kapuziner

Kapuziner is the name of the range of wheat beers from the Kulmbacher brewery group based in the small town of Kulmbach in Franconia, the brewing heartland of Germany.

There are six different varieties of wheat beer in the range, of which this classic cloudy unfiltered golden ale is the most popular. It has a fairly light aroma and flavour, making it a good straightforward refreshing summer drink. Kapuziner also comes in a filtered Kristallweiss version, a full-flavoured Schwarz (dark) version with a floral malt character, and a strong, rich winter version with a well-rounded spicy malt flavour.

SPECIFICATIONS

Brewery: Kulmbacher Brauerei
Location: Kulmbach, Franconia, Bavaria
Style: Hefe-Weizen / Weissbier
Colour: Golden orange-yellow
Alcohol: 5.4%
Serving temperature: 8°C (46.4°F)
Food: Greek salad with feta cheese and black olives

Kulmbacher Premium Pils

The Kulmbacher brewery group was formed from the merger of five independent breweries all based in the small town of Kulmbach, known as the 'capital city of beer', and Kulmbacher Premium Pils is its flagship beer, a straightforward lager with a light flavour.

Following the merger, beer production was moved to a single site, although many of the individual recipes were retained. The Kulmbacher label is applied to several famous brands, including Reichelbräu Eisbock 24, an ice-conditioned beer that was formerly a contender for the title of world's strongest beer.

SPECIFICATIONS

Brewery: Kulmbacher Brauerei
Location: Kulmbach, Franconia, Bavaria
Style: Pilsner
Colour: Pale straw yellow
Alcohol: 4.9%
Serving temperature: 6°–8°C (42.8°–46.4°F)
Food: Summer salads

Krombacher Pils

The Krombacher brewery is situated in the small town of Krombach in the Siegerland region of the North Rhine-Westphalia state, an area characterised by lushly forested valleys.

Its Pilsner, brewed with crystal clear spring waters from a natural local source, is described as 'a pearl of nature' and has a soft, creamy texture and a mild flavour with a well-balanced blend of malt and hops. Although it is slightly sweeter than some Pilsners, it has a characteristic dry, bitter hop finish. Krombacher Pils is also available in a non-alcoholic version, and the brewery also produces a dark, top-fermented altbier called Rhenania. All Krombacher beers are brewed according to Rheinheitsgebot purity regulations.

SPECIFICATIONS

Brewery: Krombacher Brauerei
Location: Kreuztal-Krombach, North Rhine-Westphalia
Style: Pilsner
Colour: Golden yellow
Alcohol: 4.8%
Serving temperature: 6°–8°C (42.8°–46.4°F)
Food: An appetising pre-dinner aperitif

Lauterbacher Hefeweizen

Founded in 1651, shortly after the end of the Thirty Years War, the Lauterbacher brewery has the motto 'Tradition is our inspiration'.

Accordingly, its classic unfiltered golden wheat beer is a sprightly top-fermented ale with a fine aroma full of banana and lemon notes characteristic of the high hop content and the individual strain of yeast, which is the same strain that the brewery has been using since 1888. The beer's flavour is balanced between grainy malt, the smoothness of wheat and the bitterness of hops. The brewery's extensive range includes nine varieties of wheat beer, including one called Bayerische Hiasl, made to an age-old recipe and named after an ancient Bavarian folk hero with a reputation similar to Robin Hood.

SPECIFICATIONS

Brewery: Privatbrauerei Lauterbach L. Ehnle
Location: Lauterbach, Hesse
Style: Hefe-Weizen / Weissbier
Colour: Golden orange-yellow
Alcohol: 5.1%
Serving temperature: 8°C (46.4°F)
Food: Steak in Stilton sauce

Maisel's Weisse Original

The town of Bayreuth is principally known for its annual Wagner opera festival, which takes place at the opera house designed by Richard Wagner himself. It is also known among beer connoisseurs for its five breweries, of which Maisel is the largest. Still owned by the Maisel family, it was established in 1874, and the former brewhouse is now a huge museum – one of the largest brewing museums in the world – housing the original brewing equipment and other artefacts ranging from massive steam engines to a mug and glass collection.

Next door to the museum is the Goldener Löwe, the brewery tap, where the full range of Maisel beers can be sampled, although they are also widely available bottled. Maisel's famous traditional speciality is its Dampfbier (steam beer), a top-fermented amber ale with a rich malty flavour. In recent years, the brewery's efforts have been concentrated on promoting its range of wheat beers, which come in six varieties. Maisel's Weisse Original is a classic unfiltered Bavarian wheat beer containing live yeast, which gives the beer a rich golden colour with a cloudy haze and allows it to continue to develop character in the bottle. It has a yeasty banana aroma and a smooth, fruity flavour with a crisp, dry hop finish. The range also includes a full-flavoured fruity dark wheat beer, a non-alcoholic version and a seasonal winter wheat beer with a rich, spicy flavour.

SPECIFICATIONS

Brewery: Brauerei Gebrüder Maisel
Location: Bayreuth, Bavaria
Style: Hefe-Weizen / Weissbier
Colour: Cloudy golden orange-yellow
Alcohol: 5.7%
Serving temperature: 8°–10°C (46.4°–50°F)
Food: Cold pork pie

Löwenbräu

Some sources date the formation of Löwenbräu (the Lion brewery) to 1383, but this view is not without controversy.

Löwenbräu was bought by Georg Brey in 1818, and under his direction it grew to become the biggest brewery in Munich, eventually merging with Spaten in 1997. Löwenbräu Original is a classic Munich lager, soft and malty with a light hoppy background. The brewery's range also includes a dry, hoppy Premium Pilsner, a non-alcoholic beer, and a golden unfiltered Bavarian wheat beer, as well as its annual seasonal speciality strong beer for the Oktoberfest.

SPECIFICATIONS

Brewery: Löwenbräu AG
Location: Munich, Bavaria
Style: Munich light lager
Colour: Golden yellow
Alcohol: 5.2%
Serving temperature: 8°C (46.4°F)
Food: Chinese noodle dishes

Paulaner Original Münchner

Since the early part of the nineteenth century Munich's breweries have been producing a distinctive local style of dark brown bottom-fermented beer, which has become known widely as Münchner.

From the 1920s onwards, many breweries switched to brewing a paler version of the Munich lager (known as Münchner helles), and the Paulaner brewery is generally credited as being the instigator of this trend. The basic version has a subtly floral hop aroma with a well-rounded malty body balanced by clean, refreshing hop bitterness. It is also available as a slightly darker Urtyp, brewed to be a bit stronger at 5.5% alcohol, with a fuller, maltier flavour.

SPECIFICATIONS

Brewery: Paulaner GmbH
Location: Munich, Bavaria
Style: Munich light lager
Colour: Golden yellow-orange
Alcohol: 4.9%
Serving temperature: 7°–9°C (44.6°–48.2°F)
Food: Lamb escalopes

Paulaner Hefe-Weissbier

The city of Munich was given its name in 1158 by Duke Henry the Lion and is derived from an old German word meaning 'Monks' Place', reflecting the fact that since the eighth century the area has been the site of many monastic communities. The Paulaner monastery was founded on a hillside on the outskirts of Munich by followers of St Francis of Paula some time in the sixteenth century. Like all monasteries it took up brewing early on, to provide liquid refreshment for the monks; the surplus was sold to local bars for public consumption.

The first official document detailing the existence of the Paulaner brewery dates from 1634. Although the brewery is traditionally known for its lagers, in recent years it has concentrated its efforts towards a popular range of wheat beers, of which it produces some of the most flavoursome examples around. The classic unfiltered golden Hefe-Weissbier has a spicy clove aroma with background honeyed sweetness and notes of banana, while the palate has a crisp, refreshing fruity flavour. The brewery also produces a dark version and a Kristallklar filtered version, and in 1987 it also launched the world's first alcohol-free wheat beer.

SPECIFICATIONS

Brewery: Paulaner GmbH
Location: Munich, Bavaria
Style: Hefe-Weizen / Weissbier
Colour: Golden orange-yellow
Alcohol: 5.5%
Serving temperature: 9°–12°C (48.2°–53.6°F)
Food: Chicken and vegetable pie

Salvator Doppelbock

Salvator from Munich's Paulaner brewery is the original Doppelbock, the one that all others look to for inspiration, not only in the beer itself, but also in the name.

The monks that originally brewed this strongly alcoholic 'liquid bread' to sustain them through Lent named it Salvator, from the Latin for 'saviour'. At one time, the name Salvator was widely adopted to indicate any beer of a similar style though eventually these beers became known as Dopplebocks (double bocks) and the name Salvator was protected by trade mark in 1894 to ensure that the Paulaner brewery could use it exclusively to designate its beer. Other breweries gave their versions names ending in '-ator', such as Optimator, Fortunator, Kulminator and Triumphator.

Salvator is still brewed annually for launch in the spring, shortly before the start of Lent. It pours with a head as thick and rich as whipped cream and gives off a complex, buttery, fruitcake malt aroma balanced with a delicate hint of hops. On the palate, a full malty flavour is characterised by notes of toffee, dark fruit and toasted bread, although the high alcohol content tempers the sweetness with a biting dryness, and the surprisingly high hop content provides a dry, bitter finish.

This exceptional beer is best enjoyed in the beer gardens of Munich in the early spring, when the frosts of winter have gone and the locals start to return to their favourite pastime of sociable drinking. Fortunately, for those that can't make it to Munich, Salvator is widely available in bottled form.

SPECIFICATIONS

Brewery: Paulaner GmbH
Location: Munich, Bavaria
Style: Doppelbock
Colour: Deep amber brown
Alcohol: 7.5%
Serving temperature: 9°C (48.2°F)
Food: A meal in itself

Pinkus Organic Hefe Weizen

The city of Münster once had over 150 breweries, but now only one remains, Pinkus Müller.

Established in 1816 by Johannes Müller as the brewhouse for the family inn, which it still serves, it has been run by the same family for five generations and was renamed after Carl Pinkus Müller, who was head of the brewery from 1944 until 1979. It still brews its beers according to the traditional methods and original recipes, although it now uses mostly organic ingredients. Its unfiltered organic wheat beer is brewed with 60% wheat malt and 40% barley malt, and has a lemony yeasty aroma, with a sharp, clean wheat flavour dominating the palate.

SPECIFICATIONS

Brewery: Brauerei Pinkus Müller
Location: Münster, North Rhine-Westphalia
Style: Organic Hefe-Weizen / Weissbier
Colour: Cloudy golden yellow
Alcohol: 5.1%
Serving temperature: 8°C (46.4°F)
Food: A pre-dinner appetiser

Plankstetten Dinkel

Founded in 1866 and now run by the fourth generation of the Krieger family, Riedenburger brewery has since 1994 concentrated on brewing exclusively organic beers.

This includes the abbey-style beers that it produces under the Plankstetten label under a licensing agreement formed in 1997 with the twelfth-century Benedictine monastery in Plankstetten. The cereals for these beers are grown on the abbey estate and include a dark lager called Dunkles, which is not to be confused with the highly unusual Dinkel. Dinkel is brewed with 50% spelt malt, for a distinctively rich, wholesome flavour with refreshing orange and apricot fruit aromas and a bread-like grain character on the palate.

SPECIFICATIONS

Brewery: Riedenburger Brauhaus
Location: Riedenberg, Bavaria
Style: Organic spelt beer
Colour: Cloudy golden orange
Alcohol: 4.9%
Serving temperature: 8°C (46.4°F)
Food: Pepperoni pizza

Plankstetten Spezial

Plankstetten Spezial is an amber-coloured beer brewed with a blend of pale and dark malts, then matured for a lengthy period to give it a smooth, spicy flavour.

Being unfiltered and unpasteurised it has a natural cloudy haze similar in appearance to Bavaria's top-fermented wheat beers, although this is a bottom-fermented lager. In addition to the Plankstetten beers, Riedenburger has a range under its own label. As well as dark and light wheat beers, a stronger 'export' wheat beer and a classic Munich-style light lager, there are a few more unusual specialities, such as the 5-Korn Urbier, which is brewed with a blend of wheat and barley malts, plus corn and spelt.

SPECIFICATIONS

Brewery: Riedenburger Brauhaus
Location: Riedenberg, Bavaria
Style: Organic
Colour: Deep amber orange
Alcohol: 5.3%
Serving temperature: 8°–10°C (46.4°–50°F)
Food: Roast beef

Rostocker Pils

Rostocker Pils is a light, refreshing golden beer with a pronounced hoppy dryness.

It comes from the historic Hanseatic Brewery of Rostock, which can trace its origins back to 1258 and was already a well-established exporter of beers by 1878, when it was taken over by Georg Mahn and Friedrich Ohlerich. It was at this point that its fortunes really took off, with the establishment of its own maltings and refrigeration plant. During World War II, the brewery was dismantled by Soviet troops, but amazingly it recovered from this setback, being rebuilt and brewing once again by 1947, and it continued to thrive despite a fire in 1967. The Rostocker brewery expanded in 2001 and now produces a range of four beers – including light and dark bock beers and a strong 'export'.

SPECIFICATIONS

Brewery: Rostocker Brauerei
Location: Rostock, Schleswig-Holstein
Style: Pilsner
Colour: Golden yellow
Alcohol: 4.9%
Serving temperature: 6°–8°C (42.8°–46.4°F)
Food: Curried rice dishes

Altenmünster Premium

'Altbier' is a German term for a top-fermenting ale, usually copper-coloured. However, this smooth, easy-drinking beer has a golden yellow appearance more typical of a light lager.

In that respect it is similar to the Kölsch ales of Cologne (only beers from Cologne itself may be called Kölsch). The aroma is rich and fruity, while the sweetly malty flavour is reminiscent of buttered toast, and the finish is soft and dry. The Sailer brewery produces a wide variety of beers in the Altenmünster range, including light and dark wheat beers and a smoked (rauch) beer.

SPECIFICATIONS

Brewery: Privatbrauerei Franz Joseph Sailer
Location: Marktoberdorf, Bavaria
Style: Altbier
Colour: Pale gold with a light, frothy head
Alcohol: 4.9%
Serving temperature: 9°–10°C (48.2°–50°F)
Food: A 'sociable' beer for drinking in company

Oberdorfer Weissbier

The original Oberdorfer brewery dates from the early sixteenth century and was originally the brewhouse for a tavern in the town from which it takes its name – Marktoberdorf in the Swabia region of Bavaria.

Oberdorfer Weissbier is available in two varieties, a dark and a light. The light version has a spicy wheat aroma with a banana yeast character, a hint of cloves and a faint herbal hop scent in the background. On the palate a crisp, slightly sour wheat character combines with a bubblegum-sweet malt flavour to create a well-balanced beer. The dark wheat beer has a richly fruity aroma with the character of grapes, bananas and apples, plus a hint of caramel and grainy malt. The palate is crisp and slightly sour, with flavours of lemon and cloves over a grainy malty sweetness.

SPECIFICATIONS

Brewery: Privatbrauerei Franz Joseph Sailer
Location: Marktoberdorf, Bavaria
Style: Hefe-Weizen / Weissbier
Colour: Pale golden yellow
Alcohol: 4.9%
Serving temperature: 9°–12°C (48.2°–53.6°F)
Food: Spicy pizza

Rauchenfelser Steinbier

Although this highly individual top-fermented wheat beer was first produced as recently as 1983, it represents the renaissance of truly ancient methods of beer production. These methods are reflected in the beer's name – Rauchenfelser means 'smoking rocks', and these are a key agent in the brewing process.

Before the introduction of copper kettles, all stages of brewing took place in wooden vessels. These vessels could not be placed directly over a fire, for obvious reasons, so in order to boil the wort (the sweet liquid drawn off after the 'mashing' of malt and water) rocks were heated in a furnace until white-hot, then placed in the brewing kettle. The hot rocks cause the wort to bubble furiously and at the same time some of the sugars in the liquid become caramelised on their surface. After fermentation the brew is allowed to mature for up to three months, still containing the sugar-coated rocks, which give the finished beer a smoky, treacly flavour and a pronounced smoky aroma.

Compared to the strongly flavoured bottom-fermented Rauchbiers (smoke beers) of Bamberg in Franconia, which are made with smoked malt and are characteristically dark, this is a light, easy-drinking beer with a lively character imparted by the relatively high levels of carbonation. The smoke and burnt caramel flavours linger through to a soft, dry finish.

SPECIFICATIONS

Brewery: Privatbrauerei Franz Joseph Sailer
Location: Marktoberdorf, Bavaria
Style: Steinbier (stone beer)
Colour: Crystal clear, reddish brown, deep creamy head
Alcohol: 4.9%
Serving temperature: 9°C (48.2°F)
Food: Barbecued meat

Jubelbier

The Franz Joseph Sailer brewery of Marktoberdorf in southern Germany produces a wide range of beers including Oberdorfer, Altenmunster, Rauchenfels Steinbier and Napoleon. Creative packaging is a key element of the brewery's marketing, and owner and brewmaster Gerd Borges has designed special bottles based on Halloween pumpkins and NASA astronauts.

Privatbrauerei Franz Joseph Sailer dates back to the 1630s, although the Sailer family name was attached to the company around 1850. In the 1960s, the company was modernized, merged with another brewery, and the rights to produce Rauchenfels Steinbier were secured in 1982.

Jubelbier is the Sailer version of the strong, malty beers brewed annually for the Oktoberfest in nearby Munich – although Jubelbier is available all year round – and is presented in a distinctive bottle with a ceramic flip-top lid. It has a rich, sweet malty aroma with a dark plummy fruit character, while on the palate it is silky smooth with an overriding caramel sweetness.

SPECIFICATIONS

Brewery: Privatbrauerei Franz Joseph Sailer
Location: Marktoberdorf, Bavaria
Style: Märzen / Oktoberfest
Colour: Dark red-brown
Alcohol: 5.5%
Serving temperature: 10°C (50°F)
Food: Roast duck or chicken

Schneider Aventinus

The Schneider brewery was formed in 1855 by the first Georg Schneider, when he took over the Weisse Hofbräuhaus in Munich and began brewing wheat beer.

It moved to its current premises in Kelheim in 1926, when the business was under the direction of the fourth Georg Schneider (the great-grandson of the first Georg). Currently in charge is the sixth Georg Schneider, who has been working at the brewery since 1982. The only family member to run the brewery who was not called Georg was Maria Schneider, wife of Georg III, who took charge following the untimely death of her husband at the beginning of the twentieth century.

During her time in charge, she was responsible for introducing this extraordinary strong 'double bock' wheat beer to the brewery's range. Its flavour is complex and richly malty, with notes of raisins, figs and plums, a spicy character reminiscent of cloves and cinnamon, and a warming 8% alcohol to give it a dry, peppery finish. It also has a remarkable natural effervescence, almost like Champagne.

Aventinus takes its name from the Aventine Strasse in Munich, where the original brewery was located. There is also a link with Johannes Thurmayr of Abensberg, a sixteenth-century Latin scholar and historian who was more commonly known as Aventinus – it is his face that is depicted on the beer's label.

SPECIFICATIONS

Brewery: Privat Weissbierbrauerei G. Schneider & Sohn

Location: Kelheim, Bavaria

Style: Wheat double bock / Weizenbock

Colour: Dark ruby red

Alcohol: 8%

Serving temperature: 9°–10° C (48.2°–50°F)

Food: Soup or pasta with a lightly flavoured sauce

Schneider Weisse

To a large extent, the history of the Schneider brewery is the history of wheat beer in Germany. When Georg Schneider took over the Weisse Hofbräuhaus in Munich in 1855 and started brewing wheat beer, this style of beer was going out of fashion and was seriously in decline by the late nineteenth century.

Then in 1872, Georg acquired the licence to brew wheat beer for King Ludwig II and thus saved wheat beer from extinction. The company rapidly expanded, acquiring the wheat beer brewhouses in Straubing and Kelheim in 1927. The latter is still the home of Schneider to this day (the original Munich brewery was destroyed during World War II) and is Bavaria's oldest wheat beer brewery, having been in continuous production since 1607. In recent years it has undergone extensive modernisation.

Brewed to the same recipe used by the first Georg Schneider around 150 years ago, Schneider Weisse is widely regarded as the definitive example of the Hefe-Weizen style, left unfiltered for the yeast sediment to give it a natural cloudiness (*hefe* is German for 'yeast'). It is a lively beer that pours with a deep, frothy head and gives off a complex aroma dominated a fruity malt character with hints of cloves, nutmeg and apple. On the palate, it tastes refreshingly clean, full-bodied and well-balanced, the fruity malt flavour giving way to a gently bitter finish and a slightly sour aftertaste.

SPECIFICATIONS

Brewery: Privat Weissbierbrauerei G. Schneider & Sohn
Location: Kelheim, Bavaria
Style: Hefe-Weizen
Colour: Amber mahogany
Alcohol: 5.4%
Serving temperature: 9°–12°C (48.2°–53.6°F)
Food: Grilled chicken

Franziskaner

The name 'Franziskaner' relates to the Franciscan monastery that stood across the street from the old wheat beer brewery in the centre of Munich.

The existence of the brewery was first recorded in 1363, when it was the Seidel Vaterstetter brewery. The two regular Franziskaner brews – Helles (light) and Dunkel (dark) – are both traditional unfiltered top-fermented wheat beers full of flavour. Wheat beers generally tend to be brewed with around 50% wheat and 50% malted barley, but unusually Franziskaner beers are brewed with 75% malted wheat.

Helles has a light fruity, spicy aroma which continues to dominate on the palate with a hint of cloves and bananas, while the Dunkel has a richer, fuller flavour with a creamy malt character and chocolate notes.

SPECIFICATIONS

Brewery: Spaten-Franziskaner-Bräu
Location: Munich, Bavaria
Style: Hefe-Weizen / Weissbier
Colour: Pale golden yellow
Alcohol: 5%
Serving temperature: 10°–12°C (50°–53.6°F)
Food: Lightly flavoured chicken

Spaten Premium Bock

Spaten's Original Munich light lager is its principal offering, but the brewery also produces two more characterful seasonal beers.

The first is an Oktoberfest beer brewed in the spring for the 'greatest folk festival in the world' – Spaten is one of the six breweries allowed to sell its beers at the official Oktoberfest in the Theresienweisen. Its other seasonal beer is the Premium Bock, a strong, lightly hopped, full-bodied malty beer brewed to celebrate the arrival of spring, when it is once again possible to enjoy sitting outside in a beer garden. Other occasional brews have included the Champagner Weisse, an original wheat beer first brewed in 1964 for the Oktoberfest.

SPECIFICATIONS

Brewery: Spaten-Franziskaner-Bräu
Location: Munich, Bavaria
Style: Bock
Colour: Deep golden yellow
Alcohol: 6.5%
Serving temperature: 8°–10°C (46.4°–50°F)
Food: Light snacks, such as peanuts and crisps

Spaten Original Munich Beer

Spaten was the first brewery in Munich to brew a Pilsner-style lager, which it launched in 1894 with the intention of exporting it to northern Germany, although it was soon made available to the local market.

This is the same beer sold today as Spaten Original Munich and has a delicately spicy aroma and a refreshing, light-bodied, mild flavour. Although its flagship beer is of such recent origin, the brewery is much older, dating back to 1397 when Hans Welser founded the Welser Prew brewery in Munich's Neuhausergasse. Over the next 125 years the brewery changed hands many times, before it entered a time of relative stability when, between 1522 and 1807, it was owned by three successive dynasties for extended periods. Of these the Spatt family, who were in charge from 1622 to 1704, from whose name the Spaten identity is derived (*Spaten* means 'spade' in German).

In 1807, the brewery was acquired by Gabriel Sedlmayer, master brewer to the royal court of Bavaria. At this time it was one of the smallest breweries in Munich, but by 1867, following a series of acquisitions and mergers, it had become the biggest, a position it retained until the 1890s. It became the biggest again in 1922 when it merged with the Franziskaner brewery, which had been owned by another branch of the Sedlmayer family. In 1997, having celebrated its 600th anniversary, the brewery merged with Löwenbräu.

SPECIFICATIONS

Brewery: Spaten-Franziskaner-Bräu
Location: Munich, Bavaria
Style: Pilsner
Colour: Clear golden yellow
Alcohol: 5.2%
Serving temperature: 6°–8°C (42.8°–46.4°F)
Food: Smoked salmon quiche

HB Münchner Kindl

The initials 'HB' stand for Hofbräuhaus and mark out this Munich institution as the official royal brewery. It was founded in 1589 by Wilhelm V, Duke of Bavaria. Until then, beers for the royal household were imported from Einbeck because those brewed in Munich were not deemed good enough.

Wilhelm's son and heir, Maximilian I, was not a fan of the brewery's brown ale, so in 1602 switched production to his preferred wheat beer.

At the same time, he banned all other breweries in Bavaria from producing wheat beer, establishing a monopoly for his own company that lasted nearly 200 years. Naturally, this had the effect of concentrating demand for wheat beer, so in 1607 the Duke built a new brewery on the town square that stands there to this day. Today, the brewery is owned by the Bavarian state and the classic wheat beer, which was revived in the 1970s, is known as HB Münchner Kindl and has a zesty, yeasty aroma and a refreshing fruity flavour. It is also available as a dark version called Schwarz Weissebier, for which the rather odd literal translation is 'Black Whitebeer'. It has a spritzy carbonation and a spicy flavour with hints of liquorice. The royal brewery was also behind the creation of Munich's famous Oktoberfest, a tradition that dates back to the marriage of Crown Prince Ludwig to Princess Therese of Saxony.

SPECIFICATIONS

Brewery: Staatliches Hofbräuhaus
Location: Munich, Bavaria
Style: Hefe-Weizen / Weissbier
Colour: Golden yellow
Alcohol: 5.1%
Serving temperature: 6°–8°C (42.8°–46.4°F)
Food: Poached or steamed white fish

Keiler Weissbier Dunkel

Lohr am Main is situated in the far northwestern corner of Bavaria, closer to Frankfurt than Munich, but the town still has a typically Bavarian character. So does its brewery, which has been run by the Stumpf family since 1878, when Pleikard Stumpf, great-grandfather of the current owner, bought the plant from Franz Stephan Vogt.

Stumpf brewery's Keiler Hell (light) wheat beer is a surprisingly complex beer with notes of bubblegum and cloves in the aroma, with background hints of lemon acidity. On the palate, the flavour is sharp and refreshing with a citrus character balanced by a touch of caramel sweetness, and the finish is intensely dry and bitter. Keiler Weissbier Dunkel, pictured here, is one of the more characterful examples of its style, presented in an appropriately individual bottle with a flip-top lid.

Vanilla, banana and bubblegum dominate the aroma, the scents being characteristic of the strain of yeast used by the brewery. On the palate, it has a smooth body and malty flavours of chocolate and caramel with underlying hints of vanilla. The brewery's range also features a lightly hopped beer with a smooth, sweet malty flavour, called Urtyp, which was first brewed in 1978 to celebrate the brewery's centenary.

SPECIFICATIONS

Brewery: Privatbrauerei Stumpf
Location: Lohr am Main, Bavaria
Style: Dunkel-Weizen / dark wheat beer
Colour: Dark red-brown
Alcohol: 4.9%
Serving temperature: 10°C (50°F)
Food: Apple strudel

Lohrer Pils

Lohrer Pils from the Stumpf family brewery is an authentic Pilsner in the traditional style, made with pale malts and a bottom-fermenting strain of yeast.

But above all it is the hops that characterise a classic Pilsner, and Lohrer Pils has hops in plentiful measure, giving it a fragrant herbal aroma and a refreshing bitterness on the palate. The brewery's extensive range also features a softer, sweeter, maltier Dortmunder Export lager with a satisfyingly full body, and a dark Märzen beer called Lohrer Schwarze, which was created in 1955 to mark three anniversaries: the 700th anniversary of the town of Lohr, the 600th anniversary of the St Maria Church, and the 50th year of the town's annual festival.

SPECIFICATIONS

Brewery: Privatbrauerei Stumpf
Location: Lohr am Main, Bavaria
Style: Pilsner
Colour: Golden yellow
Alcohol: 4.8%
Serving temperature: 8°C (46.4°F)
Food: Pasta dishes

Thurn und Taxis Pilsener

Thurn and Taxis were two royal families that merged in the mid-fifteenth century and owned two breweries, one in Regensburg, the other in a converted thirteenth-century convent in the nearby town of Schierling.

In the late nineteenth century, the brewery became the first in Bavaria to brew a Pilsner. It is a fine beer, with a fragrant hop aroma and a refreshingly dry, spicy, bitter flavour. In 1996, the brewery was acquired by Paulaner, and all brewing activities were concentrated on the Regensburg site, including the distinctive Roggen (rye beer), which has a spicy, slightly smoky flavour.

SPECIFICATIONS

Brewery: Thurn und Taxis
Location: Regensburg, Bavaria,
Style: Pilsner
Colour: Golden yellow
Alcohol: 4.9%
Serving temperature: 6°–8°C (42.8°–46.4°F)
Food: Pasta with hot, spicy sauce

Weihenstephaner

Reputedly the oldest brewery in the world, Weihenstephan is located in the university town of Freising, close to Munich in Bavaria.

It was founded in 1040 as the monastery brewery for the Benedictine monks, when Abbot Arnold obtained a licence to brew and sell beer. Over the years the monastery completely burned down four times and was ravaged on numerous other occasions by plagues, famines, wars and an earthquake. The monastery was dissolved in 1803 and ownership was passed over to the Bavarian state, although the brewery still stands on the same illustrious site on top of the Weihenstephan hill. Since 1852, it has also been home to the world's leading brewery school, where many of the world's leading brewers learned their craft.

As well as being one of the most traditional breweries in the world, it is also one of the most modern, with state-of-the-art technology in its brewing facilities. Today it produces a wide range of beers, including a mild-flavoured pale lager, which enjoys a long maturation period for a smoother flavour. It has a delicate floral aroma and a light, refreshing flavour with a dry, subtly hopped finish. Also in the range is a full-flavoured spicy, fruity Hefe-Weissbier with a naturally cloudy golden amber colour.

SPECIFICATIONS

Brewery: Brauerei Weihenstephan
Location: Freising
Style: Munich Helles lager
Colour: Slightly cloudy pale yellow
Alcohol: 5.1%
Serving temperature: 8°C (46.4°F)
Food: Rich, earthy soups and stews

Warsteiner Premium Verum

Warsteiner was founded more than 250 years ago and in many ways is a deeply traditional brewery, producing all of its beers in accordance with Germany's ancient Reinheitsgebot purity laws.

But Warsteiner also accommodates modern trends by presenting its classic Pilsner in a slim, long-necked bottle to suit the habit among young people of preferring to drink from the bottle rather than a glass. Premium Verum is an authentic Pilsner with a fragrant herbal hop aroma and a refreshingly dry and bitter flavour. It is also available in versions flavoured with cola, lemon and orange, as well as an alcohol-free version. The Warsteiner brewery also has sporting connections, sponsoring several prominent German football teams.

SPECIFICATIONS

Brewery: Warsteiner Brauerei
Location: Warstein, North Rhine-Westphalia
Style: Pilsner
Colour: Golden yellow
Alcohol: 4.8%
Serving temperature: 7°–8°C (44.6°–46.4°F)
Food: A stand-alone drink

Weltenburger

Founded in AD 610 by St Eustace, the Benedictine monastery of Weltenburg enjoys a spectacular location near the head of the Danube gorge.

It is not known when exactly the brewery was founded, but first recorded mention of it was made in 1050 – it is perhaps slightly younger than Weihenstephan; however, while that brewery became an independent business separate from the monastery in the nineteenth century, Weltenburg Brewery remains part of the monastery to this day. It produces a varied range of beers, including 'the oldest dark wheat beer in the world' and this pale version, which has a fresh, spicy yeast aroma and a well-rounded fruity flavour. Also in the range is Asam Bock, which is named after the baroque architects who redesigned the monastery in the eighteenth century.

SPECIFICATIONS

Brewery: Weltenburg Klosterbrauerei
Location: Kelheim, Bavaria
Style: Hefe-Weizen / Weissbier
Colour: Golden yellow
Alcohol: 5.4%
Serving temperature: 7°–8°C (44.6°–46.4°F)
Food: Fajitas

Wernesgrüner

Brewing arrived in the ancient town of Steinberg-Wernesgrün in 1436, when the Schorer brothers were granted brewing rights.

The town once had five breweries, but after World War II these were absorbed by the one remaining brewery, which then became Wernesgrüner. Although it is in many ways a deeply traditional brewery, it also proudly embraces modern technology. Unlike many breweries, it has just the one product, a classic Pilsner and a fine example of the style, with a big hop aroma and a mild, well-balanced flavour with malt and hops present in equal measure.

SPECIFICATIONS

Brewery: Wernesgrüner Brauerei GmbH
Location: Wernesgrün/ OT Steinberg, Saxony
Style: Pilsner
Colour: Pale golden yellow
Alcohol: 4.9%
Serving temperature: 7°–8°C (44.6°–46.4°F)
Food: Chicken tikka

Wieninger

The small picturesque Alpine town of Teisendorf is found in the far south of Germany, close to the border with neighbouring Austria.

The first recorded mention of a brewery in the town was made in the first year of the seventeenth century, when local brewer Tobias Shaidinger defaulted on tax payments which were due to the Principality of Salzburg. Eventually, in 1666, Count Guidobald of Salzburg bought the brewery and commissioned it to brew wheat beer for the royal household, which it did until 1810, when the region came into Bavarian control and the brewery was taken over by the Wieninger family. Wieninger currently brews a wide range of beers, including this traditional Bavarian unfiltered wheat ale, which has a yeasty aroma and a mildly bitter hop flavour.

SPECIFICATIONS

Brewery: Privatbrauerei Wieninger
Location: Teisendorf, Bavaria
Style: Hefe-Weizen / Weissbier
Colour: Cloudy golden yellow
Alcohol: 5.3%
Serving temperature: 6°–7°C (42.8°–44.6°F)
Food: Lentil casserole and warm bread

ABOVE

Italian wines are known the world over, but with the international spread of beers such as Peroni and Nastro Azzurro Italian skills in beer producing are steadily becoming recognised as well. The Italian brewers excel in making clean, classic pale lagers which are ideal for the easy-drinking café-bar lifestyle enjoyed by many Italian locals and visitors to Italy alike.

Italian Beers

Italy is predominantly a wine-producing country and ranks low among European countries for beer consumption. Nonetheless, certain areas of the country, particularly the north, have a strong brewing tradition, which stems from the Austrian influence exerted when the northern kingdoms of Italy were part of the mighty Hapsburg empire.

ABOVE
While wine may still predominate as the drink of choice for Italians, beer is quickly gaining in popularity among the younger and more style-conscious.

THE LOMBARDY AND VENETO REGIONS in particular saw a steady influx of Austrian merchants and businessmen who settled there and brought with them their native customs. But brewing remained a small-scale domestic activity until 1829, when Italy's first commercial brewery was established in Brescia by an Austrian, Peter Wührer. The dominant style of beer to this day is a typically Austrian easy-drinking, malty golden lager

By the end of the nineteenth century, there were around 100 commercial breweries in Italy. Then in the twentieth century large companies such as Peroni expanded, absorbing many smaller regional breweries and concentrating the brewing industry. By the 1980s, most of the major European brewers had entered the Italian market, with the Dutch giant Heineken in particular establishing a dominance over the domestic market. Carlsberg of Denmark bought Poretti, and Peroni established links with Kronenbourg of France.

While consumption is still relatively low, in recent years beer has become fashionable among younger Italians, with imported beers from England and Germany finding favour and microbreweries such as Le Baladin producing – and selling – more interesting artisanal products. Organisations such as the Slow Food movement are also having a positive influence, with many Italians rebelling against mass-produced industrial food. Despite the country's lowly status among beer-drinking nations, the future for beer in Italy is actually looking rather brighter than in many other countries with a stronger brewing tradition.

STATISTICS

Total production: 13,672,000 hectolitres (361,176,000 gallons) per year

Consumption per capita: 29 litres (8 gallons) per year

Famous breweries: Birra Peroni Industriale; Castello di Udine; Dreher; Pedavena; Poretti; Spezialbier-Brauerei Forst; Theresianer Alte Brauerei Triest

Famous brands: Birra Moretti; Crystall Peroni; Forst Sixtus; Nastro Azzurro; Pedavena; Peroni Gran Reserva; Splügen

Le Baladin Super

Super was the first beer created by Le Baladin ('The Troubadour') when owner Teo Musso Materino began brewing at his historic pub in the village of Piozzo in 1996.

Materino learned the craft of brewing in Belgium, and Super is a top-fermented 'doppio malto' (double malt) ale inspired by Belgian abbey beers. It is characterised by an intense floral aroma with apricot, ripe banana and bitter almond notes, and has a well-balanced flavour with hints of apricot and citrus fruits. It was awarded the title of Best Italian Ale on its first appearance at the Great British Beer Festival in 2000. Le Baladin also produces a range of products called Kikke Baladin, made from its beers, including a beer jelly to serve with cheeses and cold meats.

SPECIFICATIONS

Brewery: Le Baladin
Location: Piozzo, Piedmont
Style: Belgian abbey double
Colour: Amber
Alcohol: 8%
Serving temperature: 10°–12°C (50°–53.6°F)
Food: Cheeses and pastries

Le Baladin Wayan

The small village of Piozzo where Le Baladin is based lies at the heart of northwestern Italy's Le Langhe wine-growing region, close to the place from which the famous Barolo wines originate.

It is unusual among Italian breweries in that it produces only top-fermented ales. Particularly unusual is this organic beer (the first in Italy) brewed in the style of a Belgian Saison, a light, refreshing wheat beer brewed to drink in the summer. It has a soft aroma with notes of chamomile, bergamot and other citrus fruits, while a carefully selected blend of spices, including coriander, gives it a gently peppery flavour, along with a sharp hoppy bitterness.

SPECIFICATIONS

Brewery: Le Baladin
Location: Piozzo, Piedmont
Style: Belgian Saison
Colour: Pale golden straw colour
Alcohol: 5.8%
Serving temperature: 8°–10°C (46.4°–50°F)
Food: Excellent as an aperitif, or with fish or salads

Crystall Peroni

One of the most recognisable Italian premium beer brands both in Italy and abroad, Crystall Peroni is a refreshing golden lager brewed with a selected blend of malts and aromatic hops to create a beer with both a subtle aroma and a harmonious, delicate malt flavour.

Crystall Peroni is part of the 'Winning' range of premium beers from Peroni, but it also produces a range of everyday 'Picnic' beers, including its flagship Birra Peroni, which is the most popular beer brand in Italy, renowned for its sparkling character and fresh, well-balanced flavour of hops and malt.

SPECIFICATIONS

Brewery: Birra Peroni Industriale
Location: Rome, Lazio
Style: Lager
Colour: Golden yellow
Alcohol: 5.6%
Serving temperature: 7°–9°C (44.6°–48.2°F)
Food: Bread and cheese

Itala Pilsen

This classic clear golden Pilsner possesses a characteristically dry, bitter hop flavour and aroma.

It is the leading beer brand in the northwest of Italy and was originally produced by the Cappellari brewery of Padua, one of the leading independent Italian breweries of the nineteenth century that later absorbed several smaller breweries so that by 1916 it had become the fourth-largest brewing group in Italy. In the 1970s Cappellari was itself absorbed by the Peroni group, which was at the time the largest brewer in Italy, although the Itala Pilsen brand was retained as a regional speciality.

SPECIFICATIONS

Brewery: Birra Peroni Industriale
Location: Rome, Lazio
Style: Pilsner
Colour: Golden yellow
Alcohol: 4.7%
Serving temperature: 9°–10°C (48.2°–50°F)
Food: Grilled white meat or fish

Nastro Azzurro

The name Nastro Azzurro means 'blue ribbon', which signifies the status of this beer as the leading premium beer brand in Italy, as well as one of the best-known Italian beer brands outside the country.

It claimed this position following an extensive and elaborate rebranding operation in 2002, which saw the introduction of new state-of-the-art brewing equipment and the smartening up of the labels with metallic effect paper. It also benefits from an association with the Italian world motorcycling champion Valentino Rossi, as well as other sporting connections such as golf and sailing. The beer itself is a typically light, refreshing, spritzy Italian lager, with a slightly higher alcohol content than average. It is brewed with a blend of speciality malts made from superior spring-sown barley.

Nastro Azzurro was first brewed in the 1960s, although the Peroni brewery, named after its founder Francesco Peroni, was established in 1846 in the small town of Vigevano, close to Milan in northern Italy. It soon expanded and moved the bulk of its production to Rome, then spread out across Italy taking over many other smaller breweries, finally merging with Wührer in 1988, since when it has concentrated its brewing into a handful of smaller plants in Rome, Padua, Naples and Bari. Until 1996 it was the largest brewer in Italy, but was then overtaken by the merger of Dreher and Moretti, both owned by Heineken.

SPECIFICATIONS

Brewery: Birra Peroni Industriale
Location: Rome, Lazio
Style: Lager
Colour: Pale straw yellow
Alcohol: 5.2%
Serving temperature: 7°–9°C (44.6°–48.2°F)
Food: Liver paté, cured meats, dried sausages

Peroni Gran Riserva

Peroni Gran Riserva was launched in 1996 to mark the 150th anniversary of the Peroni brewery and won major awards at the International Beer & Cider Competition in 1999 and the Brewing Industry International Awards in 2000. It is presented in an elegant bottle with a gilt label bearing the picture of the brewery's founder, Giovanni Peroni, and is reputedly based on a recipe devised by Peroni himself. It is classified as a 'doppio malto' (double malt) beer, brewed broadly in the style of a German Maibock (May bock), the strong, pale amber lager which is brewed to celebrate the arrival of spring, although Peroni's version is available all year round.

It is made using exclusively Pilsner malts, which give the beer its characteristic deep golden colour, and is brewed using the complex double decoction mash process to draw off as much fermentable material as possible, before being aromatised with Saaz hops, then matured for two months. The finished product is a well-rounded, delicately balanced beer with a nutty, fruity malt character and an exceptionally smooth, firm body with light carbonation adding a spritzy touch. A slightly sweet malt flavour dominates on the palate, giving way to a late bite of hop bitterness in a crisp, clean finish with an alcoholic dryness.

SPECIFICATIONS

Brewery: Birra Peroni Industriale
Location: Rome, Lazio
Style: Maibock
Colour: Deep golden yellow
Alcohol: 6.6%
Serving temperature: 9°C (48.2°F)
Food: Savoury pork dishes, soft cheeses

Raffo

The Raffo brewery was founded in 1919 in the town of Taranto by Vintantonio Raffo, who wanted to provide the southern Mediterranean region of Italy with a brewery to rival those found in the north.

It was a popular move and Raffo beer, a classic golden lager with a fresh, hoppy aroma and a moderately bitter hop flavour, soon became established as a popular regional brand. The brewery was taken over by Peroni in 1961, but Raffo beer was maintained in the Peroni repertoire and is still the most popular beer in southern Italy.

SPECIFICATIONS

Brewery: Birra Peroni Industriale
Location: Rome, Lazio
Style: Lager
Colour: Golden yellow
Alcohol: 4.7%
Serving temperature: 8°–9°C (46.4°–48.2°F)
Food: Seafood, particularly shellfish or octopus, or grilled tuna

Wührer

This light, hoppy Pilsner has a gently herby aroma and a slightly sweet flavour leading to a dry finish.

Although the brand is currently owned by Peroni, Wührer has a strong claim to have been the first major commercial brewery in Italy, having been founded in Brescia, northeastern Italy, in 1829 by an Austrian called Peter Wührer. At the time, the Lombardy-Veneto region was part of the Hapsburg empire and was home to many Austrian immigrants. Although the area became part of the independent kingdom of Italy in 1866, beer remained popular among the local population, with Wührer maintaining its independence until 1988.

SPECIFICATIONS

Brewery: Birra Peroni Industriale
Location: Rome, Lazio
Style: Pilsner
Colour: Golden yellow
Alcohol: 4.7%
Serving temperature: 9°–10°C (48.2°–50°F)
Food: Bread with cold cooked ham, pizza

Birra Moretti La Rossa

One of the most characterful beers from Italy, Moretti La Rossa has a name meaning 'the red one', appropriately enough for its ruby red hues, which arise from the use of Vienna malt, so called after the distinctive style of beers that became popular in that city in the nineteenth century. However, it is actually classified as a 'doppio malto' (double malt) beer, brewed in the style of a German 'doppelbock' (double bock), the strong beers brewed for drinking in the spring. La Rossa has a rich, sweet aroma with notes of caramel and toffee, while on the palate it has a thick, creamy texture and a full, robust flavour with a sweet, buttery caramel malt character tempered by hints of bitter chocolate.

Its relatively high alcohol content gives it a spicy, mouth-drying finish. La Rossa was originally brewed by Moretti, which was established by Luigi Moretti in 1859 in the city of Friuli, north of Venice. The brewery remained in the ownership of the Moretti family for more than 100 years, but recently changed hands, becoming part of the Italian division of the extensive Heineken group, and was renamed Castello di Udine. Despite the changes, Heineken is commited to maintaining the historic brewery and continuing to produce its traditional range of beers.

SPECIFICATIONS

Brewery: Castello di Udine
Location: Udine, Friuli-Venezia Giulia
Style: Doppelbock
Colour: Bright amber red
Alcohol: 7.2%
Serving temperature: 9°C (48.2°F)
Food: The classic beer to serve with pizza

Birra Moretti Sans Souci

Sans Souci, which comes from the French meaning 'without a care', is the name given by the Castello brewery of Udine to its range of lagers aimed at younger drinkers, but which maintains traditional qualities in its production methods that are the hallmarks of this historic brewery.

It is very typical of the style of pale, golden lager that dominates the market in Italy and has an aroma characterised by a light, grainy maltiness with a hint of hops in the background, while on the palate the slightly sweet malt is balanced by a gentle herby hop flavour and a fine, light body with a gently spritzy carbonation. As well as regular Sans Souci, there are Sans Souci Ice and Sans Souci Export. The latter is brewed in the style of a Dortmunder Export, with a fuller flavour in which toasty malts dominate, balanced with a honeyed sweetness and a hint of dry, bitter hops. Sans Souci Ice is partially frozen before maturation, and some of the ice crystals removed, to give it a smoother body and a crisp, clean, dry flavour. The Moretti range also includes an all-malt premium lager called Baffo d'Oro, which has a citrussy yeast aroma and a satisfyingly malty flavour balanced by a pleasant hop bitterness. More unusual is its Birra Friulana, a pale golden wheat beer with a fresh, zesty aroma and a sharp, refreshing flavour with the characteristic wheat sourness.

SPECIFICATIONS

Brewery: Castello di Udine
Location: Udine, Friuli-Venezia Giulia
Style: Lager
Colour: Golden yellow
Alcohol: 5.6%
Serving temperature: 5°–7°C (41°–44.6°F)
Food: Traditional cotecchino sausage with lentils

Dreher

The first Dreher brewery was founded in Vienna in 1773 by Franz Anton Dreher, who was a member of a Bohemian family that had been brewing since the seventeenth century.

The company expanded to Italy in 1865, opening a brewery in Trieste in the north of the country. In 1974, it was taken over by the Dutch brewing group Heineken, becoming the first piece in the Heineken Italia jigsaw. Its flagship beer is a classic golden lager with a light hoppy aroma and a smooth, well-balanced flavour with a dry, slightly bitter character.

SPECIFICATIONS

Brewery: Dreher
Location: Milan, Lombardy
Style: Lager
Colour: Golden yellow
Alcohol: 4.7%
Serving temperature: 5°–7°C (41°–44.6°F)
Food: Chicken and mozzarella salad

Menabrea 150 Anniversario

First brewed in 1996 to celebrate the 150th anniversary of the brewery, this is a straightforward easy-drinking lager with a well-balanced flavour of malt and hops.

It comes from Menabrea, which proudly considers itself a Sardinian, rather than Italian, brewery. It was founded in 1846 by the brothers Gian Battista and Antonio Caraccio, who then sold it in 1854 to Jean Joseph Menabrea and Anton Zimmerman. The pair were already partners in the Zimmerman brewery in Aosta; by 1872, Zimmerman had returned to Aosta, leaving the partnership in the hands of Menabrea and his sons, since when it has gone on to become the largest brewer in Sardinia.

Brewery: Menabrea
Location: Biella, Sardinia
Style: Lager
Colour: Deep golden yellow
Alcohol: 4.8%
Serving temperature: 6°–8°C (42.8°–46.4°F)
Food: White meats and light-flavoured cheeses

Splügen

Towards the end of the 1980s, the Poretti brewery launched an aggressive marketing campaign to promote its historical Splügen range of speciality beers, which it had been brewing since 1902.

Over the course of three years, Splügen grew by around 40%, making it one of the leading premium beer brands in Italy. The growth was due not only to the intelligent advertising campaign or the introduction of innovative packaging (Splügen beers were among the first to be sold in bottles with screw-off caps), but also to the quality of its flagship beer, a classic golden Pilsner-style lager with a light grainy malt aroma and a herbal, bitter hop flavour. Poretti also brews a slightly stronger pale golden beer called Poretti Premium. More interesting, however, are its pair of bottom-fermented strong bock-style beers called Bock 1877 – Chiara (dark) and Rossa (red) – which were launched in 1961.

The success of Splügen was responsible for re-establishing Poretti, founded in 1877, as one of the leading independent breweries in Italy. It is still based in its original home town of Induno Olona, close to Varese, to the north of Milan in the Lombardy region of Italy, although it is no longer independent, having been taken over by Carlsberg of Denmark.

SPECIFICATIONS

Brewery: Poretti
Location: Induno Olona, Varese, Lombardy
Style: Pilsner
Colour: Golden yellow
Alcohol: 4.5%
Serving temperature: 7°–8°C (44.6°–46.4°F)
Food: Spicy snack dishes such as pizza

Pedavena

This golden Pilsner was first brewed by the Pedavena brewery in 1897, the year the brewery was established by the Luciani family.

It is a well-balanced beer with a fine hop aroma and a delicate hop bitterness on the palate. Located in the town of Trento, Pedavena brewery is named after the picturesque region north of Verona in the foothills of the Dolomite mountains. Since the mid-1970s, Pedavena has been part of the Dutch-owned Heineken Italia brewing group. The brewery also produces a refreshing, full-flavoured, amber-coloured, Bavarian-style 'Weizen' (wheat beer), as well as various seasonal and special occasion beers.

SPECIFICATIONS

Brewery: Pedavena
Location: Trento, Trentino-Alto Adige
Style: Pilsner
Colour: Deep golden yellow
Alcohol: 5%
Serving temperature: 4°–6°C (39.2°–42.8°F)
Food: Grilled tuna steaks

Forst Kronen

The village of Lagundo lies to the west of Merano in the mountainous Alto Adige (southern Tirol) region of the far north of Italy, an area that has historically been influenced very strongly by Austria.

This influence is notably apparent in the beers of the Forst brewery, which derives its name from the German for 'forest' and is owned by the Fuchs family, who are of Austrian descent. Forst Kronen (Kronen being from the German for 'crown') is characteristic of the typical golden style of lager popular in Vienna, with a rich, malty flavour and a light use of hops to provide balance and a refreshingly dry, gently bitter finish.

SPECIFICATIONS

Brewery: Spezialbier-Brauerei Forst
Location: Lagundo, Trentino-Alto Adige
Style: Lager
Colour: Golden yellow
Alcohol: 5.2%
Serving temperature: 8°C (46.4°F)
Food: Smoked sausages and cured meats

Forst Sixtus

First brewed in 1901, and still brewed to exactly the same recipe more than 100 years later, Forst Sixtus is a 'doppio malto' (double malt) beer named in honour of Saint Sixtus, whose statue stands in a church in Munich, Bavaria, where the Doppelbock style originates.

It has a sweet, malty aroma with brown sugar notes and a hint of peaty smokiness characteristic of the dark roasted malts used in the brewing. On the palate it has a thick, full-bodied, mouth-coating texture with sweet, earthy caramel malt flavours leading giving way to increasingly dominant hop bitterness in a long, lingering finish. Forst brews a varied range of beers, all with Austrian influences, including Forst VIP, which was first brewed in 1967 to commemorate the sixtieth birthday of the brewery's owner, Luis Fuchs, who was at the time president of the village of Lagundo. It is a classic Pilsner-style golden lager (the name stands for Very Important Pils) with a fine hoppy aroma and a refreshingly bitter hop flavour. Completing the brewery's line-up is Forst Premium, a well-balanced golden lager, which has been brewed to the same recipe since the second half of the nineteenth century and was originally known as Forster Bayrisch (Bavarian Forest). Although Forst is not a particularly large brewery, it is well known throughout Italy thanks to its enthusiastic sponsorship of sports.

SPECIFICATIONS

Brewery: Spezialbier-Brauerei Forst

Location: Lagundo, Trentino-Alto Adige

Style: Doppelbock

Colour: Dark chestnut brown

Alcohol: 6.5%

Serving temperature: 10°–12°C (50°–53.6°F)

Food: Light, nutty flavoured desserts such as almond tart

Theresianer Pale Ale

Now based in Treviso, Theresianer was established in 1766 in the cosmopolitan port city of Trieste in the far northeastern corner of Italy and takes its name from the Borgo Teresiano district of the city, which itself was named in honour Princess Maria Theresa, Empress of Austria.

Its founder was a Mr Lenz, an Austrian who arrived in the city to supply beer to the large population of Austrian merchants and businessmen. Despite the Austrian connections, Theresianer pale ale is a typically English beer of the type made popular in the mid-nineteenth century, characterised by a fruity yeast aroma and a well-balanced flavour with a refreshing hop bitterness.

SPECIFICATIONS

Brewery: Theresianer Alte Brauerei Triest
Location: Treviso, Veneto
Style: English pale ale
Colour: Amber yellow
Alcohol: 6.5%
Serving temperature: 8°C (46.4°F)
Food: Rabbit in a tomato and white wine sauce

Theresianer Vienna

This classic red Vienna-style lager has been brewed in Trieste since the start of the twentieth century. It has a smooth, easy-drinking character with a mild flavour that carefully balances malt and hops.

The Theresianer brewery produces a wide range of traditional beer styles, including a classic bottom-fermented golden Pilsner, a Bavarian-style Weizen (wheat beer), and a strong amber ale with a potent hop flavour. The symbol of the brewery, depicted on the labels of the bottles, is the Barbour lighthouse, which is also the symbol of the city of Trieste where the brewery was originally based, although it has now moved to new premises in nearby Treviso.

SPECIFICATIONS

Brewery: Theresianer Alte Brauerei Triest
Location: Treviso, Veneto
Style: Vienna lager
Colour: Copper red
Alcohol: 5.3%
Serving temperature: 8°C (46.4°F)
Food: Chocolate-based desserts

ABOVE

Kaiser Bier is Austria's best-selling lager, and is a fairly typical light Pilsner of 5% abv. Although Kaiser's alcohol content is similar to most mainstream European lagers, many Austrian beers are formidably powerful, typically ranging from 7% to 12% abv and beyond. The skill in making such potent beers is to ensure that the strength of alcohol does not overwhelm flavour or aroma.

Austrian Beers

Beers are brewed in Austria in a wide range of styles and, in many of the smaller breweries, with a good deal of skill and care. Overall, the country has 65 to 70 breweries, with the number having slightly increased in recent years due to the establishment of a few microbreweries and several brewpubs. While still to undergo the sort of new brewery revolution under way in the United States and the United Kingdom, the trend is still encouraging.

ABOVE

In every tent at an Austrian beer festival you will find 12 very strong men or women carrying steins of beer, which can contain up to 3 litres.

THE GREATEST CONCENTRATION IS in Oberösterreich, which has almost a third of the total. It borders Bavaria and has many historical and cultural links with this region, and as a consequence it is here that the strongest Austrian beer tradition is to be found, together with the biggest concentration of of local and regional breweries. In the eastern and southern parts of the country there are fewer producers, and they tend to be larger and more industrial in character – although both Vienna and Graz have recently established brewpubs.

The wide range of styles of beer encompasses most of those from South Germany, although often with subtle differences. There are also a couple which are specific to Austria, although there are no real examples of the classic Vienna amber lager, developed by Anton Dreher in the nineteenth century. Beers are only considered full-strength if brewed to at least 12% plato. Average beer strengths must be among the highest in the world, with almost nothing under 5% and beers of more than 4% labelled as 'leicht', or light.

Austrian beer has long played second fiddle to German beer in terms of reputation. This situation is unfair, and many Austrian beers are more than capable of competing with those across the border in terms of quality. While the strong pale lagers are certainly popular, there are many other more idiosyncratic Austrian styles such the unfiltered Keller or Zwickl beers, which are rewarding and interesting beers.

STATISTICS

Total production: 8,891,000 hectolitres (234,875,000 gallons) per year

Consumption per capita: 107 litres (28 gallons) per year

Famous breweries: Brau Union Österreich; Brauerei Schwechat; Brauerei Zipf; Fohrenburger; Hirter Brauerei; Ottakringer

Famous brands: Fohrenburger No.1; Gold Fassel; Hirter Privat Pils; Kaiser; Schwechater Zwick

Eggenberg Urbock 23

The Salzkammergut region of Austria is famous for its beautiful scenery of lakes, mountains and forests. At the heart of this region, at the foot of the Traunstein mountain close to the village of Vorchdorf, is Eggenberg Castle, overlooking a crystal-clear blue lake and rolling meadows.

Schloss Eggenburg is the oldest family-owned brewery in Austria. A castle has stood on this site since the tenth century, possibly even earlier, and the brewery goes back at least to the twelfth century. At that time, the castle was owned by a local order of monks. The brewery has been a commercial operation since 1681, and was taken over in the late eighteenth century by the ancestors of the current owners, the Stohr family, and was rebuilt in the nineteenth century after a fire.

Alhough the brewery has been much modernised and extended in recent years, its beers are still brewed in the traditional way, using the pure, clear waters from the castle's own spring, and matured in the castle cellars for as long as necessary. Eggenburg Urbock 23 is lagered for nine months. It has a smooth, creamy texture with a spicy citrus fruit aroma and flavour. The number 23 refers to the traditional method of measuring the strength of the beer based on its original gravity (how much fermentable material it contains). Even stronger, at around 14% abv, is Samichlaus, formerly brewed by Hurlimann of Switzerland, a beer that is brewed only once a year on 6 December and matured for 10 months.

SPECIFICATIONS

Brewery: Schloss Eggenberg
Location: Vorchdorf
Style: Double bock
Colour: Golden amber
Alcohol: 9.6%
Serving temperature: 9°–10°C (48.2°–50°F)
Food: Fruit-based desserts

Fohrenburger No. 1

Fohrenburg brewery was founded in the town of Bludenz in western Austria in 1881 by bar owner Ferdinand Gassner in order to fulfil a promise to provide his customers with good-quality beer. Immediately a success, he was already expanding the brewery within half a year of its opening, and today Fohrenburger is one of Austria's largest brewers, producing 33 million litres of beer every year, with brewing sites throughout the country, as well as in Switzerland and northern Italy. Fohrenburger also produces a wide range of fruit juices, soft drinks and spirits in addition to its extensive selection of 15 speciality beers.

Fohrenburger No. 1, also known as Jubiläum, is a strong seasonal beer brewed every spring to commemorate the brewery's anniversary, with a smooth, creamy texture and a crisp, clean, spicy hop flavour with a soft malt background. Other beers in the range include Fohrenburger Goldmärzen 1881, which is a full-bodied golden beer brewed to an original recipe as old as the brewery itself; a 7.2% abv pale golden Oktoberfest beer in the traditional Munich style; and a strong dark bock brewed with dark and caramel malts for a deep brown colour and a smooth, full-bodied malt flavour. The range also includes Kellerbier, an unfiltered lager with a spicy, yeasty aroma and flavour.

SPECIFICATIONS

Brewery: Fohrenburger
Location: Bludenz
Style: Bock
Colour: Golden yellow
Alcohol: 5.5%
Serving temperature: 10°C (50°F)
Food: Smoked ham and cured meats

Ratsherrn Trunk

Brewing has been taking place in the ancient city of Freistadt since Duke Rudolph IV granted the citizens of the town the right to brew their own beer in 1363.

In 1770, construction of a brewery was started on the outskirts of the town, to be jointly owned by the 149 households of the town and the municipal authorities, supplying beer to those households, each with a share measured as a number of buckets. This was the start of what is now known as the Bräucommune in Freistadt and as such is the oldest registered company of its kind in Europe. Its beers are still brewed using the soft water from the town's St Peter's well, hops from the local Muehlviertel region and Bavaria, and malts made from barley grown by the Zistersdorf community farmers.

The brewery produces a range of seven different beers, of which the best known is Ratsherrn Trunk, the name of which means 'drunken town councillor'. It is a described as a 'vollbier' (full beer), which is a German categorisation of beer according to strength and indicates a darkish red-gold lager with a high level of hops and a full flavour that balances hop bitterness with malt sweetness. Ratsherrn Trunk is a fine example of the style with a rich, full-bodied flavour. The brewery also produces a seasonal Weihnachtsbock (Christmas bock), a Munich-style Märzen, a soft, mild, low-strength beer called Midium, and Austria's only Rauchbier (smoke beer).

SPECIFICATIONS

Brewery: Bräucommune in Freistadt
Location: Freistadt
Style: Vollbier
Colour: Dark red
Alcohol: 5.3%
Serving temperature: 8°–10°C (46.4°–50°F)
Food: Spicy stews such as Hungarian goulash

Hirter Privat Pils

The Hirter brewery in the Karnten region of Austria, close to the historical castle city of Friesach, claims to be able to trace its origins all the way back to 1270, when it was the house brewery for the Taverna Ze Hurde in the small town of Hirt; the Braukeller bar is still operating in the town today. Hirter beers are brewed according to traditional methods and never pasteurised, instead using cold filtration to purify the end product, which ensures that the characteristic flavours of the beer are retained.

The brewery's flagship beer is its Privat Pils, produced according to an old Bohemian recipe and matured for a lengthy period to give it a smooth, well-rounded flavour with a subtle but distinct hop character, as opposed to the German style of Pilsner which has a more prominent hop profile. Hirter also produces a wide range of other beer styles. These include a dark beer called Morchl, made with dark brown and caramel malts and plenty of hops for a well-balanced easy-drinking flavour; an old-fashioned copper-coloured ale called Hirter 1270; and a naturally cloudy golden Weizen (wheat beer) made with organic wheat and hops and having a fresh, yeasty banana aroma with a clean wheat flavour on the palate. Another organic product is Hirter Biobier, made to a traditional recipe for a soft fruity malt flavour. The brewery has also created a hop-flavoured eau de vie called Braumeisterbrand.

SPECIFICATIONS

Brewery: Hirter Brauerei
Location: Hirt, Karnten
Style: Pilsner
Colour: Golden
Alcohol: 5.2%
Serving temperature: 8°C (46.4°F)
Food: Spiced lamb meatballs

Kaiser

Austria's largest brewing group started out in 1921 with the foundation of the Braubank AG, formed by the merger of several smaller regional breweries.

The group has continued to grow throughout the twentieth century by acquiring other breweries across Austria, so that today its beers account for around 33% of the Austrian domestic beer-drinking market. The main brewery is based in Linz, but has several other sites across the country that produce various regional beer brands, including Falkenstein, Göss, Kaltenhausen, Puntigam, Schwechat, Wieselberg and Zipf. Its flagship product is Kaiser Draught, the number-one-selling beer in Austria. It is a golden lager with a fruity aroma, hints of orange and a well-balanced flavour that starts off predominantly sweet and malty, but has a long dry bitter hop finish. There is also a Premium Pils with a more prominent hop profile in the aroma and a fuller, maltier flavour with hints of smoky whisky and walnuts, leading to a crisp, refreshing bitter finish. The Kaiser range also includes the complex Fasstyp with hints of pineapple balanced with floral hop notes; the fruity, spicy Goldquell with aromas of apples, pears and citrus, and a soft malty flavour balanced with a gentle hop bitterness; and the red-brown sweetly malty Doppelmalz. Among the brewery's other beer ranges are the Schladminger speciality beers from the hop-growing Styria region which are made with 100% organic ingredients.

SPECIFICATIONS

Brewery: Brau Union Österreich
Location: Linz
Style: Lager
Colour: Golden yellow
Alcohol: 5%
Serving temperature: 7°–9°C (44.6°–48.2°F)
Food: Grilled swordfish or tuna steaks

Goldfassl

The Ottakringer brewery was founded in Vienna by Heinrich Plank in 1837, taking its name from the part of the town where it was located. It was bought by the cousins Ignaz and Jacob Kuffner in 1850 and began to establish itself as one of the town's leading brewers, until it became a corporation in 1905 under the leadership of Ignaz's son Moritz. As a Jew, Moritz and the brewery suffered under Nazi rule in Austria, and the brewery was sold in 1939 to Gustav Harmer. The Kuffner family emigrated to the United States. Today, Ottakringer maintains an identity as Vienna's local brewer and is its largest remaining independent beer producing business.

Harmer introduced Goldfassl Pilsner to the brewery's range in 1967, making it the first Pilsner to be brewed in Austria. It is a light, easy-drinking beer with a fresh, floral hop aroma and a well-balanced malt flavour. The brewery also produces another stronger beer under the Goldfassl label, called Goldfassl Spezial, with a full malty flavour leading to an increasingly dry, bitter finish. The brewery's standard range of beers under the Ottakringer label include Helles, a pale Munich-style Märzen lager with a delicate, well-balanced flavour, and Dunkles, a traditional dark Vienna lager with a distinctive reddish colour and a soft, malty flavour.

SPECIFICATIONS

Brewery: Ottakringer
Location: Vienna
Style: Pilsner
Colour: Deep golden yellow
Alcohol: 4.6%
Serving temperature: 9°C (48.2°F)
Food: Roast chicken or pork

Schwechater Zwickl

Zwickl is unfiltered, unpasteurised beer, and the Schwechat version is a characteristically cloudy golden yellow with a smooth, easy-drinking flavour and a fresh hop aroma.

The Schwechat brewery also produces a traditional Vienna lager with a fruity malt character, and a beer called Hopfenperle, which has a rich, complex and intensely hoppy flavour and aroma. Schwechat is one of the oldest breweries in Austria and can trace its origins back more than 350 years, to its foundation in 1632 as the Klein-Schwechat brewery. In 1760, an ambitious waiter from Vienna named Franz Anton Dreher bought the lease on the Ober-Lanzendorf brewery, adding a second brewery to his business in 1782, then acquiring the Klein-Schwechat brewery in 1796 for the price of 19,000 Gülden, along with the brewery's attached farm. The brewery was later taken over by Franz's son Anton, who learned the craft of brewing during spells in Munich and England.

The brewery started producing a bottom-fermented lager in 1841, bringing it to Vienna, where Klein-Schwechater Lagerbier was taken up with enthusiasm by the beer-drinking population. The style of beer he created later became known as Vienna lager, and was made using a distinctive reddish malt that came to be known as Vienna malt. Following death of the last member of the Dreher family in 1921, the brewery was sold to the group that later became the Brau Union Österreich, while the Dreher name is now a brand owned by Heineken.

SPECIFICATIONS

Brewery: Brauerei Schwechat
Location: Schwechat
Style: Zwickelbier
Colour: Golden yellow
Alcohol: 5.4%
Serving temperature: 8°C (46.4°F)
Food: Pasta, rice dishes, sandwiches

Zipfer Urtyp (Original)

In 1858, the Hoffman brewery was acquired by Viennese banker Franz Schaup, and over the next five years increased its output until it was producing 10 times as much beer as when Schaup took over. The brewery closed down shortly before World War II, but was revived in the 1950s by Fritz Kretz, the great-grandson of the founder, with the successful marketing slogan 'Ein Glas heller Freude' ('A glass of clear joy'). Since 1993, Zipfer has been part of the massive Austrian brewery group Brau Union Österreich.

However, the brewery continues to produce its own beers as an independent brewing operation, and they are among the most characterful beers from the group. Zipfer Urtyp (Original in English) is a full-flavoured strong golden lager with a fragrant herbal hop aroma balanced by a fruity malt character. On the palate, it has a soft, smooth body and an initial gentle sweetness, which leads to a crisp, refreshingly dry hop finish. The brewery's full range extends to eight different beers, including a strong, pale-coloured Pils with a vigorously hoppy character, a Munich-style Märzen, and a pair of full-flavoured seasonal bock-style beers – a Christmas version named Stefanibock and a contrasting version for Easter called Josefibock.

SPECIFICATIONS

Brewery: Brauerei Zipf
Location: Zipf
Style: Lager
Colour: Golden yellow
Alcohol: 5.4%
Serving temperature: 7°–9°C (44.6°–48.2°F)
Food: Delicately flavoured fish dishes or a light herby risotto

ABOVE

Czech drinkers enjoy their beer in a pavement café. The Czech brewing industry went through some tough times in the twentieth century under the effects of two world wars and the communist takeover. However, in recent times it has reclaimed its reputation for lagers of the highest quality, and the Czech Republic is now a huge beer exporter, as well as producing beers for domestic consumption.

Czech Beers

A great deal has changed in the Czech brewing world since the collapse of the communist bloc. The industry has been completely transformed by brewery closures, new technology and foreign takeovers, and not all of these changes have turned out to be for the better.

ABOVE

Beer drinking could be classed as a national pastime in the Czech Republic, and the country's drinkers are passionate about the quality of their beers.

NO ONE CAN DENY that the quality of Czech-brewed lager is still arguably the highest in the world, and that the choice of styles is excellent. Even in a large city such as Prague, where there are several large local breweries, there is a good choice of beer from the whole of the republic. There has been criticism, however, that the quality of the Czech lagers has slipped since the industry became privatised and the old 'family' breweries were snapped up by big international concerns. In Prague, for instance, the three large breweries – Staropramen, Braník and Mestan – were in a single group, Prazské Pivovary, and had the same owner. In November 1996, when the owner increased its shareholding to 51%, that owner was the British firm Bass. When Bass decided to get out of brewing, the breweries passed to the Belgian multinational Interbrew.

The Czech brewing industry today can draw upon the country's ancient traditions of beer making. The production of hops in Bohemia is recorded as far back as AD 859, and the first Czech brewery was established at Cerhenice in 1118. The strength of the industry grew rapidly and became increasingly important to the country's infrastructure – by the early sixteenth century some towns were generating as much 80% of their municipal income from beer production. Moreover, export sales of both beer and prized Bohemian hops were booming by the end of the Middle Ages. The fortunes of Czech beer dipped during the devastating years of the Thirty Years War (1618–48) and only pulled back during the nineteenth century. The twentieth century brought more years of war and the post–World War II communist takeover, and the communist regime 'promoted' beer by making it exceptionally cheap – although the quality declined in many instances. Since the collapse of European communism in the late 1980s, Czech beer has undergone a resurgence and has regained its worldwide reputation for quality.

STATISTICS

Total production: 18,548,000 hectolitres (489,986,000 gallons) per year

Consumption per capita: 159 litres (42 gallons) per year

Famous breweries: Budejovicky Budvar; Lobkowicz; Pilsner Urquell; Pivovar Staropramen Prazské Pivovary

Famous brands: Budweiser Budvar; Lobkowicz Special; Pilsner Urquell; Staropramen

Budweiser Budvar

Budweiser Budvar, from the southern Czech town of Budejovice, is a strong golden lager with a light, smooth flavour that has more of a malty character than the classic Pilsners from the town of Pilsen in the country's north.

It is brewed using Saaz hops, Moravian barley malt and water from the brewery's own artesian wells, and matured in traditional horizontal lagering tanks for 60 days. Not to be confused with the Budweiser beer produced by the American brewer Anheuser-Busch, Budweiser Budvar takes its name from Budweis, the German form of Budejovice, the Budvar brewery's home town in the Czech Republic. Due to a bitter dispute over rights to the name, the Czech beer is known in the United States as Crystal, while the American beer is known in some European countries by its shortened form, Bud. There is some debate as to which is the 'original' Budweiser, although it seems perverse to prevent beer from Budejovice being called Budweiser.

Anheuser-Busch was founded in 1875, 20 years earlier than the Czech brewer, which was created as Cesky akciovy pivovar in 1895. However, it was formed by a collective of privileged licensed brewers who were part of a tradition that stretches all the way back to the thirteenth century, when brewing started in the town. The brewery's present incarnation dates from 1967 when the Czech ministry of agriculture formed the Budejovicky Budvar as a direct successor to Cesky akciovy pivovar. The brewery has gone on to become one of the Czech Republic's most exported brands, with almost half of its output exported to over 60 countries worldwide.

SPECIFICATIONS

Brewery: Budejovicky Budvar
Location: Ceske Budejovice, Bohemia
Style: Lager
Colour: Deep golden yellow
Alcohol: 5%
Serving temperature: 9°C (48.2°F)
Food: Roast beef and dumplings

Lobkowicz

Founded in 1466, the brewery in the Czech town of Vysoky Chlumec was bought by the Lobkowicz family eight years later in 1474 and remained in their hands until World War II, when it was confiscated by the Nazis and the family was forced into exile in Britain.

Following the war, the family returned to Czechoslovakia, but the brewery was then taken over by the communists. However, in 1992 the family finally regained control of its heritage and American-born William Lobkowicz took charge of brewing operations. Its main product is a classic dark Czech lager with a caramel malt flavour and hints of chocolate, balanced by a refreshing hop finish. It is sold in the United States as Lobkowicz Baron.

SPECIFICATIONS

Brewery: Lobkowicz
Location: Vysoky Chlumec
Style: Lager
Colour: Deep golden amber
Alcohol: 5%
Serving temperature: 8°C (46.4°F)
Food: Dried cured meats and sausages

Lobkowicz Special

Lobkowicz beers are brewed in the traditional manner in large copper brewing kettles.

The water used in producing the beer comes from the brewery's own artesian well, and the malt is produced from locally grown barley at their own maltings. Saaz hops, a particularly aromatic type of hops, are added by hand during brewing, and the finished beer is matured for several months in the cellars before it is bottled up for sale. Lobkowicz Special (which is sold in the United States under the name Lobkowicz Prince) is a strong (5.7%) bock-style lager with a smooth, creamy texture and a distinctive fruity flavour. It has a lingering sweet malty finish, and a refreshing golden yellow colour gives the beer a fine appearance.

SPECIFICATIONS

Brewery: Lobkowicz
Location: Vysoky Chlumec
Style: Lager
Colour: Golden yellow
Alcohol: 5.7%
Serving temperature: 8°C (46.4°F)
Food: Grilled veal steaks

Pilsner Urquell

Although Pilsner has come to be used as a general term for a strong, hoppy bottom-fermented golden beer, in its strictest usage it designates a beer from the Czech town of Pilsen (or Plzen). The beer that gave its name to the style is the original Pilsner Urquell.

In Czech it is called Plzensky Prazdroj, but during the nineteenth century the town of Pilsen was part of the Austrian empire and its official language was German. Hence the name comes from the German meaning 'Pilsner from the original source'. It was created in 1842 by Josef Groll. Until then, beers tended to be dark and cloudy, but the cool brewing conditions, the local water, the pale malt made from locally grown barley and the bottom-fermenting strain of yeast used by Groll combined to produce a clear golden lager that found particular popularity due to the growing trend for drinking from glass vessels instead of stone and pewter tankards. The beer was introduced to Prague three years later and soon began to be exported to Germany, where the Pilsner style was widely adopted.

Few of the imitators can match the original. The blend of Moravian malt and aromatic Saaz hops make for an extremely well-balanced beer with a crisp refreshing flavour. The aroma is dominated by a floral, spicy hop character, while on the palate an initial smooth, soft character leads to a dry, bitter finish.

SPECIFICATIONS

Brewery: Pilsner Urquell
Location: Pilsen, Moravia
Style: Pilsner
Colour: Golden amber-yellow
Alcohol: 4.4%
Serving temperature: 9°C (48.2°F)
Food: Serve as an aperitif

Staropramen

Staropramen Premium Lager is a smooth, full-bodied golden Pilsner-style beer with a refreshingly dry finish. The brewery also produces two other beers, one called Granat, a dark ruby-coloured lager with a balance of hop bitterness and caramel malt flavours, and the light-bodied Staropramen Dark, a sweet malty beer with caramel, liquorice and aniseed notes. The name Staropramen means 'old spring', but the brewery started life as the Smichov brewery, named after the Smichov district of Prague on the banks of the Vltava River, where it was situated. Building of the brewery commenced in 1869, and malting began early in 1871, with the first beers launched just a few months later.

An early customer was the nearby Ringhofer factory, where the huge demand for beer ensured that Smichov became hugely successful. Emperor Franz Joseph I visited in 1867 and left favourable comments about the beer in the guestbook, and by 1884 the brewery was exporting its beers to Vienna, Germany, Switzerland and the United States. Then in 1911, the brewery registered 16 trade marks, including Staropramen, which proved so popular that this was adopted as the brewery's key brand. The brewery grew to become one of the three largest breweries in Europe by the 1930s, but after World War II it was confiscated by the communists and did not come back into private ownership until 1950. The present company was formed in 1989, and in 2000 Staropramen became part of Interbrew. Its beers are now exported to 36 countries.

SPECIFICATIONS

Brewery: Pivovar Staropramen Prazské Pivovary
Location: Prague
Style: Pilsner
Colour: Deep golden yellow
Alcohol: 5.2%
Serving temperature: 8°C (46.4°F)
Food: Bread and cheese

ABOVE

The brewing industries of Slovenia and Croatia have struggled to rebuild themselves since the civil war resulting from the break-up of Yugoslavia in the 1990s. However, tourism to the region is once again on the increase and the countries' food and drink industries are working hard to produce quality products for the new visitors, and well as for their own people.

Slovenian and Croatian Beers

The capital of Slovenia is Ljubljana, and here the brewing industry has a tradition dating back 400 years – taxes were paid on beer as early as 1592. Ljubljana is the home to the Union Brewery, which was founded in 1864, and is today one of Slovenia's major beer producers.

Above
Croatia's beer industry was convulsed by the effects of civil war in the 1990s, but has made a remarkable recovery.

THE LARGEST BREWERY is in Lasko, and dates back to 1825, when a man called Franz Geyerset up a small brewery in what is today the Hotel Savinja. In 1924 the brewery was bought out by its competitor, the Union Brewery, only to be closed in 1927. However, a new Lasko Brewery was established in 1938, and today the Lasko Brewery controls about 50% of the Slovenian beer market.

The main brewery in neighbouring Croatia is Zagrebacka Pivovara, which as its name implies is based in Zagreb. Established in 1982, it today holds a 46% share of the country's beer market and produces a range of lager-type beers, the most popular of which is Ozujsko, named after the Croatian word for March. However, it is the second-largest concern, the Karlovacka Pivovara, based in Karlovac, which is the biggest beer supplier of the Croatian tourist region. It is also the largest Croatian beer exporter. The oldest beer producer in Croatia is the Osijek Brewery, established in 1697 in the town of that name. At that time Osijek was within the boundaries of the Austro-Hungarian empire, which consumed a high proportion of its output.

Croatian breweries were among first in the world to use microbial enzymes for brewing and clarification of the beer, and Croatian beers are of a high quality. After the indigenous brews, the most popular is Tuborg, which is brewed under licence. For the tourist, the sampling of Croatian beers can be a real revelation, and there is plenty of choice.

STATISTICS

Total production: 5,900,000 hectolitres (155,862,000 gallons) per year
Consumption per capita: 103 litres (27 gallons) per year
Famous breweries: Buzetska Pivovara; Karlovacko Pivovara; Pivovarno Lasko; Pivovara Osijek; Pivovarna Union DD
Famous brands: Crno; Favorit; Karlovacko Pivo; Premium Pivo; Zlatorog Club; Zlatorog Pivo

Termalni Desert

Lasko brewery has had an up-and-down history. It was founded in 1825 by Franz Geyer, a producer of mead and gingerbread, but in 1838 it was bought by Heinrich August Ulrich, who began distributing his beer in Trieste and exporting it to India and Egypt.

By 1867 the brewery had again changed hands, and the latest owner, Anton Larisch, moved the brewery to a new site. After the brewery became bankrupt it was rescued by Simon Kukec, who introduced the concept of using water from thermal springs in his beer production, and thus Termalni Desert was created, a rich, dark full-flavoured lager. In the past 50 years it has grown from being the fifth-largest brewer in Slovenia to become the largest. Since 1997 the brewery has also started producing soft drinks as well as a bottled blend of lemonade and beer.

SPECIFICATIONS

Brewery: Pivovarna Lasko
Location: Lasko, Slovenia
Style: Dark lager
Colour: Chestnut brown
Alcohol: 6%
Serving temperature: 8°–10°C (46.4°–50°F)
Food: Smoked fish or meat

Zlatorog Club

The original Lasko brewery was bought up by the Union Brewery in 1924, but a new company was formed in 1938 by representatives of the town's innkeepers' association. The brewery was destroyed in a World War II bombing raid in 1944, however, and production did not start again until 1946.

It was at this time that the brewery adopted the Zlatorog ('goldhorn') brand for its strong, pale Bavarian Pilsner-style lager, which has a clean, refreshing taste and a strong hop bitterness.

SPECIFICATIONS

Brewery: Pivovarna Lasko
Location: Lasko, Slovenia
Style: Dark lager
Colour: Dark golden-red
Alcohol: 5%
Serving temperature: 7°C (44.6°F)
Food: Pasta in a light sauce

Zlatorog Pivo

An unfortunate consequence of Slovenian independence was that the Lasko brewery suddenly lost 40% of its market, a blow from which it has never fully recovered – although in recent years it has enjoyed some success on the export market.

Now over 20% of its output travels outside Slovenia, while within the country the Zlatorog brand has a market share of over 50%. The various beers in the range include this low-alcohol pale lager which is now the brewery's best-selling brand. Lasko also produces a strong, full-flavoured Export Pils and a well-balanced dark, malty Munich-style lager called Netopir ('the bat').

SPECIFICATIONS

Brewery: Pivovarna Lasko
Location: Lasko, Slovenia
Style: Lager
Colour: Golden yellow
Alcohol: 2%
Serving temperature: 7°C (44.6°F)
Food: Light, fresh-flavoured vegetable dishes

Premium Pivo

Premium Pivo is the oldest beer of the Union Brewery of Ljubljana, the capital of Slovenia. A straightforward golden lager, it has a light hoppy aroma and a mild malty flavour.

Union 1864 is a slightly stronger beer, while Crni Baron is a strong, dark sweet beer with a full, malty flavour. The brewery traces its origins back to 1864, when the Kosler brewery was founded in Ljubljana. It became known as Union in 1909 when it was publicly listed, but in 1946 it came under state ownership. Then in 1991, after Slovenia gained independence from Yugoslavia, it was sold back into public ownership.

SPECIFICATIONS

Brewery: Pivovarna Union DD
Location: Ljubljana, Slovenia
Style: Lager
Colour: Golden yellow
Alcohol: 5%
Serving temperature: 7°C (44.6°F)
Food: Risotto

Favorit

The Buzetska brewery is based in the small town of Buzet on the northern Adriatic coast of Croatia.

Construction of the brewery was planned to start in the city of Rijeka in 1958, but due to problems with funding plans were suspended for 10 years until the town of Buzet stepped in to save the project. The area is a popular region with tourists and is noted for its annual folk music festival. The brewery's main product is Favorit, a light lager with a fresh hop aroma and a grainy malt flavour. The local water that is so important to the flavour of Favorit beer is also bottled and sold in its pure form.

SPECIFICATIONS

Brewery: Buzetska Pivovara
Location: Buzet, Croatia
Style: Lager
Colour: Straw yellow
Alcohol: 5.2%
Serving temperature: 6°–8°C (42.8°–46.4°F)
Food: Bread with cream cheese and ham

Karlovacko Crystal

This clear golden lager has a hoppy aroma and a light grainy malt flavour. It comes from the Karlovacko brewery, located in the city of Karlovac, which lies about 50km from the capital, Zagreb.

Beer production in the town can be traced back to 1779, but the present brewery was founded in 1854 in the town's Dubovac district, employing a man named Zisler as brewer. The brewery stopped operating in 1880, being turned into a pottery, but was relaunched in 1896 and bought by a consortium of wealthy Karlocav citizens in 1902 and renamed Karlovacko. In April 2003, Karlovacka became part of the Dutch Heineken group.

SPECIFICATIONS

Brewery: Karlovacko Pivovara
Location: Karlovac, Croatia
Style: Lager
Colour: Straw yellow
Alcohol: 4.8%
Serving temperature: 6°–7°C (42.8°–44.6°F)
Food: Serve as an aperitif

Karlovacko Pivo

Karlovacko Pivovara is the second-largest brewery in Croatia with approximately 20% of the market and Karlovacko Pivo is its most important brand, a light, crisp lager with a refreshing hop bitterness.

One of the most popular times to drink it is during the special festival known as Dani Piva ('beer day') which is held in the town square, although it can be enjoyed equally well at other times. The brewery also brews a strong winter beer called Zimsko and a full-flavoured dark lager called Crno. The range is completed by its low-alcohol beer, which is known as Rally, the first low-alcohol beer made in Croatia.

SPECIFICATIONS

Brewery: Karlovacko Pivovara
Location: Karlovac, Croatia
Style: Lager
Colour: Pale golden yellow
Alcohol: 5.4%
Serving temperature: 6°–8°C (42.8°–46.4°F)
Food: Herby rice dishes such as risotto

Osjecko Crno

Beer production began in Osijek as early as 1664, but the first known commercial brewery dates from 1695.

By 1856, the Osijek brewery was added to the ranks of the town's burgeoning brewing industry, founded by Kajetanseper who had learned his craft in Munich and the Czech Republic. In 1956, the town's breweries were merged and came under state ownership, but the Osijek brewery soon went its own way and by 1969 was the town's biggest brewer, as it remains today. The brewery's two main products are a light hoppy lager and a dark full-bodied malty beer, called Crno. Osjecko also brews the German brands Löwenbräu and Franziskaner under licence.

SPECIFICATIONS

Brewery: Pivovara Osijek
Location: Croatia
Style: Dark ale
Colour: Chestnut brown
Alcohol: 5%
Serving temperature: 8°C (46.4°F)
Food: Rich stews

Above

Asia is a region noted for the fine quality of its pale lagers, and for this reason export sales of bottled and canned beers to the United States, South America and Europe have been growing rapidly over the past 20 years. In terms of pure volume, China is the largest beer producer in the world, although individual consumption remains relatively low.

Asian Beers

The most significant markets for beer in the Far East are Japan and China, both of which rank among the world's leading beer consumers, even though neither country has a real beer brewing tradition. Beer was introduced to China by the Germans and Russians at the start of the twentieth century and now the number of breweries is approaching the 1000 mark, with businesses ranging from small, local breweries to giant state-owned industries.

JAPAN IS THE LARGEST PER CAPITA beer consumer in the Far East. Beer arrived in Japan around 50 years earlier than in China, and Kirin, the country's first commercial brewery, was established in 1870 by an American. The first Japanese-owned brewery was launched in 1876. After rapid growth in the 1890s, there was a major consolidation of breweries in 1906. Introduction of beer tax laws in 1908, which enforced a minimum production level of 180,000 litres per year, meant that smaller breweries could not survive, concentrating the industry into the hands of a few companies. The repeal of these laws in 1994 saw a sudden growth in microbreweries and brewpubs, the products of which are known as ji-biru ('local beer'). Many of the new crop of beer brewers are long-established saké brewing companies.

Brewing traditions vary widely across the rest of Asia, although as a rule beer consumption is relatively low compared to most European countries. India still feels the legacy of English colonial influence in its preference for rich, dark stouts and, of course, India pale ale, although most beer drunk in India is imported, and in certain areas of the subcontinent alcohol production and consumption are prohibited. One of the largest brewers in Southeast Asia is San Miguel of the Philippines, which has production facilities across the region. It is also one of the oldest, having been established for more than 100 years.

ABOVE

A poster for the Japanese Asahi beer. Asahi is a perfect example of a regional Asian beer capturing real export success in global markets.

STATISTICS

Total production: 396,638,000 hectolitres (10,478,067,000 gallons) per year

Consumption per capita: 10 litres (3 gallons) per year

Famous breweries: Asahi; Asia Pacific Breweries; Boon Rawd Brewery Company Ltd; Cambrew Limited; Chunghua Beer Company Ltd; Hite Company Ltd; Kirin; PT Multi Bintang Indonesia; Tsingtao

Famous brands: Angkhor; Asahi; Bir Bintang; Hite; Kingfisher; Kirin; Sapporo; Silver Sapporo; Singha; Tiger; Tsingtao

Kingfisher

Kingfisher is a very popular lager, although not to everyone's taste. It pours with a wispy little head and a tiny bit of lace.

The aroma is a pleasant mix of cereal grains and a faint yeast background. The beer is better served chilled and in a glass, while the aroma adds to the whole experience. Kingfisher's appearance is golden to yellow, and the mouthfeel is moderate, although it contains an initial bite. Kingfisher is a product of United Breweries in India. However, it is also brewed under licence in the United States and the United Kingdom.

SPECIFICATIONS

Brewery: United Breweries
Location: Bangalore, Karnataka, India
Style: Adjunct lager
Colour: Pale yellow
Alcohol: Not listed
Serving temperature: Chilled
Food: Curries, especially coconut-based

Bengal Tiger

A rather sugary-sweet lager, Bengal Tiger is nevertheless becoming an increasingly popular choice in Indian restaurants in Europe.

Straw gold, it has a light malt aroma. The bottled lager is produced by Mysore Breweries of Bangalore. In common with other Indian bottled lagers, Bengal Tiger should be served chilled and drunk with spicy oriental food to be appreciated fully, and many drinkers consider it to be too bland for their palates.

SPECIFICATIONS

Brewery: Mysore Breweries
Location: Mysore, Karnataka, India
Style: Adjunct lager
Colour: Straw gold
Alcohol: 5%
Serving temperature: Chilled
Food: Curries, especially coconut-based

Zhong Hua

The Chung Hua beer company, like Tsingtao, was originally founded by German settlers in the coastal province of Zhejiang in eastern China, an area that was subject to German colonial rule until the early twentieth century, in much the same way that Hong Kong was under British rule.

Today both the region and the brewery are under Chinese ownership. Although less well known outside China than Tsingtao, Zhong Hua beer is one of the country's leading exported beers, mainly available in areas with large Chinese communities and often served in Chinese restaurants. It is a straightforward, light, easy-drinking pale golden lager with a modest hop profile.

SPECIFICATIONS

Brewery: Chunghua Beer Company Ltd
Location: Chunghua, Zhejiang Province, China
Style: Lager
Colour: Pale blonde
Alcohol: 5%
Serving temperature: 8°C (46.4°F)
Food: Simple vegetable and rice-based dishes

Tsingtao

Founded in 1903 by German settlers in the port of Tsingtao (now Qingdao), Tsingtao (pronounced 'ching-dow') was one of the first commercial breweries in China and is currently one of its largest.

Its flagship golden lager is the best-selling beer in China and by far the best known Chinese beer worldwide, first introduced to the United States in 1972 and today accounting for around 80% of Chinese beer exports. Produced using spring water from the Laoshan mountains, and malt and yeast imported from Canada and Australia, it has a light hoppy aroma and a well-balanced flavour.

SPECIFICATIONS

Brewery: Tsingtao
Location: Qingdao, Shandong Province, China
Style: Lager
Colour: Pale yellow
Alcohol: 4.8%
Serving temperature: 8°C (46.4°F)
Food: Steamed or poached fish

Lion Stout

The Ceylon brewery takes its name from the former identity of Sri Lanka, where it has been based since 1881.

The original brewery was built in the hillside town of Nuwara Eliya, among the tea plantations near the holy city of Kandy, with the purpose of supplying British-style beers to the colonial plantation owners. This remote location is reached by steep, narrow, winding roads, which causes many difficulties with the delivery of the ingredients used in brewing, so in 1998 the company built a new brewing plant in the capital city, Colombo.

Until the 1960s, the most popular beer in the region was an English-style India pale ale. This style has become unfashionable and the company's main product is now a golden lager, but like many breweries in the region it has maintained the tradition of brewing a stout for those who prefer a beer with a fuller flavour. It is one of the best examples of a stout made in Asia, having an intense fruity aroma with hints of coffee, while on the palate it has a dense, treacly body and starts with a rich, dark, sweet malt flavour that becomes increasingly dry and bitter with the character of roasted coffee and bitter chocolate. Although the beer is these days pasteurised, it is still bottled unfiltered. It is fashionable in Sri Lanka to drink it with a shot of the local coconut-based spirit called arrack.

SPECIFICATIONS

Brewery: Ceylon / Lion Brewery Limited
Location: Colombo, Sri Lanka
Style: Tropical stout
Colour: Black
Alcohol: 8.2%
Serving temperature: 13°C (55.4°F)
Food: Chocolate cake

Bir Bintang Pilsner

Bir Bintang is a German-style Pilsner with a well-balanced flavour of malt and hops. It comes from the largest brewery in Indonesia, which was founded in 1929 under the name Nederlandsch Indische Bierbrouwerijen.

The company was taken over by Heineken in 1936 and started brewing Heineken beer. However, Heineken withdrew from the region in 1957 and prohibited the use of its brand name, so the beer was renamed Perusahaan Bir Bintang. When Heineken resumed brewing in Indonesia in 1967, the beer was relaunched as Bintang Baru. It has been known as Bir Bintang since 2002. The brewery also produces Guinness under licence.

SPECIFICATIONS

Brewery: PT Multi Bintang Indonesia
Location: Surabaya, Indonesia
Style: Pilsner
Colour: Golden yellow
Alcohol: 4.8%
Serving temperature: 8°C (46.4°F)
Food: Goes well with spicy Indonesian food

Singha

The first and still the largest brewery in Thailand, Boon Rawd was founded in 1933 by Phraya Bhirom Bhakdi, using German technology to produce Pilsner-style beers.

Today, Boon Rawd is a diverse company with product lines including bottled water, tea and coffee, as well as its three beer brands, Singha, Leo and Thai Beer. Singha is a full-bodied all-malt lager with a prominent herbal hop character. Also available is Singha Gold Light, a low-calorie and low-alcohol version of Singha with a light, refreshing flavour. Leo is a standard light, golden lager, while Thai Beer is a slightly stronger beer.

SPECIFICATIONS

Brewery: Boon Rawd Brewery Company Ltd
Location: Bangkok, Thailand
Style: Lager
Colour: Golden yellow
Alcohol: 6%
Serving temperature: 6°–8°C (42.8°–46.4°F)
Food: Fish and seafood

Tiger

Tiger Beer is the best-selling beer in Singapore, an all-malt golden lager brewed with malt imported from Europe and Australia, and hops imported from Germany.

The yeast strain is also European, developed exclusively for the brewery in the Netherlands by Heineken. It is the leading brand of the Asia Pacific Breweries company, which was founded in 1931 under the name Malayan Breweries Limited as a joint venture between Heineken and Fraser & Neave. Although the brewery uses imported ingredients, all its beers are brewed exclusively at the two plants in Singapore and Kuala Lumpur, Malaysia, unlike many other Asian beers which are brewed under licence in Europe and the United States.

Despite this, it is one of the best-known Asian beers in the west, largely thanks to the fact that it was very popular with Allied troops stationed in the Far East during World War II and was first introduced to the west by soldiers who took bottles home with them. Tiger beer is now exported to more than 50 countries worldwide. The English writer Anthony Burgess spent time in the Far East during the 1950s and even named one of his books after the Tiger advertising slogan 'Time for a Tiger'. Asia Pacific Breweries also makes a seasonal beer for New Year called Tiger Classic, a golden lager with a smooth, soft malt flavour, as well as several other brands such as Anchor (or Anker) Pilsner.

SPECIFICATIONS

Brewery: Asia Pacific Breweries
Location: Alexandra Point, Singapore
Style: Lager
Colour: Pale straw yellow
Alcohol: 5%
Serving temperature: 6°–8°C (42.8°–46.4°F)
Food: Spicy oriental dishes

Angkor Beer 

Most beers drunk in Cambodia are imported brands such as Tiger, San Miguel and Heineken, but the country has its own national beer, Angkor, produced in the port city of Sihanoukville by Cambrew, which was founded in 1990.

It is named after the majestic Angkor Wat temple, which is depicted on the labels on the bottle, and was built by the Khmer empire which ruled in the ninth and tenth centuries AD. The beer is a typically European-style golden lager with a full body, a soft bitterness and a light, hoppy aroma.

Angkor beer has enjoyed a steadily growing popularity overseas in recent years, and is becoming a more common sight in the bars and specialist drink shops of Europe and the United States, with major export markets in Japan and Canada. It comes in a variety of formats: 640ml bottles, 320ml bottles, 320ml cans and also as a draught.

The Cambrew range of brands includes Bayon Beer (named after the statues at the Angkor Wat temple) which, according to company publicity, is 'essentially catered to Asian drinkers with a smooth and hoppy aroma to give a pleasant after taste'. Cambrew also makes Black Panther Stout, a powerful drink of between 8% and 8.3% alcohol containing a flavourful bitterness.

The Cambrew brewery was originally of French ownership established in the mid-1960s, and taken over and refurbished by Cambrew in 1992. Cambrew itself was founded in 1990, and its growth through its three brands has been impressive. In 2004 its brewery had an output of 500,000 hectolitres.

SPECIFICATIONS

Brewery: Cambrew Limited
Location: Sihanoukville, Cambodia
Style: Lager
Colour: Golden yellow
Alcohol: 5.2%
Serving temperature: 6°–8°C (42.8°–46.4°F)
Food: Amocfish (fish soup with coconut milk)

Hite Beer

Beer first came to Korea in 1933, when the Chosun Beer Company was founded, at first owned by the government, but becoming a private company in 1952.

Throughout the 1980s, Hite expanded its range, introducing a light version of its beer in 1982, and a non-alcoholic malt drink in 1984. Since 1986 it has also brewed Carlsberg beers under licence, and in 1989 it created Super Dry. Despite its diversification into other beer brands, the flagship product remains Hite Beer, a crisp-tasting beer made using a three-stage process to control the temperature during fermentation.

SPECIFICATIONS

Brewery: Hite Company Ltd
Location: South Korea
Style: Pilsner
Colour: Golden yellow
Alcohol: 4.5%
Serving temperature: 8°–10°C (46.4°–50°F)
Food: Spicy fish and seafood dishes

San Miguel Dark

San Miguel Dark is simply a darker version of San Miguel Corporation's flagship Pale Pilsen, brewed with darker malts to create a Munich-style lager with a well-rounded fruity, toffee malt flavour and also containing hints of roasted coffee and bitter chocolate.

It is known in its home country as Cerveza Negra (Spanish for 'black beer'), where it has a reputation as the beer chosen by connoisseurs. Most of the beers drunk in Asia are of the light variety, so the Dark Lager also carries a reputation for distinction. San Miguel also brews several other beers that are not so well known outside their home country. These include Red Horse Beer, which was the first extra-strong beer to be produced in the Philippines, and Golden Eagle Beer, a pale amber lager with a smooth body and a delicate hop aroma.

SPECIFICATIONS

Brewery: San Miguel Corporation
Location: Manila, Philippines
Style: Munich dark lager
Colour: Light amber-brown
Alcohol: 5%
Serving temperature: 8°–10°C (46.4°–50°F)
Food: Any meat dish with a rich, spicy sauce

San Miguel Pale Pilsen

After being granted royal permission to commence brewing, La Fabrica de Cerveza de San Miguel was founded in 1890 in the centre of Manila, in premises that stood next door to the colonial mansion of the Spanish governor-general. The brewery's inauguration was timed to coincide with the festival of San Miguel (St Michael) the Archangel, and despite a few hiccups, including the weather causing the ceremony to be postponed, the brewery was named in the saint's honour.

San Miguel's flagship product, San Miguel Pale Pilsen, is by far the biggest-selling beer in the Philippines, with a share of over 90% of the market, which also makes it one of the top three beer brands in the whole of Asia. It has a bready malt aroma with yeasty notes and, although it is designated as a Pilsner, it has a fairly light hop profile, with just a hint of floral hops in the aroma, and a subtle balancing bitterness on the malt-dominated palate. The San Miguel Corporation, as it is now known, has expanded across the region and has more than 100 brewing facilities across the Philippines, Southeast Asia, China and Australia, making it by far the largest brewer in the region, and in 2002 entered into a partnership with Kirin of Japan.

SPECIFICATIONS

Brewery: San Miguel Corporation
Location: Manila, Philippines
Style: Pilsner
Colour: Golden yellow
Alcohol: 5%
Serving temperature: 7°–8°C (44.6°–46.4°F)
Food: Spicy fish stew

Asahi Super Dry

The leading Japanese brewery was founded in 1889 as the Osaka brewery, and launched the first Asahi beer in 1892. In 1906, Asahi merged with two other breweries – Japan Beer Brewery Ltd and Sapporo Beer Company – to form the Dai Nippon Breweries Company.

The company quickly expanded, building several regional brewing plants. Then in 1949, the government's economic decentralisation act forced the giant Dai Nippon to separate into two companies, of which Asahi was the smaller. It remained the smaller company until the late 1980s, when it launched Asahi Super Dry. The huge success of this beer – not only in Japan, but also around the world – saw the company rocket from a relatively modest 10% market share to not far short of 50%, making it the second-largest brewing company in Japan.

Asahi Super Dry's success is down to its smooth, light flavour, which was formulated following extensive market testing. The smoothness and lightness are achieved through a longer maturation period, allowing it to ferment fully and giving it a higher alcohol content. In this respect, it is similar to a classic German Pilsner, although it has a much lighter hop profile, with just a hint of bitter, herbal hop character. The result is an astringently dry beer with a delicate flavour. Asahi also brews several beers with a more interesting character, including Asahi Draft Beer Fujisan, which is brewed exclusively using water drawn from the springs of Mount Fuji, while Asahi Super Malt is a low-alcohol, low-calorie all-malt lager.

SPECIFICATIONS

Brewery: Asahi
Location: Tokyo, Japan
Style: Lager
Colour: Golden yellow
Alcohol: 5%
Serving temperature: 6°–7°C (42.8°–44.6°F)
Food: Traditional Japanese cuisine, especially sushi

Asahi Black

Inspired by German Schwarzbier (black beer), Asahi Black has more of a reddish brown colour than its name suggests, albeit of a very dark shade.

The beer's rich aroma is redolent of dark, smoky caramel malts (Asahi avoids using roasted barley in the recipe), and has notes of sweet caramel and coffee, while similar characteristics dominate the palate, along with hints of buttery toffee and bitter chocolate. Asahi does also make a genuinely black-coloured beer, its Stout, which was first launched in 1935. This beer, like English porters, does use roasted barley, which gives it a rich, bitter coffee-ish flavour. It is also noted for its exceptionally smooth satin-like texture, and with a potent 8% abv it evokes Irish and British stouts.

Asahi Black and Stout are just two of a very extensive range of beers produced by the Asahi company. Asahi Edomae is a classic German Pilsner-type lager, and the Asahi brewery specialises in a variety of beers of this type, with other brands including Asahi Fujisan, Asahi Minori Zanmai and Asahi Honnama. More specialist beers include Asahi Point One, a low-alcohol lager. Asahi also makes a range of fruit beers, these being available in apple, grapefruit and raspberry flavours.

Asahi is one of the dominant players in the Japanese marker, but export sales to Europe and the United States are also strong, particularly of its Super-Dry brand.

SPECIFICATIONS

Brewery: Asahi
Location: Tokyo, Japan
Style: Dark lager
Colour: Dark red-brown
Alcohol: 5%
Serving temperature: 8°–10°C (46.4°–50°F)
Food: Chocolate and fruit-based desserts

Kirin Ichiban

Kirin's 'other' beer was launched in 1990 as Ichiban Shibori, which translates literally as 'first pressing'.

It earns its name because it is brewed using only the first run of wort – usually the malt is re-used to brew a second batch of wort, which is weaker than the first and contains a higher level of bitter-tasting tannin. Subsequently, Kirin Ichiban had a higher alcohol content and a milder, purer flavour, which made it instantly popular among Japanese beer drinkers. Kirin Ichiban also helped the brewery to establish an international reputation and in recent years the company has expanded outside Japan, acquiring a major share in New Zealand's Lion Nathan group in 1998, and investing in San Miguel of the Philippines in 2001.

SPECIFICATIONS

Brewery: Kirin
Location: Tokyo, Japan
Style: Lager
Colour: Golden yellow
Alcohol: 5.5%
Serving temperature: 8°–10°C (46.4°–50°F)
Food: Sushi, sashimi and tempura

Kirin Beer

Kirin Beer is a crisp, golden Pilsner-style lager flavoured with Saaz and Hallertau hops for a refreshing floral bitterness. It is also matured in cold cellars for up to two months to give it a smoother, lighter body and a richer, fuller flavour.

In Japan, it is bottled unpasteurised and unfiltered, although when it is exported to other countries it tends to be sold in a filtered form. Kirin beers are also brewed under licence in the United States by Budweiser and in Europe by the English brewer Charles Wells. The brewery, originally known as Spring Valley, was founded in Yokohama in 1869 and can claim to have been one of the earliest commercial breweries in Japan. While Kirin Beer has been the best-selling beer brand in Japan continuously since 1888, Kirin only became the country's leading brewer in 1954; however, it is a position the brewery has held on to ever since.

SPECIFICATIONS

Brewery: Kirin
Location: Tokyo, Japan
Style: Pilsner
Colour: Golden yellow
Alcohol: 4.9%
Serving temperature: 8°C (46.4°F)
Food: Sushi, sashimi and tempura

Hitachino Nest Lacto Sweet Stout

The Kiuchi brewery came into existence in 1823, initially producing saké to use up the spare rice collected as tax from local farmers.

It only began to brew beer as recently as 1996, but quickly established a reputation for high-quality beers brewed to traditional styles, as well as beers with a special Japanese character. The Lacto Sweet Stout is a typical example of this. It has notes of caramel and chocolate in the aroma, with a hint of lactic sourness, which comes from the use of milk-derived sugars in the brewing. On the palate, it has a full body with a lively carbonation and an astringently bitter roasted malt character, balanced by a smooth, creamy sweetness.

SPECIFICATIONS

Brewery: Kiuchi Brewery
Location: Naka-gun, Ibaragi, Japan
Style: Milk stout
Colour: Dark brown, almost black
Alcohol: 3.9%
Serving temperature: 10°–12°C (50°–53.6°F)
Food: Shellfish and other seafood

Hitachino Nest Red Rice Beer

This distinctive beer has a grainy malt aroma with subtle floral hop notes and an underlying yeasty fruitiness, with notes of cherries, oranges, pears and apples.

The slightly hazy orangey colour comes not from the malts used, as you might expect, but from the use of red rice, which also gives the beer a crisp, clean, refreshing character with a slightly sweet edge, similar to a saké. There is also a delicate hint of bitter, citrussy hops in the flavour, while the high alcohol content gives it a spicy, mouth-drying tang and a pleasant warmth in the finish.

SPECIFICATIONS

Brewery: Kiuchi Brewery
Location: Naka-gun, Ibaragi, Japan
Style: Belgian abbey double
Colour: Dark amber-orange
Alcohol: 8.5%
Serving temperature: 8°–10°C (46.4°–50°F)
Food: Yakitori-style grilled chicken

Hitachino Nest Weizen

This German-style naturally cloudy golden wheat beer has a sweet, yeasty banana and orange fruit aroma with hints of spiciness, particularly black pepper, cloves and coriander.

On the palate, a refreshing wheaty tartness dominates, the mouthfeel is refreshing, and a fruity, acidic touch of lemon is evident in the finish. The wide range of beers from Kiuchi also includes Japanese Classic Ale, matured in cedar casks which give the beer a distinctive spicy, resiny flavour; Cascade Ale, an English-style pale ale with well-balanced hop and malt flavours; and a German-style Eisbock with a whopping 9% alcohol.

SPECIFICATIONS

Brewery: Kiuchi Brewery
Location: Naka-gun, Ibaragi, Japan
Style: Hefe-Weizen / wheat beer
Colour: Hazy straw yellow
Alcohol: 5%
Serving temperature: 8°–10°C (46.4°–50°F)
Food: Sushi

Sapporo Yebisu Stout Draft

Yebisu beer was first brewed in 1890 by the Japan Brewing Company, which was set up in Tokyo in 1887 by a group of local entrepreneurs, following a recipe for all-malt golden lager created by a German brewer on behalf of the company.

Japan Beer Company later became Kirin, then part of Dai Nippon, and the Yebisu brand died out, but it was revived in 1971 by Sapporo, making it the first German-style all-malt beer to be brewed in post-war Japan. 'Stout' in the name does not refer to the style of the beer, but to the rich, malty flavour, which is similar to a Dortmunder Export beer. Sapporo's dark Munich-style lager is called Yebisu Black Beer.

SPECIFICATIONS

Brewery: Sapporo Breweries Ltd
Location: Hokkaido, Japan
Style: Dortmunder / export
Colour: Golden yellow
Alcohol: 5%
Serving temperature: 8°–10°C (46.4°–50°F)
Food: Spicy dishes such as chilli chicken noodles

Silver Sapporo

In Japan, the flagship beer of the Sapporo brewery is usually sold in bottles and is known as Sapporo Black Label, after its distinctive black label that bears the brewery's silver star emblem.

Elsewhere the bottled beer is known as Sapporo Premium, but it also comes in stylish silver cans as either Silver Sapporo or Sapporo Draft. Wherever it is sold, it is a light, refreshing golden lager with a soft, malty aroma and a gently bitter hop flavour. It was launched in Japan in 1977, but the Sapporo brewery has a history that stretches back to 1876, when Seibei Nakagawa, who had recently travelled to Germany to learn the art of brewing, was employed by the Japanese government to oversee the construction of a brewery in Hokkaido. Before the end of that year the Kaitakushi brewery was open, producing Bavarian style beers.

The company was renamed Sapporo in 1886, then in 1906 it became part of the Dai Nippon group, with its beers brewed in Tokyo, but regained independence when that company was split up in 1949. At that time it renamed itself, Nippon Breweries Ltd, but bowing to popular pressure was eventually again renamed Sapporo in 1956 and also resumed brewing in Hokkaido.

SPECIFICATIONS

Brewery: Sapporo Breweries Ltd
Location: Hokkaido, Japan
Style: Lager
Colour: Golden yellow
Alcohol: 4.5%
Serving temperature: 6°–8°C (42.8°–46.4°F)
Food: Light pasta or rice dishes

ABOVE

Foster's lager is undoubtedly one of the world's best-known beer brands, a brand which is backed by a strikingly efficient advertising campaign. Alongside Castlemaine XXXX, Foster's has given Australia a worldwide presence on the beer markets, but New Zealand is also claiming an increased market share through quality premium beers such as Steinlager (produced under the giant Lion Nathan Group).

Australian and New Zealand Beers

Brewing in Australia and New Zealand started with the arrival of European settlers in the late eighteenth century – the first record of brewing in Australia dates from 1794, when John Boston produced a beer using maize imported from India (instead of barley) and the stems and leaves of cape gooseberries as a bittering agent.

ABOVE

Part of the reason for the major success of Australian beers in export is the Australian identity itself.

ASIDE FROM THE DIFFICULTY of obtaining ingredients, early brewers also had to deal with an unfavourable climate. The effect of the heat on the top-fermenting yeast used to produce English-style ales meant that brewing was an unpredictable business, and even when attempts were successful the beer would not keep for very long.

By the late nineteenth century, the introduction of refrigeration by brewing pioneers such as the Foster brothers meant that ales had been mostly replaced by bottom-fermenting golden lagers, which remain the most popular style. Meanwhile, in New Zealand, where the climate was similar to that of northern Europe, ales could be brewed successfully and remained popular even after the introduction of lagers.

The domestic market in Australia is dominated by two giant companies, Carlton and United Breweries (a division of the international Foster's Brewing Group) and New Zealand's Lion Nathan. Beer is still hugely popular, although since the early 1980s it has been in steady decline due to the increasing popularity of wine. Brewing in New Zealand has historically been severely affected by the influence of the temperance movement. Lion Nathan was formed in 1923, when 10 of the country's largest breweries merged in order to survive.

STATISTICS

Total production: 20,300,000 hectolitres (536,270,000 gallons) per year

Consumption per capita: 82 litres (22 gallons) per year

Famous breweries: Castlemaine Perkins; Foster's Brewing Group Ltd; Lion Breweries; Malt Shovel; Swan Brewery; Tooheys

Famous brands: Castelmaine XXXX; Foster's; James Squire Original Amber Ale; Steinlager; Swan Draught; Tooheys New

Castlemaine XXXX

Castlemaine XXXX is a pale malty lager brewed with whole hops for a refreshing bitter flavour. Castlemaine Brewery was founded in Castlemaine, Victoria, in 1859 by brothers Nicholas and Edwin Fitzgerald.

In 1877 they took over an ailing distillery in the Brisbane suburb of Milton where they started brewing Castlemaine XXX Sparkling Ale. This was joined by Castlemaine XXXX Sparkling Ale in 1894, but the Queensland heat caused problems in the brewing process. In 1920, an Austrian brewer, Alois Wilhelm Leitner, was called in, and he developed a lighter bottom-fermented recipe that was launched as XXXX Bitter Ale. Castlemaine later merged with Perkins Brewery of Brisbane and in 1992 became part of New Zealand's Lion Nathan group.

SPECIFICATIONS

Brewery: Castlemaine Perkins
Location: Brisbane, Queensland
Style: Lager
Colour: Pale golden yellow
Alcohol: 4.8%
Serving temperature: 6°–8°C (42.8°–46.4°F)
Food: Spicy food such as Thai curries

James Squire Original Amber Ale

The original Malt Shovel brewery was founded in 1795 by James Squire, a brewer, publican and convicted highway robber who was deported to Australia.

James Squire Original Amber Ale is an imitation of the English-style pale ales that were brewed by the first Malt Shovel brewery. It is brewed with a blend of crystal and caramel malts to give it a distinctive coppery colour and a rich, sweet, nutty malt flavour, while late hopping with Willamette hops gives a refreshingly bitter citrussy grapefruit finish. The brewery also produces a heavily hopped Pilsner with a fragrant herby, floral aroma balanced by a mellow malt flavour.

SPECIFICATIONS

Brewery: Malt Shovel
Location: Sydney, New South Wales
Style: English pale ale
Colour: Copper red
Alcohol: 5%
Serving temperature: 10°C (50°F)
Food: Lamb, beef or game dishes

Foster's Lager

Australia's original lager has a smooth texture and a well-rounded malty flavour on the palate, with a light hop presence in the finish. It was originally brewed in 1887 in Melbourne by two brothers from New York. Although the brewery still bears their name, their involvement with the company ended after just 18 months when they returned to New York, but not before they had introduced an innovative refrigeration process that enabled the brewing of lighter European-style golden lagers in the harsh Australian climate.

Fosters is now Australia's best-known beer brand, available in more than 150 countries worldwide. This is largely the result of a phase of massive international expansion throughout the 1980s after it was taken over by Elders IXL (later becoming Foster's Brewing Group), which saw the company buy Courage in England and Carling in Canada – although by the late 1990s the company was forced to sell off both of these foreign interests. At the same time the company also diversified by staking a claim in the enormous Australian wine market. But Foster's still produces a wide range of beers, including notable brands such as Victoria Beer (VB), Carlton Draught and Crown Lager, all of which are well known in the domestic market.

SPECIFICATIONS

Brewery: Foster's Brewing Group Ltd
Location: Melbourne, Australia
Style: Lager
Colour: Pale golden yellow
Alcohol: 4.9%
Serving temperature: 5°–7°C (41°–44.6°F)
Food: Salads, shellfish

Swan Draught

The first commercial brewery in Perth, founded in 1837, was called Albion. The original Swan brewery came later, in 1857, formed by Frederick Sherwood, who settled in the area now known as Sherwood Court.

The brewery was leased to Captain John Ferguson and William Mumme, whose expertise in German beer styles greatly enhanced the quality of Swan beers. It later came under the sole ownership of Mumme, who in 1928 also acquired ownership of Albion, which by then was known as Emu. Today the Swan brewery is part of the huge Lion Nathan Group of drinks producers. Swan Draught is its flagship brand and the leading lager in Western Australia. It is a smooth, easy drinking beer with a malty flavour balanced by a gentle bitterness provided by Tasmanian hops.

In 1983 Swan added to its Draught beer a new drink, Swan Stout, which it brews using traditional methods to produce a drink of full body and rich flavour backed by a powerful 7.4% abv content.

SPECIFICATIONS

Brewery: Swan Brewery
Location: Perth, Western Australia
Style: Lager
Colour: Golden yellow
Alcohol: 4.8%
Serving temperature: 6°–8°C (42.8°–46.4°F)
Food: Barbecued sausages

Tooheys New

Tooheys New is a straightforward pale golden lager with a crisp, clean flavour. It has been brewed by Sydney's Tooheys brewery since 1931 and was originally launched as Tooheys Draught. It changed its name to Tooheys New in 1998, although the beer is still brewed to the same recipe as it always has been. Until the 1930s, the company had brewed an English-style dark, mild top-fermenting ale, which became known as Tooheys Old. This is a rich, malty beer with chocolate notes on the palate and a low hop content.

Tooheys now produces a wide range of beers, including a pair of darker lagers called Amber and Red, an ice beer called Blue Label and a hoppy German-style Pilsner. The most recent addition to the range, launched in 2001, was Tooheys Maxim, a full-strength, lower-calorie lager. The history of Tooheys brewery starts in 1869, when Irish Catholic immigrant John Thomas Toohey acquired his brewing licence. Three years later he and his brother James bought the Darling brewery in Cockle Creek, Sydney, which was later renamed Darling Harbour. Tooheys became a public company in 1902, and in 1985 was bought by the Bond corporation along with Swan Brewery. In 1992 it became an independent brewery again under the umbrella of the international Lion Nathan Group, which is based in New Zealand, and moved to a brand new state-of-the-art brewhouse in Auburn in 1994.

SPECIFICATIONS

Brewery: Tooheys
Location: Sydney, New South Wales
Style: Lager
Colour: Pale golden yellow
Alcohol: 4.6%
Serving temperature: 6°–8°C (42.8°–46.4°F)
Food: Spicy food such as Thai curries

Steinlager

Steinlager is the Pilsner-style lager made by Lion Breweries. It has a distinctive grassy aroma and clean, crisp hop bitterness on the palate leading to a dry, astringent finish.

Lion was formed in 1923 when eight of New Zealand's leading breweries merged in a bid to fight off prohibitive legislation. The new company was called New Zealand Breweries, but was renamed Lion after one of its strongest brands in 1977. Prior to the merger, Lion beers had been brewed by the Great Northern Brewery, which had been founded in 1860.

Lion Breweries is a division of the Lion Nathan Group, which is a major producer of wines and beers throughout New Zealand and Australia. Other popular brands from the Group include Lion Red, a full-bodied malt-flavoured beer which has become the leading beer in New Zealand, Speight's Amber Ale (described by the company as 'traditionally brewed with choice Nelson hops, the finest Canterbury barley and water to produce a full-strength ale, more bitter than other mainstream draught beers'), Hahn Premium Light and the mid-strength XXX Gold.

SPECIFICATIONS

Brewery: Lion Breweries
Location: Auckland, New Zealand
Style: Pilsner
Colour: Pale golden yellow
Alcohol: 5%
Serving temperature: 6°–8°C (42.8°–46.4°F)
Food: An appetising aperitif

Index

Page numbers in **bold** refer to main entries.

Picture Acknowledgments

Many thanks to all the Breweries which have contributed to preparation of this book.

With special thanks to:
Adrian Matthew, www.newbelgium.com
Anthony Crewe
Corey and Nate, www.beerlabels.com
Miller Brewing Co
Dave Hoffmann at New Jersey Climax Brewing Company
The Boston Beer Company
The Staff at Cambrew Ltd, Phnom Penh, Cambodia
www.schlenkerla.de

PICTURE CREDITS

All pictures © Istituto Geographico DeAgostini Italy, with the exception of:

www.beerlabels.com, 169, 193

Corbis: End papers, 6, 10, 13, 26, 70, 71, 78, 79, 82, 90, 91, 98, 99, 112, 113, 128, 129, 132, 133, 144, 145, 190, 191, 202, 203, 208, 209, 256, 257, 270, 271, 280, 281, 286, 287, 292, 293, 308, 309

Getty Images: 83

Amber Books: 15, 23B (Both), 25B (Both), 33,34T (Both), 38T (Both), 41T (Both), 49, 50, 58B, 62T (Both), 63, 72B (Both), 74T (Both), 118, 123B (Both), 206B (Both), 240, 247, 285, 294B (Both), 296, 297, 300T (Both), 313

Oland Brewer/Interbrew, 14T; **Amsterdam Brewing Company**, 14B; **Big Rock Brewery**, 16T (Both); **Brick Brewing Co.**, 16B (Both), 17; **Creemore Springs**, 18T (Both); **McAuslan Brewing**, 19B (Both), 20; **Molson Breweries**, 12, 21; **Moosehead Breweries Ltd**, 22T (Both); **Sleeman Brewing & Malting Co.**, 22B (Both); **Upper Canada Brewing**, 25T (Both); **Anchor Brewing Co.**, 28, 29; **Alaskan Brewing Company**, 30T; **August Schell Brewing Co.**, 31; **Bear Republic Brewing Co.**, 32; **Breckenridge Brewery**, 34B (Both); **Brooklyn Brewery**, 35; **BridgePort Brewing Company**, 36; **Coors Brewing Company**, 11, 38B, 39T; **Full Sail Brewing Co.**, 39B; **Great Lakes Brewing Co.**, 40; **Hale's Ales Brewer & Pub**, 41B; **Hair of the Dog Brewing Co.**, 42; **Left Hand & Tabernash Brewing Co.**, 43; **Jacob Leinenkugel Brewing Company**, 44T (Both); **MacTarnahan's Brewing Company**, 44B (Both) 45; **Anheuser-Busch**, 46B; **SAB Miller**, 47, 48T; **North Coast Brewing Co.**, 48B (Both), 51; **Odell Brewing Company**, 52; **Old Dominion Brewing Company**, 53; **Brewery Ommegang**, 54; **Pabst Brewing Company**, 55; **Pensylvania Brewing Company**, 56; **Pete's Brewing Company**, 57; **Pike Pub and Brewery**, 58T; **Brooklyn Brewery**, 59; **Redhook Ale Brewery**, 60T; **Rogue Ales**, 60B, 61; **Saint Arnold Brewing Company**, 62B; **Boston Beer Company**, 64; **Sierra Nevada**, 65; **Stone Brewing Company**, 66, 67T; **Stoudt's Brewing Co.**, 67B, 68T; **Privatbrauerei Sudwerk Hubsch**, 68B; **Victory Brewing Company**, 69; **Especialidad Cerveceras**, 72T; **Beamish and Crawford**, 92T; **Belhaven Brewer Company Ltd**, 100; **Caledonian Brewery**, 108, 109; **Adnams Ltd**, 114; **Batemen's**, 116; **Fuller, Smith & Turner Plc**, 119, 120, 121T; **George Gale & Co**, 121B, 122T; **Brouwerij Haacht NV**, 161B; **Brauerei Eichhof**, 204B, 205, 206T; **Bürgerbräu**, 212B; **Berliner Kindl Brauerei**, 215T; **Binding Brauerei**, 215, 216T; **Bitburger Brauerei**, 217; **DAB**, 218, 219T; **Brauerei P.J. Fruh**, 225T (Both); **Heller-Brau**, 227; **Friesisches Bauhaus**, 229B (Both); **Spaten-Franziskaner-Bräu**, 238 top; **Brauerei Pinkus Muller**, 241T (Both); **Rostocker Brauerei** 242 bottom; **Privat Weissbierbrauerei G. Schneider & Sohn**, 246; **Thurn und Taxis**, 252B; **Wernesgrüner** 255 top; **Braucommune in Freistadt**, 274; **Brau Union Österreich**, 276; **Brauerei Schwechat**, 278; **Brauerei Zipf**, 279; **United Breweries**, 294T (Both); **Asia Pacific Breweries**, 9, 298; **Cambrew Ltd**, 299; **San Miguel Corporation**, 300B; **Asahi**, 303; **Kuchi Brewery**, 305, 306T (Both); **Sapporo Breweries Ltd**, 306; **Malt Shovel**, 310B (Both); **Swan Brewery**, 312

CLAUSTHALER
CLASSIC
PREMIUM ALKOHOLFREI
Gutmann
Andechser
LÖWENBRÄU
Premium Pils
PAULANER
Hefe-Weißbier
PAULANER
Hefe-Weißbier
KULMBACHER
Mönchshof
Original
PILS
Seit 1887
Leikeim
AUS ALTENKUNSTADT
Schöfferhofer
SCHNEIDER WEISSE
HELL WEIZENBIER
Original